ACCESS

Building Literacy Through Learning™

Science

Great Source Education Group

a division of Houghton Mifflin Company

Wilmington, Massachusetts

www.greatsource.com

AUTHORS

Dr. Elva Durán holds a Ph.D. from the University of Oregon in special education and reading disabilities. Durán has been an elementary reading and middle school teacher in Texas and overseas. Currently she is a professor in the Department of Special Education, Rehabilitation, and School Psychology at California State University, Sacramento, where she teaches beginning reading and language and literacy courses. Durán is co-author of the Leamos Español reading program and has published two textbooks, *Teaching Students with Moderate/Severe Disabilities* and *Systematic Instruction in Reading for Spanish-Speaking Students*.

Jo Gusman grew up in a family of migrants and knows firsthand the complexities surrounding a second language learner. Gusman's career in bilingual education began in 1974. In 1981, she joined the staff of the Newcomer School in Sacramento. There she developed her brain-based ESL strategies. Her work has garnered national television appearances and awards, including the Presidential Recognition for Excellence in Teaching. Gusman is the author of *Practical Strategies for Accelerating the Literacy Skills and Content Learning of Your ESL Students*. She is a featured video presenter, including "Multiple Intelligences and the Second Language Learner." Currently, she teaches at California State University, Sacramento, and at the Multiple Intelligences Institute at the University of California, Riverside.

Dr. John Shefelbine is a professor in the Department of Teacher Education, California State University, Sacramento. His degrees include a Master of Arts in Teaching in reading and language arts, K–12, from Harvard University and a Ph.D. in educational psychology from Stanford University. During his 11 years as an elementary and middle school teacher, Shefelbine has worked with students from linguistically and culturally diverse populations in Alaska, Arizona, Idaho, and New Mexico. Shefelbine was a contributor to the California Reading Language Arts Framework, the California Reading Initiative, and the California Reading and Literature Project and has authored a variety of reading materials and programs for developing fluent, confident readers.

EDITORIAL: Developed by Nieman Inc. with Phil LaLeike
DESIGN: Ronan Design

Printed in the United States of America

International Standard Book Number: 0-669-50895-0

3 4 5 6 7 8 9—RRDW—10 09 08 07 06

CONSULTANTS

Shane Bassett
Mill Park Elementary School
David Douglas School District
Portland, OR

Jeannette Gordon
Senior Educational Consultant
Illinois Resource Center
Des Plaines, IL

Dr. Aixa Perez-Prado
College of Education
Florida International University
Miami, FL

Dennis Terdy
Director of Grants and Special
  Programs/Newcomer Center
Township High School
Arlington Heights, IL

TEACHER GROUP REVIEWERS

Sara Ainsworth
Hannah Beardsley
  Middle School
Crystal Lake, IL

Walter Blair
Otis Elementary School
Chicago, IL

Vincent Egonmwan
Kilmer Elementary School
Chicago, IL

Ann Hopkins
Albany Park
  Multicultural Academy
Chicago, IL

Heather Pusich
Field Middle School
Northbrook, IL

Dana Robinson
Northwestern University
Evanston, IL

Nestor Torres
Chase Elementary School
Chicago, IL

RESEARCH SITE LEADERS

Carmen Concepción
Lawton Chiles Middle School
Hialeah, FL

Andrea Dabbs
Edendale Middle School
San Lorenzo, CA

Daniel García
Public School 130
Bronx, NY

Bobbi Ciriza Houtchens
Arroyo Valley High School
San Bernardino, CA

Portia McFarland
Wendell Phillips High School
Chicago, IL

RESEARCH SITE SCIENCE REVIEWERS

Kristen Can
Edendale Middle School
San Lorenzo, CA

Delores King
Warren Elementary School
Chicago, IL

Dania Lima
Lawton Chiles Middle School
Hialeah, FL

Elizabeth Tremberger
Bronx, NY

Jackie Womack
Martin Luther King, Jr.
  Middle School
San Bernardino, CA

SCIENCE TEACHER REVIEWERS

Said Ahmed
Sanford Middle School
Minneapolis, MN

Kellie Danzinger
Carpentersville Middle School
Carpentersville, IL

Jean Garrity
Washington Middle School
Kenosha, WI

John Kimsey
Carpenter School
Chicago, IL

Anna Kong
Stone Academy
Chicago, IL

Jill McCarthy
Auburndale, MA

Donna O'Neill
Fairfax County Public Schools
Fairfax, VA

Kevin Smith
North Welcome Center
Columbus, OH

Nancy C. Svendsen
J. E. B. Stuart School
Falls Church, VA

Jill M. Thompson
Roosevelt Middle School
Blaine, MN

STANDARDS *Lesson 1:* Students should understand concepts of time and size relating to Earth processes. Students should understand that different kinds of questions suggest different kinds of scientific investigations. They should realize that science advances through legitimate skepticism. Students should communicate the logical connection among hypotheses, science concepts, tests conducted, data collected, and conclusions drawn from evidence. They should think critically and logically to relate evidence and explanations.

CONTENTS

STANDARDS *Lesson 2:* Students should know Earth is composed of layers and that many land features result from gradual changes, such as plate tectonics. Students should know that major geological events, such as earthquakes, volcanic eruptions, and mountain building, result from plate motions. *Lesson 3:* Students should be able to analyze and predict the sequence of events in the rock cycle. Students should know that the rock cycle includes the formation of new sediments and rocks and that the rocks are often found in layers, with the oldest generally on the bottom. *Lesson 4:* Students should know that mechanical and chemical activities shape and reshape Earth's land surface by eroding rock and soil in some areas and depositing them in other areas.

UNIT 2

EARTH SCIENCE

STANDARDS *Lesson 5:* Students are expected to know that global patterns influence local weather. Students should be able to explain how incoming solar radiation, ocean currents, and land masses affect weather and climate. They should know that changes in pressure, heat, air movement, and humidity result in changes of weather. *Lesson 6:* Students should be able to describe patterns of daily, monthly, and seasonal changes in their environment. Students should be able to relate Earth's movements and the moon's orbit and explain tides and eclipses.

CONTENTS

STANDARDS *Lesson 7:* Students should know that when fuel is consumed, most of the energy is released as heat. They should know that most of the energy used today is derived from burning fossil fuels. Students should be familiar with different natural energy and material resources and should know how to classify them as renewable or nonrenewable. *Lesson 8:* Students should know that human decisions and activities have had a profound impact on the physical and living environments. They should be able to make inferences and draw conclusions about the effects of human activity on Earth's resources, analyze how natural and/or human events may have contributed to the extinction of some species, and project population changes when habitats are altered or destroyed.

STANDARDS *Lesson 9:* Students should identify the general climate of the major biomes. Students should know that all populations living together and the physical factors with which they interact compose an ecosystem. They should be able to describe the flow of energy and matter through food chains and identify the relationship among producers, consumers, and decomposers in an ecosystem. *Lesson 10:* Students should know that all organisms must be able to obtain and use resources, grow, reproduce, and maintain stable internal conditions while living in a constantly changing external environment. Students should develop systematic observation abilities and base their explanations on what they observe. Students should know that all organisms are composed of cells. They should distinguish between single-cell organisms and multicellular organisms and understand that specialized cells perform specialized functions in multicellular organisms.

CONTENTS

STANDARDS *Lesson 11:* Students should know the differences between plant and animal cells and understand that some functions are unique to certain types of cells. Students should know that mitochondria liberate energy for the work that cells do and that chloroplasts capture sunlight energy for photosynthesis. Students should know the processes of division, growth, and maturation that occur during the cell cycle. They should know that cells divide through the process of mitosis, which results in two daughter cells with identical sets of chromosomes. *Lesson 12:* Students should know that living systems demonstrate the complementary nature of structure and function at all levels, including cells, organs, tissues, organ systems, whole organisms, and ecosystems. Students should know that each type of cell, tissue, and organ has a distinct structure and set of functions that serve the organism as a whole.

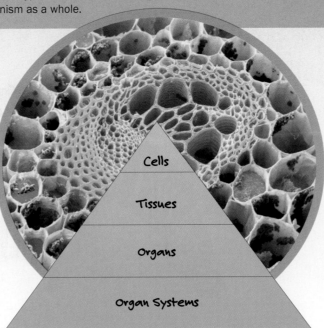

Cells

Tissues

Organs

Organ Systems

TABLE OF

STANDARDS *Lesson 13:* Students should know that cells take in nutrients. They should be able to describe photosynthesis. Students should know that living things are made of carbon, hydrogen, nitrogen, oxygen, phosphorus, and sulfur and that living organisms have many different kinds of molecules. *Lesson 14:* Students should know that regulation of an organism's internal environment involves sensing the internal environment and changing physiological activities to keep conditions within the range required to survive. They should be able to identify responses in organisms to internal and external stimuli. Students should know that disease is a breakdown in structures or functions of an organism, sometimes as the result of infection by other organisms.

CONTENTS

STANDARDS *Lesson 15:* Students should know that reproduction is a characteristic of all living systems and be able to distinguish between sexual and asexual reproduction. They should know that variations within a species are the result of genetic information being passed from parent to offspring. Students should know the difference between mitosis and meiosis. They should know that DNA is the genetic material located in the chromosome of each cell. They should be able to use a Punnett square to predict the results of crosses and to distinguish between dominant and recessive traits.
Lesson 16: Students should understand that genetic variation and environmental factors are causes of evolution and diversity of organisms; that differences within a species may give individuals an advantage in surviving and reproducing; and that variations relate to survival. Students should understand that the fossil record provides evidence of changes that have occurred over time. They should know that extinction occurs when the environment changes and the adaptive characteristics of a species are insufficient for its survival.

STANDARDS *Lesson 17:* Students are expected to define matter and energy and describe the structure and parts of an atom. Students should understand that protons and neutrons are located in the nucleus of the atom, while electrons exist in areas of probability outside of the nucleus, and that most of the atom is empty space. *Lesson 18:* Students should know the states of matter. Students should be able to describe changes in states of matter and develop their own mental models to explain them. They should be able to describe and measure how the interactions of energy with matter effect changes of state. Students should know that a substance has characteristic properties, such as density. They should know how to calculate density from measurements of mass and volume.

CONTENTS

STANDARDS *Lesson 19:* Students should know how to use the periodic table and how to identify regions corresponding to metals, nonmetals, and inert gases. Students should know that substances can be classified by their properties and should know how to identify substances by those properties. *Lesson 20:* Students should know that, in chemical reactions, the total mass is conserved. They should understand the difference between a physical change and a chemical change, know that chemical changes result in new substances with different characteristics, and know how to use clues to determine whether a change is chemical or physical. They should be able to describe energy changes related to chemical reactions and describe situations that support the principle of conservation of energy.

TABLE OF

STANDARDS *Lesson 21:* Students should be able to identify forms of energy, explain that they can be measured and compared, and observe how one form of energy can be transformed into another form in common situations. Students should be able to describe situations that support the principle of conservation of energy. Students should be able to compare conduction, convection, and radiation of heat. They should explain heat in terms of kinetic molecular theory. *Lesson 22:* Students should be able to measure force, explain the dimensions of force graphically, compare common examples of balanced or unbalanced forces, and examine frictional forces in common examples. They should know that gravity is a universal force that every mass exerts on every other mass. Students should know that the motion of an object can be described by its position, direction, and speed and distinguish between speed and velocity. They should be able to compare common situations to each of Newton's three laws of motion.

CONTENTS

STANDARDS *Lesson 23:* Students should be able to diagram how sound and light energy are detected by humans and other organisms. Students should observe and be able to describe variations in wavelength and frequency in terms of the source of the vibrations that produce them. Students should understand that visible light is a small band within a very broad electromagnetic spectrum. *Lesson 24:* Students should know the appearance, general composition, relative position and size, and motion of objects in the solar system, including planets, planetary satellites, comets, and asteroids. They should understand the vast size of our solar system and know how to use light years to measure distance. Students should know that stars are the source of light for all bright objects in outer space and should examine the effects of the sun's gravitational force in the solar system.

Being a
Scientist

Here you'll learn about how to think and work as a scientist. You'll also learn how to use the science process and practice relating evidence and explanations.

Building Background

▲ My grandparents took me to a beach like this once. I wonder what the brown things are.

■ **What do you think these people are doing?**

■ **What questions would you ask them?**

■ **What does this make you think of?**

When you work as a scientist, you ask questions. Scientists usually use 4 steps to find answers to their questions. The answers often lead to new questions.

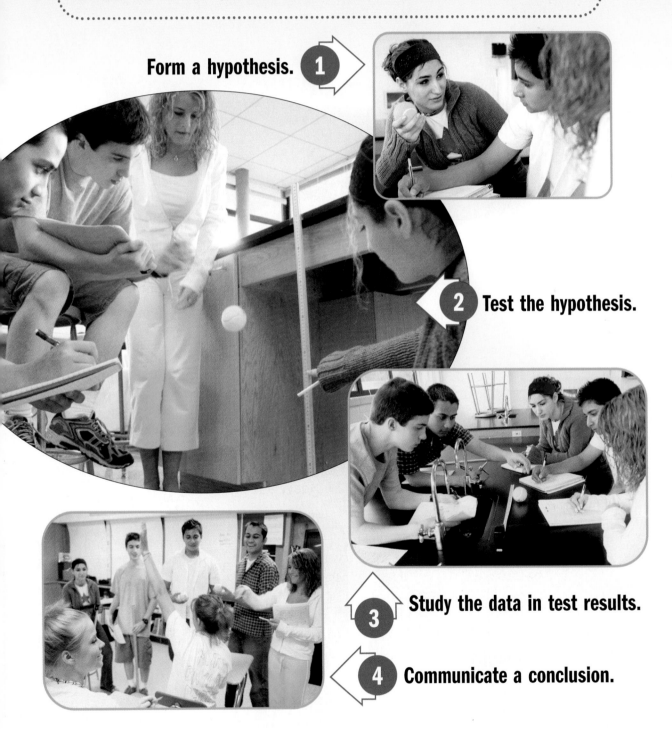

Form a hypothesis. **1**

2 Test the hypothesis.

3 Study the data in test results.

4 Communicate a conclusion.

Key Concepts

hypothesis   test   result   supports

A **hypothesis** is an idea you can **test.**

The **result** of your test is what happens. If the result is what you thought it would be, the result **supports** your hypothesis.

Measuring

Scientists measure many different things. These are just a few examples.

Size
Large and small

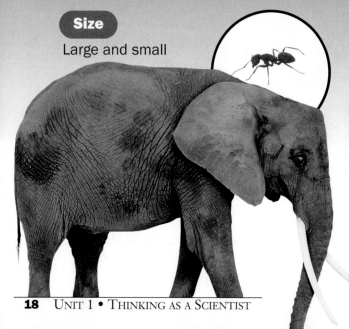

Weight
Heavy and light

Use the Science Process

In the science process, you test a hypothesis. Imagine that your hypothesis is "A frozen ball will not bounce as high as a ball at room temperature." Here is an experiment you can use to test this hypothesis.

A Model Experiment

Procedure

1. Hang the tape measure from the flat surface. The starting end of the tape measure should touch the floor.

2. Roll the ball off the end of the flat surface next to the tape measure.

3. Observe and record how high the ball bounces. Do this 4 times the same way.

4. Put the same ball in a freezer overnight.

5. Roll the frozen ball off the end of the same flat surface 4 times and record how high it bounces. Wait 10 minutes and repeat the experiment 4 times. Record the results.

6. Wait 20 more minutes. Do the experiment 4 more times. Record the results.

Materials
- One tennis ball
- One tape measure
- A flat surface such as a counter or table, 36 inches (91 cm) or higher
- A pencil and paper
- A freezer

As a scientist, you will probably use measuring tools such as scales, balances, rulers, and thermometers.

Age
Old and young

Temperature
Hot and cold

Being a Scientist

Scientists ask questions about the world around them. They find answers by forming a hypothesis, testing the hypothesis, studying the data in test results, and communicating a conclusion. What they learn often leads to new questions.

From Question to Hypothesis

Look around you. You use your **senses**—sight, taste, touch, smell, and hearing—to **observe** the world.

You may have questions about what you observe. Do you wonder how things work or why things happen? What kind of bird is that? What makes lightning? You might ask, "Does temperature **affect** how high a ball will **bounce?**"

Scientists ask all kinds of questions. How do they find answers?

When you are a scientist, you use your observations. ▶

VOCABULARY
senses—sight, taste, touch, smell, and hearing
observe—notice
affect—change
bounce—spring back after hitting something

THINK OF AN EXPLANATION

A scientist thinks of possible answers to questions. The answers can be possible **explanations** for what the scientist observes. Explanations give the reasons something happens.

When you have an idea that you think explains what you observe, you have a **hypothesis.** A hypothesis must be an explanation you can test. You test a hypothesis to see how well your explanation really works.

Here is one hypothesis for the ball question: "A frozen ball will not bounce as high as a ball at room temperature."

MAKE A PREDICTION

Based on your hypothesis, you can make a **prediction,** or a guess about what will happen. You make a prediction by using what you already know. State your prediction using the words *if* and *then.* For example: *If I freeze a tennis ball, then it will not bounce as high as it bounced before freezing.*

Language Notes

Signal Words: Cause-Effect
These words are clues to discovering why something happened.

- ☐ affect
- ☐ reasons
- ☐ explains
- ☐ based on
- ☐ depends on
- ☐ results

TALK AND SHARE
With your partner, describe a prediction and give some examples.

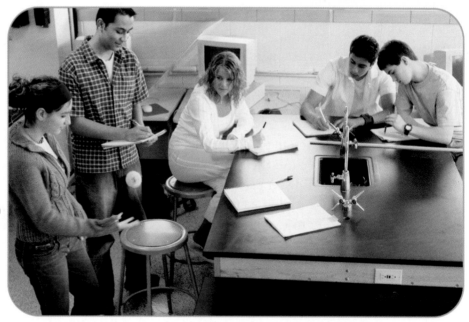

You make a prediction before you test your hypothesis. ▶

VOCABULARY

explanations—statements that give reasons or make a topic easier to understand
hypothesis—an idea you can test that explains what you observe
prediction—a guess about what will happen

Designing a Test

As a scientist, your next job is to test the hypothesis. You can do different kinds of tests.

CHOOSE A METHOD

The **method** you use to test a hypothesis depends on your question. You can make observations, which means you write down what you observe. You can build a **model** or do a **survey.** You can also test your hypothesis with an **experiment.** Always **design** an experiment so that other people can repeat it.

◄ You design your test so that other people can do it exactly the same way.

Science, Technology, and Society

What Is Technology?

Science and **technology** depend on each other. Science deals with knowledge. Some people use their knowledge to create new products. For example, Thomas Edison used his knowledge to invent the light bulb. Any invention—a tool, machine, material, or method—that solves a problem is due to technology. New technology can lead to new knowledge. For example, the invention of the microscope led to new knowledge about cells.

Microscope ►

VOCABULARY

method—a way of doing something
model—a copy of something
survey—the process of asking a set of questions and collecting answers
experiment—a set of steps for testing a hypothesis
design—plan
technology—the use of science to solve problems

PARTS OF AN EXPERIMENT

When you design an experiment, you identify **variables.** Variables are all the things, or **factors,** that can affect the **results** of your experiment. As a scientist, you decide which single variable to change. You change just one thing so that you can learn the effect of that single change. In the ball experiment, you change the temperature of the ball.

Most factors in an experiment do not change. For example, you use the same ball and drop it from the same height. These factors are called **controls.** Controls do not affect what happens.

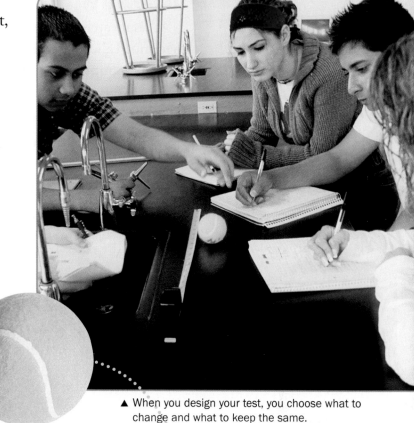

▲ When you design your test, you choose what to change and what to keep the same.

Parts of the Bouncing Ball Experiment

Controls (do not change)	▢ Same ball
	▢ Same drop height
	▢ Same floor
Variable (to change)	▢ Temperature of ball
Results	▢ Measurements of how high the ball bounces

(TALK AND SHARE) **Talk with your partner about what you think the terms *factors*, *variables*, and *controls* mean.**

VOCABULARY

variables—factors in an experiment that can change
factors—things that can affect what happens
results—things that happen
controls—factors in an experiment that are kept the same

Dealing with Data

As you watch what happens in your experiment, you gather **evidence** called **data.** Data can be numbers, **measurements,** or observations. Carefully record your data. The data are the results of your experiment.

Scientists **organize** their data to study them. They make graphs, tables, and diagrams to show their data.

When you organize your data, it is easy to see what happened in the experiment. As a scientist, you **analyze** the data by thinking about them and deciding what they mean.

TALK AND SHARE Explain to your partner what the data would be in the ball experiment. Together, decide how you could show the data.

▲ You record, organize, and analyze data.

Some Ways to Organize Data

You can show data in graphs, such as bar graphs, line graphs, and pie charts. You can also use data tables and drawings. ▼

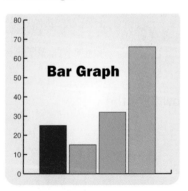

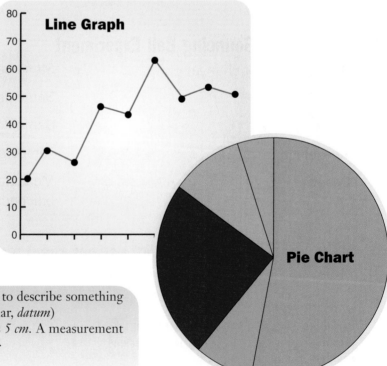

VOCABULARY

evidence—information and facts you can use to describe something
data—facts collected in an experiment (singular, *datum*)
measurements—numbers plus units, such as *5 cm.* A measurement must always have both a number and a unit.
organize—put in order
analyze—think about data and decide what they mean

Concluding and Communicating

Finally, you make a **conclusion** about your experiment and tell it to other scientists. The conclusion tells what happened. It also compares the results to the hypothesis. For example, if the frozen ball does not bounce as high as the ball at room temperature, your prediction was correct. The results of the experiment **support** your hypothesis.

Sometimes the results *do not* support your hypothesis. That is all right. In your conclusion, explain how the results are different from what you expected. Your conclusions may lead to new questions and give you ideas for new experiments.

How the Ball Bounces

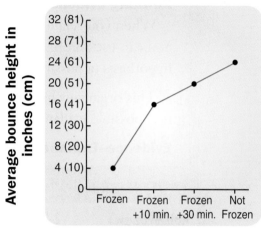

▲ This line graph shows that the ball bounced highest when it was not frozen. The data here support the hypothesis.

(TALK AND SHARE) **Tell your partner why scientists communicate their conclusions.**

Summary

You work as a scientist when you ask questions you can test. What you learn may lead to new questions.

VOCABULARY
conclusion—a report of what happened
support—make stronger

Relating

Relating Evidence and Explanations

When you relate pieces of information, you show how they are connected. You can use an organizer to help you relate your results (evidence) to your hypothesis (a possible explanation).

This organizer lists some data from the bouncing ball experiment. It also lists possible explanations.

Evidence–Explanation Organizer

Temperature	Height of Bounce	Explanation
not frozen	24 inches (61 cm)	
frozen	4 inches (10 cm)	Freezing makes a tennis ball bounce less.
+10 minutes	16 inches (41 cm)	
+30 minutes	20 inches (51 cm)	The warmer the tennis ball gets, the higher it bounces.

Practice Relating

1. Draw Make a graph or use an organizer to show the data from your own bouncing ball experiment. Show your work to your partner or group. Use it to explain what happened in the experiment.

2. Write Write a conclusion about your experiment. Words from the Word Bank can help you.

- State your hypothesis and tell whether or not the data from your experiment support your hypothesis.

  - Explain the evidence and relate it to your prediction.

    - Include any ideas for follow-up experiments.

Word Bank

predict
support
explain
learn
repeat
affect

hypothesis
experiment
prediction
result
observation

Activities

Grammar Spotlight

Using est When you add *est* to an adjective, you can relate 3 or more things. Adding *est* means "the most."

Adjective	*est* Form	Example
high	highest	*This ball bounces the highest.*
big	biggest	*He is the biggest boy.*
large	largest	*This plant is the largest.*

Now practice using *est* in one or two sentences of your own. Write about what happens to the ball after it is in the freezer.

Hands On

Measuring Challenge Have each person in your group use a tape measure to measure the width of a desk. Are the measurements the same? Discuss the results with your group. Why do you think you got these results? Then list some rules you could use to make sure measurements come out the same.

Partner Practice

Predicting Think about your own bouncing ball experiment. Now imagine that you put the tennis ball into hot water for 10 minutes. What do you think will happen? Tell your prediction to your partner. Listen to your partner's prediction. Be sure to include the words *if* and *then*.

Oral Language

Use the Science Process With your partner or group, talk about a new experiment you could do with the tennis ball. Talk about the *variable* you would change and predict the *results*.

Understanding

Earth

Here you'll learn about Earth and how it changes. You'll also learn how to analyze evidence and practice summarizing evidence.

▲ I've lived on two continents, South America and North America. Someday, I want to go to a third continent— Australia.

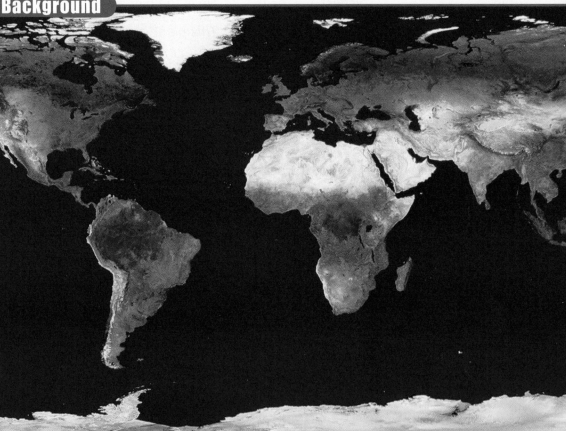

■ **What do you see between South America and Africa?**

■ **How could South America and Africa fit together?**

■ **How does Earth remind you of a puzzle?**

Earth has 3 layers. Under the surface, rock is hot enough to become soft. When soft rock rises toward the surface, it can move plates. When plates move, continents and oceans move, and volcanoes and earthquakes can form.

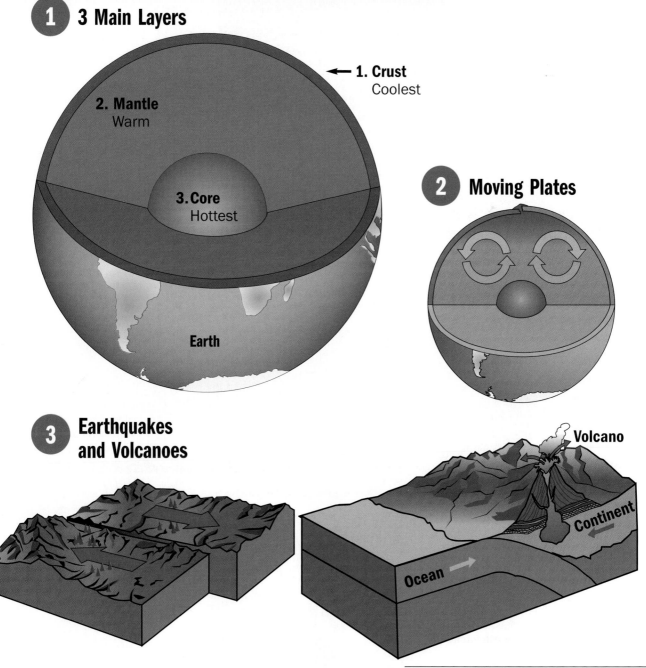

1 **3 Main Layers**

← 1. **Crust**
Coolest

2. **Mantle**
Warm

3. **Core**
Hottest

Earth

2 **Moving Plates**

3 **Earthquakes and Volcanoes**

Volcano

Continent

Ocean →

Key Concepts

crust   plates   mantle   core

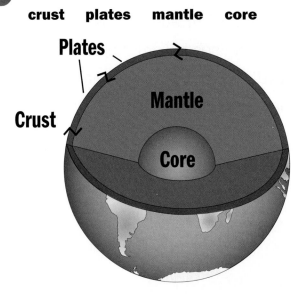

Plates

Mantle

Crust

Core

Earth has an outer layer called the **crust** that is made of pieces called **plates.** The crust is cool compared to the mantle.

Earth has a middle layer called the **mantle.** The mantle is warm.

Earth has a center layer called the **core.** The core of Earth is very hot.

History of Earth

Earth is very, very old. This timeline shows Earth's history, from its beginning to the present.

600 million years ago
First evidence of living organisms appears in rocks.

200 million years ago
Atlantic Ocean starts opening; Appalachian Mountains form.

4 billion years ago
Oldest known rocks

4.6 billion years ago
Earth forms.

Analyze Evidence

Evidence is data about something that happened. Scientists analyze evidence to form a theory. For example, scientists observed things they could see on the surface of Earth. They analyzed their observations to form the theory of plate tectonics. Look at the Web.

When you analyze evidence, you decide what it means. Here is one way to do this.

1. Think about what one piece of evidence means and write down your idea.

2. See if other evidence means the same as the first piece. If it does not, revise your idea.

Evidence
Most earthquakes occur in certain places on Earth's surface.

The Theory of Plate Tectonics

Evidence
Many volcanoes are found on the edges of continents.

Evidence
Some continents look like they could fit together.

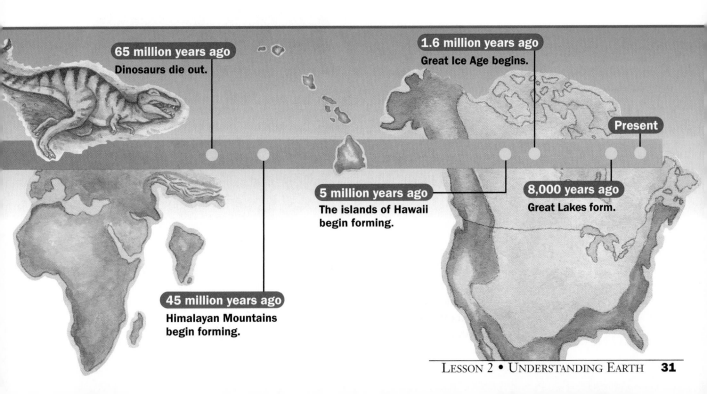

65 million years ago
Dinosaurs die out.

1.6 million years ago
Great Ice Age begins.

Present

5 million years ago
The islands of Hawaii begin forming.

8,000 years ago
Great Lakes form.

45 million years ago
Himalayan Mountains begin forming.

Understanding Earth

E arth has 3 different layers. The inside layers are hot. This heat makes rock soft. Plates move because the soft rock is moving. This can cause volcanoes and earthquakes to form.

The Structure of Earth

Earth has 3 main layers. Oceans and continents make up its top **layer.**

THREE MAIN LAYERS

The **crust** is Earth's outside layer. It is the layer where we live. Compared to the other layers, the crust is thin and cool. Cool **rock** is strong.

The **mantle** is Earth's thick middle layer. Rock in the mantle is softer than rock in the crust. That's because the mantle is hot enough to melt rock. Hot rock can bend and move.

The **core** is at Earth's center. The core is the hottest layer of Earth.

▲ A picture of Earth taken from outer space shows South America and parts of Central America and North America.

Earth has 3 layers. ▶

Crust

Mantle

Core

Language Notes

Multiple Meanings
These words have more than one meaning.

■ rock
1. a solid material
2. move back and forth
3. a kind of music

■ plates
1. pieces of Earth's crust
2. dishes to eat on
3. parts of a baseball diamond

VOCABULARY

layer—one thickness that lies on top of or under another one
crust—the outside layer
rock—a hard material that makes up Earth's crust and mantle
mantle—Earth's thick middle layer
core—Earth's hot center

OCEANS, CONTINENTS, AND PLATES

Oceans are big areas of salty water. They cover most of Earth's **surface**. **Continents** are very big areas of land.

Plates are under the oceans and continents. Plates are thick pieces of the crust that can move. Earth's surface is broken into 11 big plates and 10 to 20 small plates. A continental plate has a continent on it. An ocean plate has an ocean on it.

TALK AND SHARE With your partner, talk about how the crust of Earth is different from the other layers of Earth.

▲ A view from space shows the eastern part of the North American continent and part of the Atlantic Ocean.

Earth's Plates

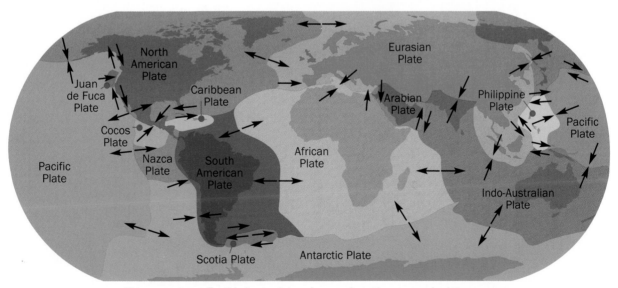

▲ This map shows Earth's large plates. Arrows show the way each plate moves.

How Plates Move

There are **mountains** on the surface of Earth. Mountains are beneath the ocean water, too. There are **trenches** in the ocean bottoms. Trenches are deep, low areas that are very long.

What makes mountains and trenches? Scientists developed a **theory** that answers this question.

THE THEORY

A theory is an idea that explains how or why something happens. A theory must have **evidence** to **support** it.

The theory of **plate tectonics** explains how mountains and trenches are made. It states that the plates on Earth do not stay in one place. Heat in the mantle causes the plates to move.

Mountains may form where plates meet. ▼

Warm, soft rock rises.

Cooler rock sinks.

VOCABULARY

mountains—parts of Earth's crust that are taller than the surrounding crust
trenches—deep, long, low areas of land
theory—an explanation with evidence to support it
evidence—the information and facts you can use to describe something
support—make stronger
plate tectonics—the way Earth's plates move

EVIDENCE FOR THE THEORY

When two plates bump together, Earth's surface **wrinkles.**
This makes mountains. The Himalayan Mountains north
of India are evidence that two continental (land) plates
bumped together.

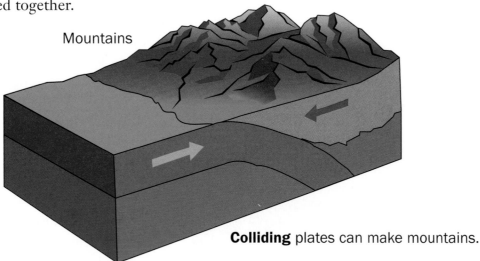

Mountains

Colliding plates can make mountains.

Sometimes an ocean plate bumps into a continental plate. The
ocean plate is pulled under the continental plate. A trench forms
when the ocean plate is pulled down. The trench is evidence that
one plate is going under another plate. Mountains may form on
the continental plate when this happens.

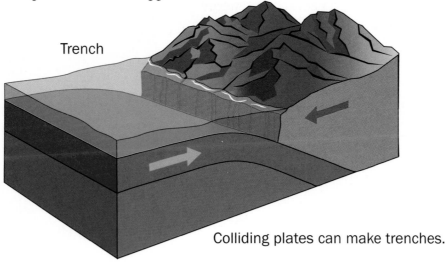

Trench

Colliding plates can make trenches.

(TALK AND SHARE) **Tell your partner how
plates change the way Earth looks.**

Volcanoes and Earthquakes

Volcanoes and earthquakes are caused by changes inside Earth. Some places have a lot of earthquakes and volcanoes. These places are on the edges of plates.

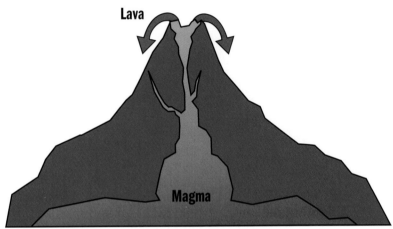

▲ Magma rises to the surface of Earth in volcanoes.

VOLCANOES

A **volcano** forms above cracks in Earth's surface. Heat below the surface melts rock. Melted rock inside Earth is called **magma.**

Magma rises toward the surface. When magma **spills** onto the surface, it is called **lava.** Lava cools as it moves away from the volcano. Cooled lava turns into hard rock.

Science, Technology, and Society

Geothermal Energy

When water boils, it becomes steam. People can use steam to make electricity and heat. Steam that comes from volcanoes is called geothermal energy. *Geothermal* means "earth heat."

Geothermal energy starts when water flows into cracks in a volcano. The volcano's magma heats the water. It turns into steam. Power companies catch the steam in pipes. The pipes carry the steam to places where people use it for energy.

A geothermal energy plant in Iceland catches steam that is used as energy. ▶

VOCABULARY

volcano—a place where melted rock comes out on Earth's surface
magma—melted rock inside Earth
spills—falls out
lava—magma on the surface of Earth

EARTHQUAKES

An **earthquake** is a sudden release of energy caused by moving rock. Many earthquakes happen where two plates **scrape** against each other. The movement makes energy build up until the rock breaks. A crack where rock breaks and moves is called a **fault.**

The ground shakes in an earthquake. After a big earthquake, the ground may shake for days or weeks. Each shake gets a little weaker. When rock along the fault completely **settles** into its new position, the shaking stops.

(TALK AND SHARE) **Ask your partner why earthquakes happen in some places and not in other places.**

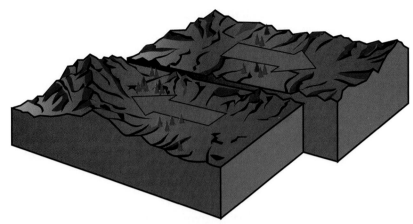

▲ Scraping plates can cause earthquakes.

▲ Earthquakes can destroy homes.

Summary

Earth has 3 layers. The heat inside Earth makes rock move. Moving rock near Earth's surface makes plates move. When plates move, mountains, trenches, earthquakes, and volcanoes can form.

VOCABULARY

earthquake—a sudden release of energy caused by breaking and moving rock
scrape—rub hard
fault—a crack where rock breaks and moves
settles—comes to rest

Summarizing

Summarizing Evidence

When you summarize evidence, you tell it again in fewer words. You only tell the important points and leave out the small details.

A Web can help you collect your evidence and make a summary about it. The Web below summarizes the evidence for the theory of plate tectonics.

Web

Evidence
Earthquakes release energy from inside Earth.

Evidence
Volcanoes form above cracks in Earth's surface.

Evidence
Continents fit like puzzle pieces.

Plate Tectonics
Plates on Earth do not stay in one place. When plates move, Earth's surface changes.

Evidence
Many mountains are near the edges of continents.

Practice Summarizing

1. Draw Make a Web using pictures. Include at least one mountain, one trench, one volcano, and one earthquake. Then talk with your group about how each of these things supports the theory of plate tectonics.

2. Write Think about volcanoes and make a new Web. Write *volcanoes* in the center. Include facts about volcanoes in each outer circle. Use your Web to write a paragraph that summarizes what you have learned about how volcanoes form. Words from the Word Bank can help you.

Word Bank

flows
rises

rock
magma
crust
mantle

soft
melted

Activities

Grammar Spotlight

Using *there is* and *there are* The words *there is* and *there are* call attention to a noun later in the sentence. You need to find the noun so you can decide whether to use *there is* or *there are*.

Rule	Example	Explanation
Use *there is* when the noun is singular.	*There is a volcano in Japan.*	One volcano
Use *there are* when the noun is plural.	*There are 11 big plates.*	More than one plate

How many volcanoes are in your state? Give a sentence with the answer. Use either *there is* or *there are* in your answer. (Hint: If your state does not have any volcanoes, use *there is no* or *there are no* in your sentence.)

Partner Practice

Analyze Evidence Look at the picture on page 28. Then draw the shape of South America. Next, draw the shape of Africa. Cut out the shapes and give one to a partner. Try to fit the shapes together. What happens? Talk about the result and what it may mean.

Hands On

Plate Crash Take one piece of construction paper and give another piece to your partner. Think of the pieces of paper as two plates. Push the two pieces of paper together. Do you get a mountain? Do you get a trench? Talk about what happens.

Oral Language

North America In a small group, talk about mountains and earthquakes on the continent of North America. Pick out things you know that give evidence for the theory of plate tectonics. As a group, summarize all the evidence you can think of for plate tectonics in North America.

All About

Rocks

Here you'll learn about 3 kinds of rock and how they form. You'll also learn how to make observations and practice interpreting observations.

Building Background

▲ I've never been on a highway so close to the ocean.

- **What does this remind you of?**
- **When have you seen or visited a place like this?**
- **What do you think made these rocks?**

Rock can form on Earth or below its surface. Earth has 3 kinds of rock. Each kind of rock can turn into another kind. The rock cycle shows how rock changes.

Igneous Rock 1
forms in Earth's crust when magma cools and hardens.

Sedimentary Rock 2
forms on Earth's surface when bits and pieces of rock and other things get stuck together.

Metamorphic Rock 3
is formed when any rock is changed by heat and pressure within Earth.

Key Concepts

sedimentary   igneous   metamorphic

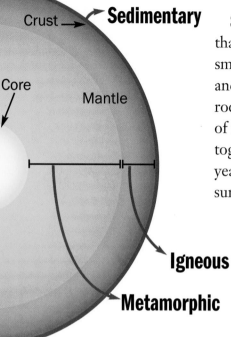

Crust

Core

Mantle

Sedimentary

Igneous

Metamorphic

Sedimentary is a word that relates to sediment, or small pieces of rock, shell, and bone. Sedimentary rock is made of small pieces of rock that get pressed together over millions of years. This happens on the surface of Earth.

Igneous is a word that relates to fire. Igneous rock is made of melted rock that cools and hardens. This usually happens on or near the surface of Earth.

Metamorphic is a word that relates to change. Metamorphic rock comes from the actions of heat and pressure on other kinds of rock. This always happens deep inside Earth.

How Magma Turns into Rock

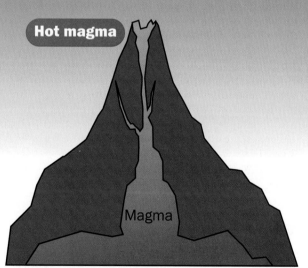

Hot magma

Magma

Rock deep inside Earth is soft and hot.
It may melt and become magma.

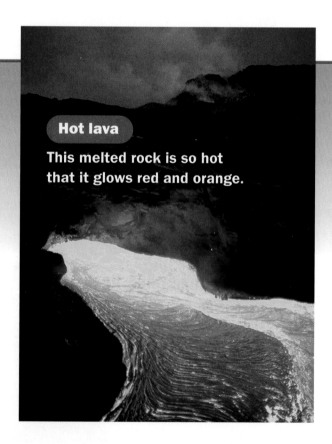

Hot lava

This melted rock is so hot that it glows red and orange.

Make Observations

When you make observations, follow these steps.

1. Use your five senses—sight, touch, hearing, taste, and smell—to study something carefully.

2. Write down your observations.

The list to the right shows some observations about the rock in the picture. The details you observe can help you decide what kind of rock this is.

◄ Limestone is a sedimentary rock.

Observations

1. The rock contains seashells.

2. The rock is a blue-gray color.

3. The rock is rough, not smooth.

Cooling lava

Lava cools when it meets the air. The surface of this lava is black and crusty.

Cooled rock

The black rock on this beach formed when lava flowed into cold water. The lava cooled so fast that it exploded into pieces.

All About Rocks

Rocks form in different ways, either on or below Earth's surface. Earth has 3 kinds of rock: igneous, sedimentary, and metamorphic. The rock cycle shows how they can change from one kind to another.

Where Rock Forms

Rock can form deep inside Earth. Rock also forms on Earth's surface. It can form on dry land as well as under ocean water.

ON LAND

Water, wind, and ice can break rock into pieces. They can carry the pieces to new places.

Water may mix with the pieces of rock. The water usually has other things in it, such as **chemicals** from the air and from living things. Over time, the water goes away. The chemicals are left behind and hold the pieces of rock together. As a result, new hard rock forms.

Volcanoes add new rock to Earth's crust. Heat melts hard rock into **magma.** The magma rises and **lava** flows from the volcano. The lava cools and hardens into rock.

▲ A view from space shows the tops of volcanoes on the Galapagos Islands, near Ecuador.

Geologists are scientists who study Earth. These geologists stand on fresh lava in Hawaii. The lava is still hot enough in some places to melt their shoes. ▼

VOCABULARY
chemicals—materials found in Earth and around Earth
volcanoes—places where melted rock comes out on the surface of Earth
magma—melted rock inside Earth
lava—melted rock on the surface of Earth

UNDER THE OCEAN

There are volcanoes under the oceans. Some underwater volcanoes form a **mid-ocean ridge.** Mid-ocean ridges form along the edges of **plates.** In these places, the plates are moving away from each other.

Magma rises in a mid-ocean ridge. Lava flows out and cools. More magma rises behind it. The rising magma puts **pressure** on the cooling lava. It forces the lava to spread away from the mid-ocean ridge.

This process is called **seafloor spreading.** Seafloor spreading makes new rock on the ocean floor.

(TALK AND SHARE) **With your partner, use the diagram to explain how seafloor spreading takes place.**

Language Notes

Confusing Word Pairs
These words are easily mixed up.

◻ **form:**
1. a verb meaning to shape or become shaped
2. a noun meaning shape or structure

◻ **from:** a preposition used with a place, a time, a beginning, a source, or a cause

Seafloor Spreading

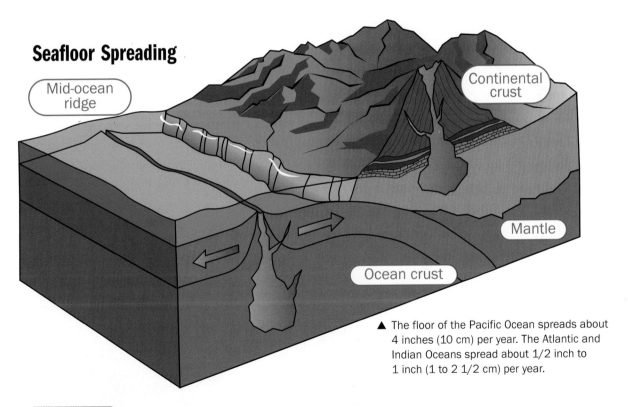

Mid-ocean ridge

Continental crust

Mantle

Ocean crust

▲ The floor of the Pacific Ocean spreads about 4 inches (10 cm) per year. The Atlantic and Indian Oceans spread about 1/2 inch to 1 inch (1 to 2 1/2 cm) per year.

VOCABULARY

mid-ocean ridge—a line of volcanoes on the bottom of an ocean
plates—large, thick pieces of Earth's crust that move
pressure—a push
seafloor spreading—the way rock is added to Earth's crust on the bottom of an ocean

Three Kinds of Rock

You can put any rock into one of three groups—igneous, sedimentary, and metamorphic.

IGNEOUS ROCK

Igneous rock forms when magma cools. If magma cools slowly, tiny **crystals** form. A crystal has flat sides and **angles.** Crystals can be many sizes and colors. Some igneous rocks contain crystals. For example, granite is an igneous rock with many crystals.

Obsidian is a kind of igneous rock called volcanic glass. It forms when magma cools very fast. There is no time for crystals to form.

SEDIMENTARY ROCK

Sedimentary rock is made from **sediment.** Sediment consists of small pieces of rock, shell, and bone.

Water, wind, and ice move sediment. The sediment **settles** in a new place. Over time, it makes a **layer.** Many layers may settle on top of the first layer. The top layers put pressure on the bottom layers. Over many, many years, the sediment is **compressed,** or squeezed together. It hardens and becomes rock. Limestone is a sedimentary rock. It often has bits of shells in it.

▲ This sedimentary rock contains a shark's tooth.

▲ Obsidian

VOCABULARY

igneous rock—the kind of rock that forms when magma cools
crystals—tiny structures with flat sides and angles
angles—corners
sedimentary rock—the kind of rock made when small pieces of rock, shell, and bone are squeezed together
sediment—small pieces of rock, shells, and bone
settles—comes to rest
layer—one thickness, like a sheet, that lies on top of or under another one
compressed—squeezed, or pressed, together

METAMORPHIC ROCK

Metamorphic means "shape change." A **metamorphic rock** is one that has been changed by heat and pressure. Heat inside Earth may slowly change a rock. Earth's crust is heavy, which means that it creates a lot of pressure. Pressure under the crust slowly changes old rock into new metamorphic rock.

For example, heat and pressure may change limestone. When this happens, limestone changes to a metamorphic rock called marble. Another metamorphic rock is slate. People make roofs out of slate.

(TALK AND SHARE) **With your partner, make a chart that shows and describes the three different types of rock.**

These homes have roofs made of slate. ▼

▲ This sedimentary rock contains pieces of igneous rock.

The Rock Cycle

A **cycle** is a **pattern** of events that occurs over and over. The **rock cycle** is a pattern of the events that change rock.

The rock cycle is like a big circle. Look at the diagram on the next page. You can start with sedimentary rock. Sedimentary rock may change if it gets buried. Heat and pressure change it into metamorphic rock. Metamorphic rock can melt and become magma. The magma cools and hardens. It is now igneous rock.

Water, wind, and ice break rock apart. When they do, we say rock is being **weathered.** The process of **weathering** breaks rock into small pieces.

The cycle continues when the pieces mix with other sediment. Slowly, water and **minerals** in the ground **cement,** or glue, the sediment together. It hardens into sedimentary rock.

Science, Technology, and Society

Minerals and Gems

Minerals are hard, nonliving substances made in Earth. Rocks are made of minerals.

People make things with minerals. For example, graphite is a mineral. The part of a pencil that leaves a mark is made of graphite.

Some minerals, called **gems,** are especially valuable to people because of their beauty. Gems include diamonds, emeralds, rubies, and sapphires.

▲ A blue sapphire from Thailand

VOCABULARY
cycle—a set of events that repeats again and again
pattern—a repeating order
rock cycle—the way rocks change and become different rocks
weathered—broken apart by water, wind, or ice
weathering—the process of being broken apart
minerals—hard, nonliving substances made in Earth
cement—stick together
gems—minerals valued for their beauty

The Rock Cycle

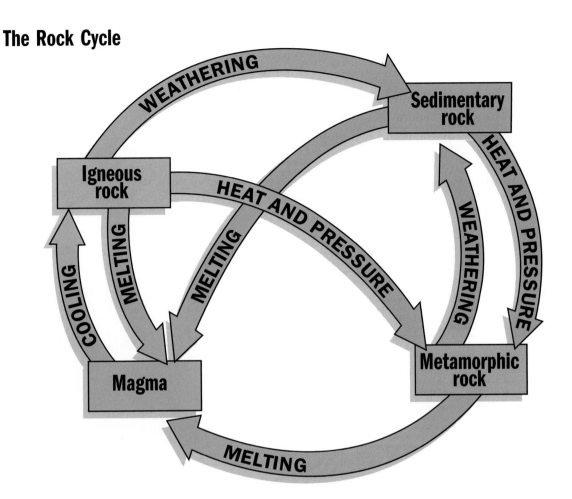

Sedimentary rock can also melt into magma. It can break apart and make new sedimentary rock. Igneous rock can turn into metamorphic rock. Any rock can break apart and become sedimentary rock. All of these processes usually take thousands of years.

TALK AND SHARE With your partner, talk about at least 3 ways rock changes during the rock cycle.

Summary

Rock can form on or below Earth's surface. The 3 types of rock on Earth are igneous, sedimentary, and metamorphic rock. Each type of rock can change into other kinds of rock. The rock cycle shows how this happens.

Interpreting

Interpreting Observations

When you interpret, you decide what something means. For example, when a geologist interprets something, the geologist begins to understand what he or she sees. You can interpret observations about rock. A journal can help you organize and interpret observations.

Observation Journal

Observations
1. This rock has shiny parts.
2. Parts of the rock have flat sides.
3. The lumps in the rock look like crystals.

Interpretation
This is an igneous rock.

Quartz ▶

Practice Interpreting

1. Draw Look at a rock. It can be on a building, on the ground, or in a piece of jewelry. Draw what you see. With a partner, decide whether the rock is igneous, sedimentary, or metamorphic. Explain your interpretation.

2. Write Now use your journal to record observations you make about a rock that you see. Is it rough or smooth? Does it have layers? Are there shiny places? Is there sediment in the rock? When you are done recording, interpret your observations. Write a paragraph that tells about your rock. Include details that helped you decide if the rock was igneous, sedimentary, or metamorphic. Words from the Word Bank can help you.

Word Bank

color
crystals
pieces

rough
shiny
smooth

observe
feel

Activities

Grammar Spotlight

Using Active and Passive Verbs A verb is active if a subject *does* the action in the sentence. A verb is passive if the subject *receives* the action. A passive verb uses a form of the verb *be* plus a past participle. Try to use active verbs instead of passive verbs as much as you can.

Verb Type	Example	What to Notice
Active	*Water moves sediment.*	*Water* does the action.
Passive	*Sediment is moved by water.*	*Sediment* receives the action.

Rewrite this sentence to make it active.

Rock is changed by heat and pressure.

Partner Practice

Building with Rock Imagine that you and your partner are going to build a house out of rock. Together, decide if you will build it from igneous rock, sedimentary rock, or metamorphic rock. Why would you use that kind of rock?

Oral Language

Make Observations Look at the pictures of rock on page 41. Tell your partner what you observe in each picture. Then ask your partner to make more observations about each picture.

Hands On

Rock Cycle Poster Make your own poster showing the rock cycle. Collect pictures of rocks to show the different kinds. Create labels to tell what happens as rock changes.

The Changing
Surface of Earth

Here you'll learn about how the surface of Earth changes every day. You'll also learn how to organize data and practice comparing and contrasting changes.

Building Background

▲ In the summer, my brothers and I swim in a river by our house.

■ **How do you think this river is changing the surface of Earth?**

■ **How did these rocks form?**

■ **How is this river like ones you have visited?**

The surface of Earth changes every day. Wind, water, gravity, and even living things cause weathering, erosion, and deposition. These changes can be fast or slow.

1 ## Weathering and Erosion

Over millions of years, the Colorado River slowly carved out the Grand Canyon.

2 ## Deposition

Wind carries sand and puts it down. On a windy day, the pattern in the sand can change quickly.

Key Concepts

weathering   erosion   deposition

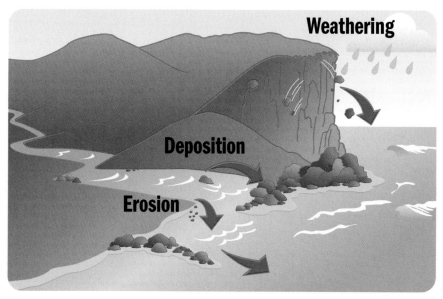

Weathering

Deposition

Erosion

Weathering breaks rocks apart.

Erosion moves rocks from place to place.

Deposition puts rocks down in a new place.

Water on Earth

Earth

Oceans

Glaciers

Water covers almost 75% of Earth's surface.

Oceans hold 97% of Earth's water. Each day ocean water moves tons of sediment.

A little more than 2% of Earth's water is frozen in glaciers. Glaciers change the surface of Earth when they move.

Organize Data

As part of the science process, you organize data, or put it in order. One way to organize data is by making a Venn Diagram. A Venn Diagram shows how two things are alike (similar) and how they are different. To make a Venn Diagram, follow these steps.

1. Draw two circles that overlap. Label each circle.

2. Put similarities in the middle part. Put differences in the outside parts.

Look at this Venn Diagram. It shows data about two groups of mountains. Notice the age of each set of mountains.

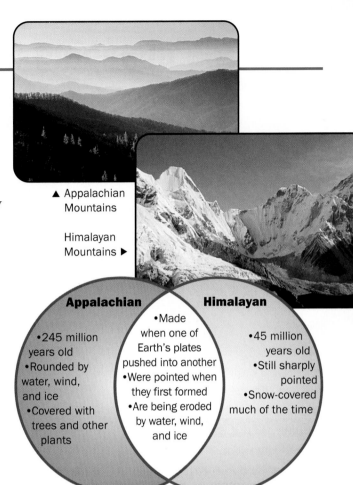

▲ Appalachian Mountains

Himalayan Mountains ▶

Appalachian
- 245 million years old
- Rounded by water, wind, and ice
- Covered with trees and other plants

- Made when one of Earth's plates pushed into another
- Were pointed when they first formed
- Are being eroded by water, wind, and ice

Himalayan
- 45 million years old
- Still sharply pointed
- Snow-covered much of the time

Freshwater

About 1% of Earth's water is the freshwater found in lakes and rivers or flowing underground.

Caves

Underground water may hollow out caves.

The Changing Surface of Earth

The surface of Earth changes by weathering, erosion, and deposition. Heat, cold, wind, water, and gravity cause these processes. The changes can happen quickly or slowly.

▲ Soil includes small pieces of rock.

Weathering

Weathering breaks rocks into pieces. Weathering happens in two ways.

CHEMICAL WEATHERING

Chemical weathering changes the **chemicals** inside rocks. For example, salt is a chemical in some rocks. If water **dissolves** the salt, the rock starts to break apart.

Some rock has **iron** in it. Iron will **rust** when water and air touch it. The rock falls apart if it gets too rusty.

Chemical weathering helps create **soil.** When water weathers rock, small pieces mix with the water and air. Plants grow in this mixture.

Chemical weathering caused these iron-rich rocks to rust and turn a reddish color. ▶

VOCABULARY

weathering—the process of being broken apart by wind, water, ice, and living things
chemical weathering—the process that changes the materials that make up rock
chemicals—materials found in Earth and around Earth
dissolves—breaks apart in a liquid
iron—a metal chemical
rust—change by reacting with air or water
soil—a mixture of rock pieces, water, and air in which plants can grow

MECHANICAL WEATHERING

Mechanical weathering changes the size and shape of rock. Heat, wind, water, ice, and living things can cause mechanical weathering.

- Hot objects **expand,** or get bigger. Rock breaks if it expands too much.

- Water flows into cracks in rock. In freezing weather, ice forms in these cracks. Ice pushes against the sides of the crack and widens the crack. If the crack gets too wide, pieces of rock break off.

- Living things can break rock apart, too. Plant roots can grow into cracks and make rock break apart. Animals and insects break rock as they dig holes in the ground.

- Water, ice, and wind move **sediment.** Moving sediment will wear away rock.

▲ These ferns in the Grand Canyon are causing mechanical weathering.

(**TALK AND SHARE**) **Tell your partner some of the ways weathering changes the surface of Earth.**

Science, Technology, and Society

Chalk

Most chalk formed about 100 million years ago. It formed on ocean bottoms. Tiny shells and crystals stuck together and became sedimentary rock.

Mechanical weathering easily breaks chalk. Because it breaks easily, chalk is useful. Chalk is so soft that tiny pieces break off when you write with it. They stick to the chalkboard or sidewalk. People use chalk when they make some kinds of cement. Even some powders that help clean teeth have ground-up chalk in them.

VOCABULARY

mechanical weathering—the process that changes the size and shape of rock
expand—get bigger
sediment—a mixture of small pieces of rock, bone, and shell

Erosion

Erosion moves rock. Erosion happens on mountains, in fields, on beaches, and even under water. Erosion by wind, water, and **gravity** can completely change the way the surface of Earth looks.

WIND AND WATER

Wind sweeps up sediment. In some places, it may carry all the sediment away, leaving only **bare** rock.

Rivers wash against the land. The water pulls sediment from the land. It falls loose into the water and turns the water brown.

Waves crash onto land. Waves pick up sediment, including sand. The waves carry the sediment out into the water. Some waves carry sediment back to the beach. That's why a beach changes shape over time.

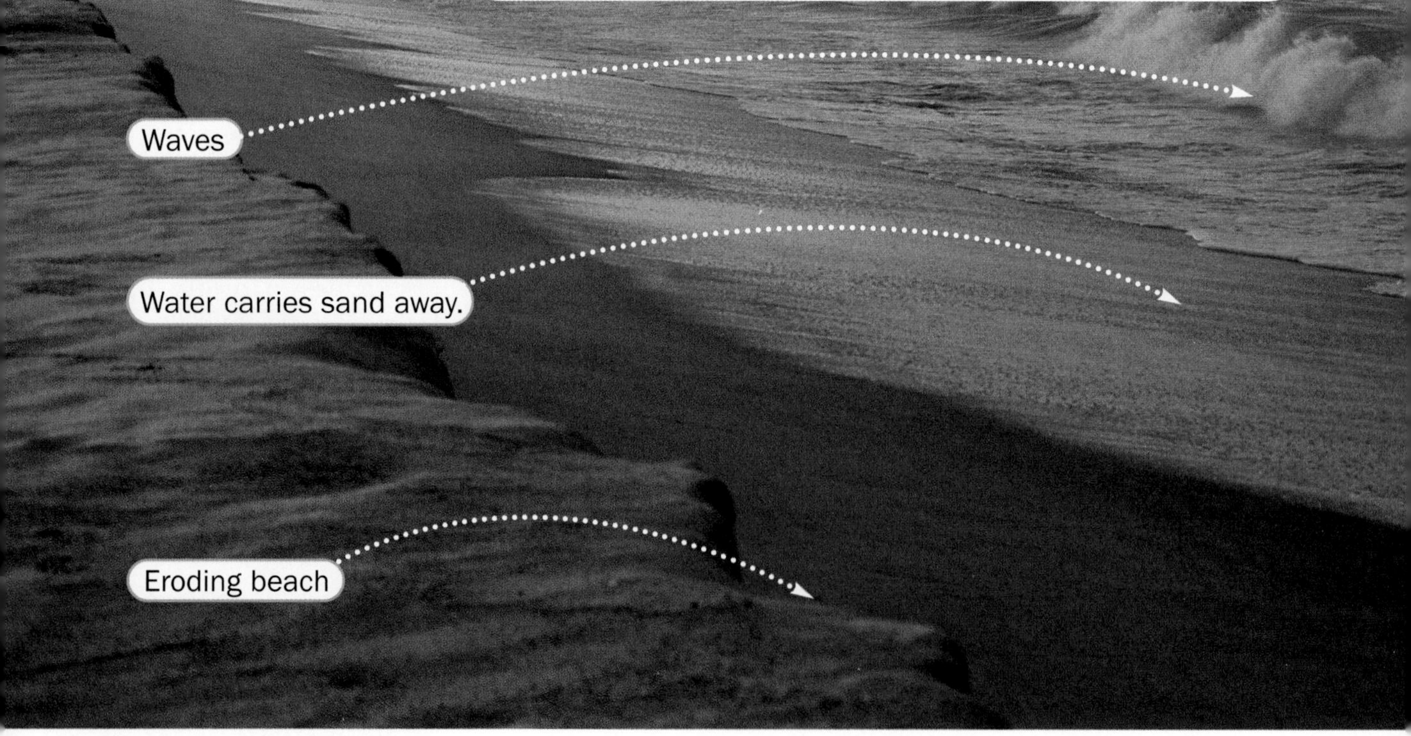

Waves

Water carries sand away.

Eroding beach

▲ Waves carry sand into water through the process of erosion.

VOCABULARY

erosion—the process of moving rock from place to place
gravity—a force that pulls things together
bare—not covered

Landslide

Gravity

▲ A landslide caused damage in El Salvador in 2001. An earthquake caused the landslide.

GRAVITY

Gravity is the **force** that pulls things together. It keeps your feet on the ground. Gravity is also the reason rock falls down a mountain, not up. Gravity pulls the rock from high places to lower places.

Gravity can move a lot of rock at one time. A **landslide** happens when gravity pulls many rocks down a hill. One rock may slip out of place. Gravity pulls it down. On its way down, it may crash into other rocks. If they pull loose, they fall. Erosion caused by a landslide can quickly change the way a mountain looks.

(TALK AND SHARE) **With your partner, talk about ways the wind, water, and gravity can change the surface of Earth.**

VOCABULARY

force—a push or a pull
landslide—many rocks moving fast down a hill

Deposition

Deposition builds up the surface of Earth. Water, wind, and ice leave behind, or deposit, **layers** of sediment. The layers can be thick or thin.

When loose sediment is deposited on top of a rock, a new layer of **sedimentary rock** begins to form. It forms on top of the older rock. **Geologists** have a name for the layers of sedimentary rock in a single place. Geologists call each set of layers a **bed.**

One at a time, new layers are deposited on top of older layers. Each new layer is younger than the ones beneath it. The oldest layer of rock is on the bottom of the bed. The youngest layer lies on top.

Layers are not always easy to see. They are often under the ground. You may see them if they get pushed up from Earth's crust. You may also see them where erosion has cut into the ground.

(**TALK AND SHARE**) **Ask your partner how deposition can change the surface of Earth.**

▲ This **delta** formed when a river deposited sediment. A delta is the area of sediment that a river leaves at its mouth, the place where it empties into a lake or an ocean.

Sediment layers are not always the same color. When the colors are different, you can see where one layer stops and another begins. ▶

VOCABULARY

deposition—the process of building up the surface of Earth by putting down rock

layers—pieces, like sheets, that lie on top of or under other pieces

sedimentary rock—the kind of rock made when pieces of rock, bone, and shell are squeezed together

geologists—scientists who study the whole Earth

bed—one set of layers of sedimentary rock

delta—a large area of sediment put down where water flows into a lake or an ocean

Fast Changes and Slow Changes

Rivers and **glaciers** cause weathering, erosion, and deposition. These processes may be fast or slow.

FAST CHANGES

Fast-flowing rivers wash away sediment. Fast-moving water with rock in it cuts into Earth. It makes a V-shaped **valley.** The steep valley may form in hundreds or thousands of years. That is a short time in the history of Earth.

Floods happen when a river spills over its sides. Fast-moving floodwater can wash soil away from a field.

▲ Rivers can flow very fast.

SLOW CHANGES

Glaciers slowly dig into the surface of Earth. A glacier has time to make a U-shaped valley. It may take tens of thousands of years to make a glacier valley.

Rivers and glaciers also deposit sediment on the surface of Earth. Sediment slowly makes the surface higher. Deposits from melting glaciers can make hills and ridges, but this takes thousands and thousands of years.

(TALK AND SHARE) **Talk with your partner about how rivers, floods, and glaciers change the surface of Earth.**

◄ A glacier meets a lake in British Columbia. Glaciers move very slowly.

Summary

Weathering, erosion, and deposition change the surface of Earth. The changes may happen quickly or may take thousands of years.

VOCABULARY

glaciers—big areas of ice and snow that do not melt each year
valley—a low place between hills or mountains
floods—water spilling over the sides of a river

Comparing and Contrasting

Comparing and Contrasting Change

When you compare and contrast, you study two things. You see how they are alike and how they are different.

At times, the surface of Earth changes quickly. Other changes take thousands or millions of years. Study this Venn Diagram to compare and contrast speeds of change.

Venn Diagram

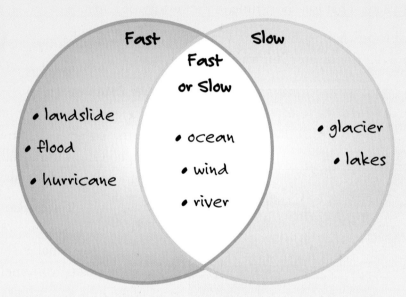

Fast

Slow

Fast or Slow

• landslide
• flood
• hurricane

• ocean
• wind
• river

• glacier
• lakes

Practice Comparing and Contrasting

1. Draw With a partner, make a Venn Diagram that shows slow changes and fast changes in sand. Think about hot beaches and crashing waves. Talk about how you can compare the different speeds of change.

2. Write In a paragraph, compare and contrast fast changes caused by water and slow changes caused by water. Think about glaciers and rivers. Tell how the slow changes and fast changes are alike and how they are different. Exchange paragraphs with a partner and check each other's paragraphs with the Check Your Writing checklist.

Check Your Writing

Make sure you
- ☐ Use complete sentences.
- ☐ Use a period at the end of each sentence.
- ☐ Spell all the words correctly.

Activities

Using *much* to Make a Comparison Stronger Use *much* to compare two things when you want one thing to seem greater or stronger than the other.

Comparison	Strong Comparison
A flooding river carries more sediment than a calm river.	*A river carries much more sediment than a puddle.*
Mud slides down a hill more slowly than small rocks.	*Mud slides down a hill much more slowly than large rocks.*

   Think of a sentence that compares rivers and glaciers. Use the word *much* in your sentence. Write it in your notebook.

Sand Slide   Get a dish of sand from your teacher. With a partner, take turns moving the sand. You may use your hands, a tool, or some water. First, use the sand to show erosion. Next, use it to show deposition. Talk with your partner about what you see each time.

Organize Data   With your partner, make a Venn Diagram that compares chemical weathering and mechanical weathering. Include an example of each kind of weathering in your diagram.

Observe!   Use a magnifying glass or a hand lens to look at a small pile of sand. Observe the colors, sizes, and shapes of the different pieces. Talk with your partner or your group about everything you see in the sand. Compare and contrast the different pieces of sand you observe.

Climate and

Weather

Here you'll learn about climates and weather patterns. You'll also learn how to look for patterns and practice predicting the weather.

▲ What a crowded beach! I wonder where it is.

■ **What makes a day hot?**

■ **How can you predict what the weather will be tomorrow?**

■ **What do you do to be more comfortable on a hot day?**

Energy comes to Earth from the sun. Earth has different climate zones because its surface is curved. Energy from the sun also powers Earth's water cycle and creates weather patterns.

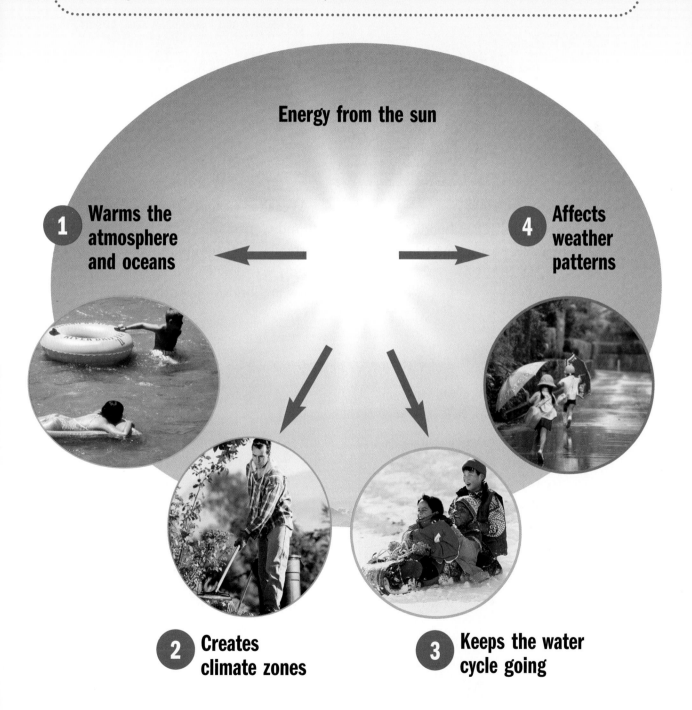

Energy from the sun

1 **Warms the atmosphere and oceans**

4 **Affects weather patterns**

2 **Creates climate zones**

3 **Keeps the water cycle going**

Key Concepts

climate   weather   temperature   precipitation

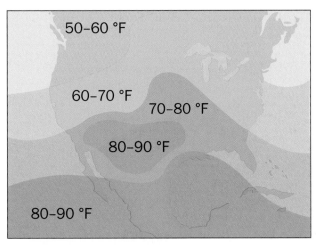

50–60 °F

60–70 °F

70–80 °F

80–90 °F

80–90 °F

Climate

A **climate** is the general pattern of weather in an area for a long time.

RAIN	P. SUN	SUNNY	P. SUN	CLOUDY
50°	58°	65°	62°	60°
M	T	W	TH	F

Weather

Weather includes **temperature,** humidity, **precipitation,** and wind at a particular time and place. Temperature is how warm or cool it is. Rain and snow are kinds of precipitation.

Hot Air and Cold Air

Hot air is lighter than cold air.

Air is heated.

Hot air rises.

The hot air inside the balloon rises up through the cooler air surrounding it.

Look for Patterns

Patterns are groups of actions or events that are repeated. For example, weather happens in patterns. When you look for patterns, follow these 3 steps.

1. Find events that happen over and over.

2. Record the events on a chart.

3. Describe the way events repeat.

What pattern can you see here?

Weather Chart

	Monday	Tuesday	Wednesday	Thursday	Friday	Saturday	Sunday
High Temperature	45 °F	43 °F	41 °F	29 °F	35 °F	33 °F	28 °F
Low Temperature	32 °F	33 °F	34 °F	26 °F	29 °F	24 °F	24 °F
Precipitation and Clouds	rain	cloudy	cloudy	none	none	none	cloudy

Hot air stays up.

Cool air comes down.

Air inside the balloon loses heat as the balloon rises. The balloon stays up because the pilot adds heat with a flame.

To land, the pilot lets the air inside the balloon lose heat. As the air inside cools, the balloon sinks to Earth.

Climate and Weather

Energy from the sun warms the curved surface of Earth. The curve of the surface creates different climate zones. Energy from the sun also powers Earth's water cycle and creates weather patterns.

Sun, Atmosphere, and Ocean

Energy from the sun is called **solar energy.** Solar energy heats Earth.

Earth's **atmosphere** is made of air. This air keeps Earth warm, like a blanket. Rocks, water, and soil are all heated by the sun. They help keep the air warm, too.

Oceans can hold heat. It takes a long time for the **temperature** of water to change. Oceans near the **equator** are usually warm. Oceans near the poles are usually cold.

(TALK AND SHARE) **With your partner, talk about how the sun affects the temperature of Earth.**

Science, Technology, and Society

Temperature Inversions and Smog

Earth is usually warmest close to the surface. However, sometimes air close to the ground can be colder than air higher up. This is called a temperature **inversion.**

In cities such as Los Angeles and Mexico City, temperature inversions sometimes make the air dangerous. The cool air keeps **smog,** a combination of smoke and fog, close to the ground. Mountains around the city stop the low, cool air and smog from blowing away. The smog stays until the cool air becomes warm. Then the smog rises and blows away.

▲ Smog over Mexico City

VOCABULARY

energy—the power to make something change
solar energy—energy from the sun
atmosphere—the layer of air that surrounds Earth
temperature—amount of heat

equator—an imaginary line around Earth's middle
inversion—the condition of being upside down
smog—dirty air made of smoke and fog

Climates of the World

A **climate** is a long-term pattern of air temperatures and **precipitation.** Earth has 3 major climate **zones** on each side of the equator: tropical, temperate, and polar. Look at the diagram of Earth on the right.

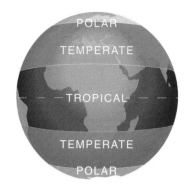

- ■ **Tropical** climates are always warm. They are near the equator, where the sun shines directly on Earth. Warm ocean water helps heat the air.

- ■ **Temperate** climates are between the tropical climates and the North and South Poles. The surface of Earth is curved away from the sun, so the sun does not shine directly on it. At different times during the year, Earth tips toward or away from the sun. This changes the amount of solar energy that reaches a particular location. Temperate climate zones have both hot and cold seasons.

- ■ **Polar** climate zones are cold all the time. The least amount of solar energy reaches them. The ocean water stays cold all year, which keeps the air cold.

Oceans and mountains affect the climate within each zone. In temperate climates, ocean water can keep nearby air from being very hot or cold. Mountains near an ocean can block ocean winds. The climate on the side of the mountains away from the ocean is hot and dry, because no **moisture** reaches it from the ocean winds.

(TALK AND SHARE) **With your partner, talk about why some climates are cooler than others and describe the 3 climate zones.**

Tropical climate

Temperate climate

Polar climate

VOCABULARY

climate—the general pattern of weather for a long time in a big area
precipitation—water that falls in the form of fog, rain, snow, or sleet
zones—areas or regions that have special characteristics

tropical—warm and wet
temperate—having a cycle of cold and hot temperatures
polar—cold and dry
moisture—wetness

The Water Cycle

Water moves around Earth in a constant **cycle.** In the atmosphere, **clouds** are made of tiny drops of water or pieces of ice. Precipitation from clouds falls on the land and into rivers, lakes, and oceans. Water then **evaporates** back into the air. This pattern is called the **water cycle.** Look at the diagram below.

WATER ON EARTH

Oceans hold 97 percent of Earth's water. Almost all of the other water on Earth is in rivers, lakes, and glaciers. Some water **seeps** into the ground. It moves under the surface of Earth. Someday the water might reach the surface again as a **spring,** but this may only happen after thousands of years.

Water that moves over the ground instead of seeping in is called **runoff.** This water moves from the land into rivers, lakes, and oceans.

The Water Cycle

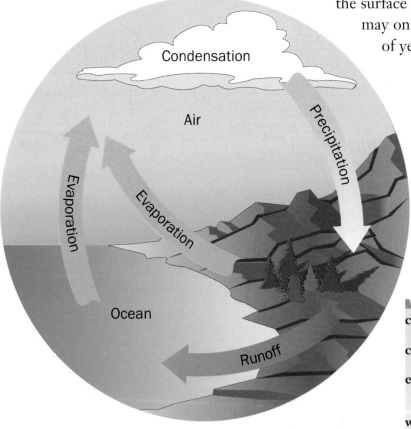

Condensation

Air

Precipitation

Evaporation

Evaporation

Ocean

Runoff

VOCABULARY

cycle—a set of events that repeats over and over

clouds—groups of tiny water drops or pieces of ice that hang in the air

evaporates—turns from a liquid to a vapor, or gas. This process is called *evaporation.*

water cycle—the pattern of water moving between the air and the ground

seeps—drips down slowly

spring—a place where underground water flows to the surface of Earth

runoff—water that moves over the top of the ground

EVAPORATION

Evaporation puts water into the air. Solar energy changes water into **vapor.** The vapor rises into the air. You can see something similar when water **boils.**

Water evaporates all the time from oceans, lakes, and rivers. Wind helps evaporation happen even faster. People measure the amount of water vapor in the air. This measurement is called **humidity.**

CONDENSATION AND PRECIPITATION

Precipitation forms when water vapor cools in the air. The vapor *condenses*, or turns back into liquid water. This process is called **condensation.** In the process, very small water drops form and group together into clouds. When the drops get too heavy, rain, snow, or sleet falls out of the clouds as precipitation.

The water cycle is balanced. This means that, overall, the amount of water that evaporates equals the amount of precipitation that falls.

▲ Water evaporates from a hot spring in Yellowstone National Park, Wyoming.

◄ Precipitation may fall to Earth in the form of rain.

TALK AND SHARE **With your partner, describe the water cycle and how it works.**

VOCABULARY

vapor—a gas, such as air
boils—heats to a high temperature. When water *boils*, it changes into water vapor.

humidity—a measure of the amount of water in the air
condensation—the process of turning from a vapor, or gas, to a liquid

Weather Patterns and Problems

Weather is different from climate. A climate stays the same for many years. **Weather,** however, can change from one minute to the next.

HOW WEATHER CHANGES

An **air mass** is a big area of air that has the same temperature and amount of water (humidity). An air mass can be cold or warm. Sometimes cold air masses meet warm air masses. The places where air masses meet are called **fronts.** Weather changes along fronts.

A **cold front** happens when cold air pushes under a warm air mass. It pushes the warm air up quickly. Water condenses as the warm air cools. It brings tall clouds and thunderstorms.

A **warm front** happens when warm air blows into cold air. The warm air moves up slowly over the cold air. Water condenses into a long line of clouds. The rain that follows is a gentle rain with soft winds.

Each pattern of weather has its own kind of clouds. High, thin white clouds are a sign of good weather. So are puffy white clouds. Big gray clouds are a sign that precipitation is on the way.

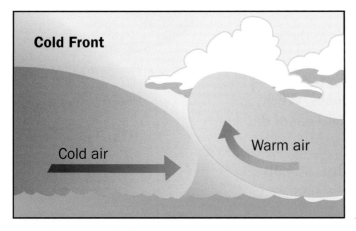

Cold Front
Cold air
Warm air

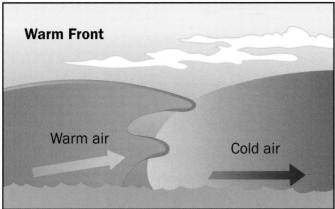

Warm Front
Warm air
Cold air

VOCABULARY

weather—the temperature, humidity, precipitation, and wind at a particular place and time

air mass—a large area of air that has the same temperature and amount of water (humidity)

fronts—the places where cold and warm air masses meet

cold front—a place where cold air pushes up warm air

warm front—a place where warm air moves over cold air

DANGEROUS WEATHER

When air masses mix, big storms can occur. **Tornadoes** are caused when two air masses meet and form twisting clouds. The wind in a tornado can be faster than 300 miles (480 km) per hour. A tornado can rip buildings to pieces. The central part of the United States has the most tornadoes on Earth.

Hurricanes are powerful storms that start over an ocean. They can have winds as fast as 160 miles (260 km) per hour. They are dangerous when they hit land. Their winds tear apart buildings and push ocean waves high onto land. A lot of rain falls during a hurricane and can cause floods. Many lives can be lost if people stay where a hurricane happens.

▲ Tornado in South Dakota

(TALK AND SHARE) **With your partner, list some differences between tornadoes and hurricanes.**

Summary

Earth has tropical, temperate, and polar climate zones. They are caused by the curve of Earth's surface, which means that solar energy reaches Earth in different amounts. Solar energy also keeps the water cycle going. Weather can change quickly in each climate.

VOCABULARY

tornadoes—twisting storms with very fast winds
hurricanes—swirling storms that start over an ocean

Predicting

Predicting the Weather

You are predicting when you say what you think will happen in the future. A scientific prediction is not just a guess. It has evidence to support it. You can make a prediction based on patterns of evidence.

- Study this Weather Chart. It shows how you can keep track of temperature and precipitation patterns in your area.

- Many factors affect the weather. A Weather Chart like this can give you evidence that may help you predict the weather.

Weather Chart

	Monday	Tuesday	Wednesday	Thursday	Friday	Saturday	Sunday
High Temperature	45 °F	43 °F	41 °F	29 °F	35 °F	33 °F	28 °F
Low Temperature	32 °F	33 °F	34 °F	26 °F	29 °F	24 °F	24 °F
Precipitation and Clouds	rain	cloudy	cloudy	none	none	none	cloudy

Practice Predicting

1. Draw Refer to the Weather Chart above and look for patterns. Draw a picture of what you think the weather will be on the next Monday. Trade pictures with your partner and talk about your predictions.

2. Write Make a chart of the weather in your area for one week. Look for patterns in temperature, precipitation, and any other measurements or events you record. Then write your prediction of the weather for the next day. In a paragraph, explain the pattern that helps you make the prediction. Words from the Word Bank can help you.

Word Bank

sunny
cloudy
snowy
rainy
worse
better

pattern
chance
degrees
temperature

Grammar Spotlight

Using *will* to Talk About the Future   *Will* is usually used with another verb. It tells you that the action in the verb has not happened yet. It signals an action that is going to take place in the future.

Example	What It Means
If I don't wear boots, the rain will wet my shoes.	Rain hasn't wet the shoes yet, but it is going to in the future.
The newspaper says it will snow tonight.	It hasn't snowed yet, but it is going to snow during the coming night.

Write a sentence about weather for tomorrow that uses the word *will*. Read your sentence to your partner.

Oral Language

Rain Saving   Many people collect rainwater. They use the rainwater for everything from drinking to washing clothes. Talk with your partner or your family about how you could collect rain. Then discuss how you could use the rainwater you collect.

Partner Practice

Water Cycle   With a partner, talk through each part of the water cycle. Explain to your partner how evaporation works. Then have your partner explain how condensation works. Draw diagrams and use arrows to help explain the cycle. If you can, create study notes for your whole class to use.

Hands On

Look for Patterns   Find out your climate zone. Use the library, the Internet, or other sources. Talk about your climate zone with a partner. Look for weather patterns in the zone. Then make a poster about the temperature and precipitation in your climate zone. Use pictures from newspapers to show what the weather in your climate zone is like. Finally, prepare a 30-second talk about your climate zone for the class.

Earth, Sun, and Moon

Here you'll learn about Earth, the sun, and the moon and how they move. You'll also learn how to use a model and practice describing a model.

▲ I usually see the sun set, but I don't wake up early enough to see it rise!

- ■ **Why does the sun rise and set?**
- ■ **Why isn't the moon big and round every night?**
- ■ **Where does the moon go during the day?**

Earth moves around the sun, and the moon moves around Earth in a pattern. Their movements explain night, day, and the seasons. The pattern of movements also explains how the moon looks to us and how eclipses happen.

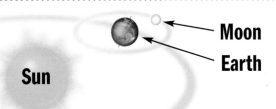

Moon

Earth

Sun

This pattern of movements explains

1 Day and night

2 Seasons

3 How the moon looks

Key Concepts

rotates   axis   revolves

Axis

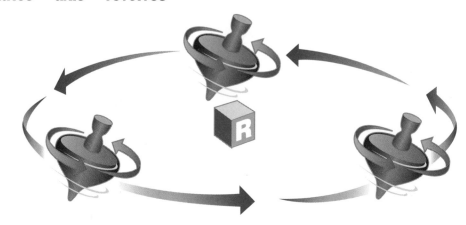

Rotates

When something **rotates,** it spins on an axis. An **axis** is an imaginary line straight through something.

Revolves

When something **revolves,** it moves in a path around another object.

Phases of the Moon

Why does the shape of the moon seem to change? Light from the sun bounces off one side of the moon's surface.

Waxing Crescent

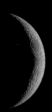

Waxing means "getting bigger." A crescent is a thin, curved slice.

First Quarter

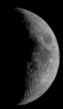

You see half of the moon's lighted surface.

Waxing Gibbous

Gibbous means "hump shaped." The lighted area is much larger.

Use a Model

A model is a copy of an object or a system. A system is a set of objects that work together. Using a model helps you think about how the parts work together. When you understand how the model works, you will better understand how the real object or system works.

Hundreds of years ago, some people thought the sun revolved around Earth. Their models had Earth in the center. Today we know Earth revolves around the sun. Our model puts the sun in the center. Look at today's model. To use this model, follow these steps.

1. Study the model until you can imagine the movements of Earth and the moon.

2. As you learn about day, night, and the seasons, decide how the model helps you understand what you learn.

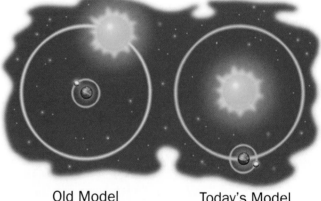

Old Model   Today's Model

The shape we see changes as the sun lights up different parts of that side.

| Full Moon | Waning Gibbous | Third Quarter | Waning Crescent |

Earth, Sun, and Moon

O ur Earth, moon, and sun are parts of the same system. The relationship among them explains day and night, the seasons, and how the moon looks from Earth.

▲ Earth rotates on its axis once each day.

Day and Night

Earth has **alternating** light and dark times. We call these times day and night. When it is day on one side of Earth, it is night on the other side. We have day and night because Earth spins around.

24 Time Zones

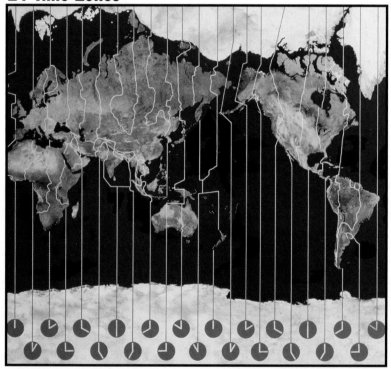

▲ Earth is divided into 24 time zones to represent the 24 hours in a day.

ROTATION

Earth spins, or **rotates,** on its **axis.** Think of the axis as an imaginary stick. The axis goes straight through Earth. One end sticks out at the North Pole. The other end sticks out at the South Pole.

Earth rotates once on its axis every 24 hours. One day is equal to one complete turn of Earth on its axis.

VOCABULARY

alternating—taking turns or changing back and forth
rotates—turns in place, spins
axis—an imaginary line through the center

Sunrise

DAY STARTS

Some part of Earth is always facing the sun. You have daytime when the part of Earth where you live faces the sun. Have you ever seen the sun rise? The sun is not moving. Earth is. At sunrise, the part of Earth where you live is rotating toward the sun. All morning this part of Earth turns a little bit more toward the sun. At about noon, this part of Earth completely faces the sun.

DAY ENDS

In the afternoon, the part of Earth where you live starts to turn away from the sun. As this part of Earth rotates away from the sun, afternoon turns into evening. The day gets darker. By nighttime, the part of Earth where you live is facing away from the sun.

(TALK AND SHARE) **Explain to your partner why Earth has a regular pattern of day and night.**

Sunset

Spring

Summer

Fall

Winter

Seasons

Earth **revolves** around the sun. We say it **orbits** the sun. It takes Earth one year to go all the way around the sun. People divide a year into 4 periods of time called **seasons.** Each season lasts a few months.

The axis of Earth is **tilted.** It remains tilted as Earth orbits the sun. Some part of Earth is always tilted toward the sun. The tilt and Earth's location in its orbit determine what season it will be.

SUMMER AND WINTER

Look at the diagram on page 83. Find the picture of Earth that is marked June. Below is a close-up. The north end of the axis is tilting toward the sun. That means the northern half of Earth is getting a lot of direct sunlight. The sun's energy heats the air and the ground. This hot season is called summer. Summer happens where Earth tilts toward the sun.

Look again at the picture. Notice that the south end of the axis tilts away from the sun. The southern half of Earth gets less direct sunlight. As a result, the air and the ground are cool. The season there is the opposite of summer. It is winter.

Now look at the picture of Earth marked December. The north end of Earth's axis tilts away from the sun. Here the northern half of Earth gets less sunlight. The season in Earth's northern half is not summer anymore. What do you think the season is? (Yes, it's winter.)

VOCABULARY

revolves—travels around something
orbits—revolves in a way that is controlled by gravity
seasons—spring, summer, fall, and winter
tilted—slanted; tipped

SPRING AND FALL

Now look at the picture of Earth that is marked March. It shows spring in North America. Find the picture of Earth that shows fall in North America.

In spring and fall, neither end of Earth's axis tilts toward the sun. The north and south parts of Earth receive about the same amount of sun.

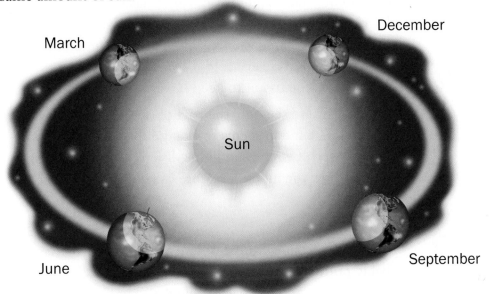

March

December

Sun

June

September

(TALK AND SHARE) **Ask your partner to explain to you how it can be summer and winter on Earth at the same time.**

Science, Technology, and Society

Calendars

A calendar is a tool that people invented to keep track of time. Our calendar for a year has 365 days. That is just a little less than the time it takes Earth to revolve around, or orbit, the sun one time. Every 4 years, the calendar has 366 days.

Calendars help us. They let people know what kind of weather to expect. Farmers use calendars to decide when to plant seeds. Scientists and travelers plan trips to different climates based on calendars.

▲ The rocks in Stonehenge possibly were used as an ancient calendar. Stonehenge was created sometime between 3000 B.C. and 1000 B.C. in England.

Low tide

▲ Mont St. Michel at low tide. At low tide, people can walk to this island off the coast of France.

High tide

▲ At high tide, Mont St. Michel cannot be reached by foot, except by a bridge.

The Moon

Just as Earth revolves around the sun, the **moon** revolves around Earth. **Gravity** causes the moon to orbit Earth. Gravity is the pulling **force** that keeps you on the ground. The gravity of Earth also pulls on the moon.

MOON AND SUN

The moon rotates and, like Earth, it has morning and night. One day on the moon lasts about 15 Earth days. One night is also 15 Earth days. During the day, the moon is hot. At night, the moon is very cold, because there is no atmosphere on the moon to keep it warm.

From Earth, we see only the part of the moon that is lit by the sun. The moon seems to change shape, because as it rotates and revolves, the sun lights different parts. These changes in how the moon looks are called its **phases** (see pages 78–79).

TIDES

Have you ever been to the ocean? If you have, you have probably noticed that the water is low during part of the day and high during another part of the day. These changes in the water level of the ocean are called **tides.**

Tides on Earth are mostly caused by the gravity of the moon. At high tide, the ocean is pulled toward land. The beach becomes a narrow strip of sand. At low tide, the ocean is pulled away from the shore and the beach is much wider.

(TALK AND SHARE) **With your partner, talk about some of the ways the moon is different from Earth.**

VOCABULARY
moon—an object that orbits a planet
gravity—a force that pulls things together
force—a push or a pull
phases—regular changes in how the moon looks from Earth
tides—daily changes in the height of water along coasts

Eclipses

Sometimes the position of the moon makes it seem as though the sun has disappeared. Sometimes the position of Earth makes it seem as though the moon has disappeared. However, the sun and moon do not really disappear. Instead, they are in shadows. The moon and Earth can both make shadows. These shadows are called **eclipses.**

SOLAR ECLIPSES

You make a shadow when the sun shines on you. Your body blocks the sun and your shadow is on the ground. The moon can make a shadow, too.

Sometimes the moon comes between Earth and the sun. The moon partly blocks the sun. Earth gets darker because the moon blocks sunlight. This is called a **solar eclipse.**

LUNAR ECLIPSES

Sometimes Earth is between the moon and the sun. At these times, Earth makes a shadow on the moon. This is a **lunar eclipse.** A little sunlight bends around Earth and reaches the moon. That little bit of light makes the moon look red.

(TALK AND SHARE) **Talk with your partner about what happens during a solar eclipse and during a lunar eclipse.**

Solar Eclipse

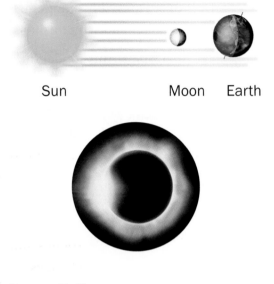

Sun   Moon   Earth

Lunar Eclipse

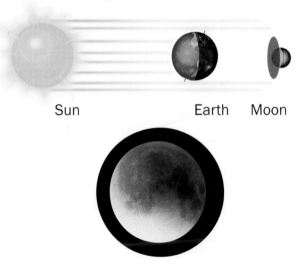

Sun   Earth   Moon

> ### Summary
> Earth, the sun, and the moon are part of a system. This system explains day and night, the seasons, how the moon looks, and eclipses.

VOCABULARY

eclipses—shadows caused by Earth or the moon
solar eclipse—the shadow made on Earth when the moon comes between Earth and the sun
lunar eclipse—the shadow made on the moon when Earth comes between the moon and the sun

Describing

Describing a Model

When you describe something, you tell about it. You can describe a model of seasons. This model will help you understand how the position of Earth changes and why this makes seasons change.

Look at this model of Earth and the sun. To describe it, you would include details like these.

Season Model

Sun

June

- The model shows the sun and Earth.

- Part of Earth is tilted toward the sun and part is tilted away from the sun.

- In the diagram, it is summer in Earth's northern part.

- It is winter in Earth's southern part.

Practice Describing

1. Draw Work with a partner and draw a model like the one above to show the season you are in now. Put Earth and the sun on your model. Add any labels you want. With your partner, talk about what your model shows.

2. Write Make the model described under Draw. Write a paragraph that describes what your model shows. Describe the locations of the sun and Earth. Also describe the season you are in right now and how it fits with your model. Then exchange papers with a partner. Check your partner's paragraph using the Check Your Writing checklist.

Check Your Writing

Make sure you
- ☐ Use complete sentences.
- ☐ Use a period at the end of each sentence.
- ☐ Spell all the words correctly.

Activities

Grammar Spotlight

Adding *ing* to a Verb   Sometimes when you add *ing* to a verb, the spelling of the original verb changes a little bit. Here are two ways you can check your spelling.

Kind of Verb	Examples	*ing* Rule	Examples
Verb that ends in *e*	*rotate* *shine*	Drop the *e*, add *ing*	*rotating* *shining*
Consonant + vowel + consonant (one-syllable verb)	*tip* *spin*	Double the consonant and add *ing*	*tipping* *spinning*

Write two sentences. In the first, add *ing* to the verb *stop*. In the second, add *ing* to the verb *use*.

Hands On

Use a Model   With a small group, create models to show the positions of the sun, the moon, and Earth for each of the examples below. Use items in your classroom to show light and shadows. Try different objects and talk about what works best and why.

- Daytime in North America
- Spring in South America
- A solar eclipse
- A night with a full moon

Oral Language

Pattern Rhyme   With a partner, read this rhyme aloud:

> *Earth revolves around the sun.*
> *It takes one year before it's done.*
> *Different places have different seasons.*
> *Earth is tilted—that's the reason!*

Now work with a partner to write a rhyme about the way Earth moves in a pattern. Here are some rhyming words to help you: *sun, run, fun, one, done—night, sight, right, light—spin, pin, begin, in—place, space, race—rotate, locate—repeat, meet—season, reason—day, say, way.*

Natural
Resources

Here you'll learn about natural resources, the things we take from Earth to help us live. You'll also learn how to use math to organize data and practice summarizing data.

Building Background

▲ I wonder where these places are. I saw a dam like that in Nevada once.

■ **What do these pictures make you think about?**

■ **What resources can you see?**

■ **How could you use these resources?**

A resource is something humans use to help make life better. Earth has two kinds of natural resources. Renewable resources never get used up. Nonrenewable resources can get used up.

1 → Natural Resources

2

Renewable Resources
Wind energy makes these windmills turn. Wind is a renewable resource.

Nonrenewable Resources
The coal being mined here will run out. Coal is a nonrenewable resource.

3 Conservation
When we use resources wisely, they last longer.

Key Concepts

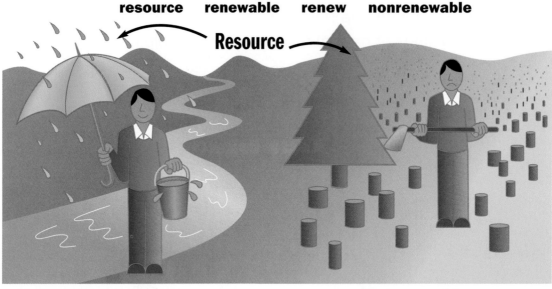

resource   renewable   renew   nonrenewable

Resource

Renewable   Nonrenewable

A **resource** is anything you use, like coal, oil, water, or the wind. A resource is **renewable** if it cannot run out. **Renew** means *to make new.*

A resource is **nonrenewable** if you can run out of it.

What Are Fossil Fuels?

Fossil fuels are sources of energy. Energy is stored in dead plant material.

Coal

Broken plants fall to the ground and pile up in layers.

In time, the dead plants start to rot. The partly rotted dead plants are called peat.

Over many years, heat and pressure change peat into coal. Most coal is sedimentary rock that can burn.

Skill Building

Use Math to Organize Data

When you work as a scientist, you may need to use math when you organize data. One way to organize data is with a pie chart.

Making a pie chart means using math. A circle has 360 degrees. Look at the example below. Out of all the electricity in Canada, 75 percent comes from hydroelectric power and 25 percent comes from other resources. To make a pie chart for these data, you would follow these steps.

1. Multiply 360 degrees by 25 percent (360 x 0.25 = 90).

2. Draw a circle. Use a protractor to make an angle of 90 degrees inside the circle.

3. Check your work: Multiply 360 degrees by 75 percent (360 x 0.75 = 270).

4. Measure your angles and make sure you have a 270-degree wedge and a 90-degree wedge in the pie chart.

5. Color in the wedges, label them, and add a title.

Canadian Electricity Sources

Other resources 25%

90°

270°

Hydroelectric power 75%

Petroleum

Dead ocean plants pile up in layers. Over millions of years, these layers turn into a thick liquid called petroleum.

Gasoline and oil are fossil fuels that come from petroleum. A car engine burns gasoline and oil.

Natural Resources

People need resources, such as water, to live.

People use electricity every day to light buildings, cook food, and play music. ▼

R esources are things that people use to meet their needs. Natural resources on Earth can be renewable or nonrenewable.

Natural Resources

Natural resources are part of Earth. We use them to make energy, grow food, build things, and make clothing.

ENERGY RESOURCES

People use many natural resources to create **energy**, the power to make something change.

- We use **solar energy** to heat buildings and to heat water for cooking. People collect solar energy in equipment that holds it as heat or that turns it into **electricity.**

- People also use wind and water to make electricity. Windmills can pump water from deep inside Earth up to the surface. The moving water spins water wheels. Most water wheels are used to make electricity.

- We burn **coal** and **petroleum** to get electricity and heat. Petroleum fuels machines such as furnaces, airplanes, and cars. People also make products like plastic from petroleum.

VOCABULARY

natural resources—things found on Earth that people use to meet their needs
energy—the power to make something change
solar energy—energy that comes from the sun
electricity—a source of power used for heat, light, and equipment
coal—a resource that comes from land plants
petroleum—a resource that comes from ocean plants

OTHER RESOURCES

Not all natural resources are used for energy. People use resources to grow food and to make things.

▲ People all over the world use cotton to make pants and shirts.

- Plants supply us with food. We use them to make cloth, such as cotton. Wood comes from trees. People use wood as a building **material** for homes.

- Some animals supply us with food and clothing. People also use some animals, such as horses and camels, to help do work.

- Rocks are also resources. People use granite and limestone for building. People need **soil** to grow crops, and rocks help form soil. **Minerals** are another type of natural resource that comes from rocks. People use minerals to make glass, steel, and **fertilizer.**

- Diamonds, gold, and silver are natural resources, too. People use them to make the small parts inside many **machines.**

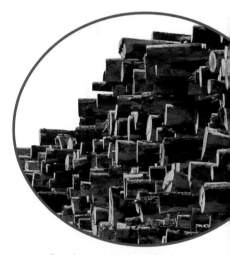

▲ People use wood, such as these logs, to build houses and to make fires.

(**TALK AND SHARE**) **Talk with your partner about the kinds of natural resources you use every day in your homes.**

◀ Many people use cows to get milk, for food, and for clothing.

Language Notes

Verb Phrases
These phrases have special meanings.

- **used up:** burnt, spent, or consumed completely

- **run out:** have no more

Renewable and Nonrenewable Resources

You can divide all of Earth's resources into two groups. One group is **renewable resources.** The other group is **nonrenewable resources.**

RENEWABLE RESOURCES

Nature or people can replace renewable resources in a short time. Nonliving natural resources, such as the wind, sun, water, and air, are always around us. They will not run out.

All living resources together are called **biomass.** People can **manage** biomass to keep a supply available. For example, they can raise more farm animals to replace older ones that die.

By using resources **wisely,** people can manage renewable resources. That way the resources will be here when people need them.

Science, Technology, and Society

Using the Wind

Wind is a renewable source of energy. Windmills make electricity from the wind. Each windmill in this picture has 3 flat blades called *rotors*. The rotors are at the tops of tall towers. When wind spins the rotors, the rotors make energy.

The energy travels into a machine that turns it into electricity. Power lines carry the electricity to places where the electricity gives people power for light and heat.

VOCABULARY

renewable resources—things that can be used again and again without running out
nonrenewable resources—things of which there is a limited supply, so that if you run out there is no more
biomass—renewable resources that come from living things
manage—control or give direction
wisely—carefully and thoughtfully

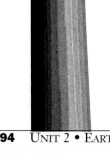

NONRENEWABLE RESOURCES

People cannot replace nonrenewable resources when they have been used up. **Fossil fuels** are one kind of nonrenewable resource. The oil, gas, and coal we use today formed millions of years ago. Although new fossil fuels are forming in **swamps** and oceans today, they will not be ready to use for a very long time. They cannot be easily renewed.

People cut wood from forests all over Earth. Forests with trees that are hundreds of years old cannot grow back within a human lifetime.

Nuclear energy is power that comes from a change to **atoms** in uranium, a rock. This rock takes thousands of years to form. People cannot make more of it.

In 2003, more than 90 percent of electricity in the United States was made using nonrenewable resources. If we keep using the amounts we are using now, we could run out of some of these resources. Some scientists predict we will use up the oil and gas supply on Earth in about 35 years!

▲ Fossil fuels may form in swamps like this one. However, the process takes thousands of years.

Renewable Resources	Nonrenewable Resources
Wind energy	Oil
Geothermal energy	Coal
Water energy	Natural gas
Solar energy	Nuclear energy
Biomass (living things)	Very old forests

(TALK AND SHARE) **With your partner, compare and contrast renewable and nonrenewable resources. Give a few examples of how you use each kind.**

▲ Nuclear energy from this nuclear power plant is a nonrenewable resource.

Human Resource Use Today

People use electricity in homes and places where they work. Fossil fuels and other resources supply the energy to make electricity. Look at the pie chart below. It shows how the United States made electricity in the year 2003.

FOSSIL FUELS

People burn fossil fuels to make electricity. Coal, **natural gas,** and petroleum are all fossil fuels. In 2003, the United States made 71 percent of its electricity by burning coal, natural gas, and petroleum.

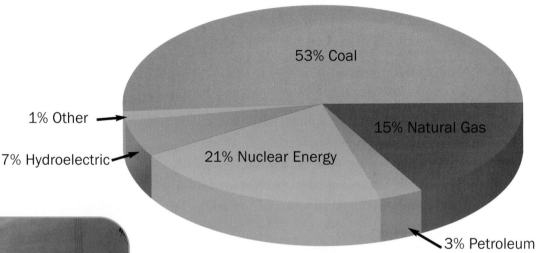

53% Coal

1% Other

7% Hydroelectric

21% Nuclear Energy

15% Natural Gas

3% Petroleum

NUCLEAR ENERGY AND HYDROELECTRIC POWER

Nuclear energy is made from an **element** called uranium. Uranium forms inside Earth. We make nuclear energy by splitting apart the **nucleus,** or center part, of a uranium atom. A small amount of uranium can make a lot of energy.

People use fast-moving water to make **hydroelectric power.** Dams create fast-moving water that spins a wheel. Machines collect the energy made by the spinning wheel and change it into electricity.

▲ Dams create fast-moving water that is used for energy.

VOCABULARY

natural gas—a fossil fuel that is invisible like air
element—one of the basic materials that make up Earth
nucleus—the center part
hydroelectric power—energy that comes from fast-moving water

CONSERVING RESOURCES

Conserving a resource means using it wisely. Good conservation takes planning. When you run in a race, do you plan ahead? Sure you do. You plan to save a little energy for the end of the race so you can finish strong. When you plan ahead like this, you are conserving your resources.

People must plan to conserve Earth's resources, too. Nonrenewable resources will run out some day, but we can do things to make them last longer.

We can start using more renewable resources, such as solar energy. There is an unlimited supply of sunlight. Scientists predict the sun will shine brightly for 5 billion more years.

Geothermal energy comes from heat inside Earth. It is a renewable resource that does not pollute the air by burning fuel. However, geothermal energy must be used close to volcanoes and other places that make heat in Earth's crust. It cannot be used everywhere.

Hydroelectric power is also a clean, renewable source of energy. Canada gets 75 percent of its electricity from hydroelectric power.

(TALK AND SHARE) **Talk with your partner about what you can do to conserve resources today.**

▲ Water and steam are renewable sources of energy found naturally inside Earth's crust. A geothermal power station changes this natural energy into electricity.

Summary

Humans use Earth's natural resources every day to make life better. We can use up nonrenewable resources. We cannot use up renewable resources.

VOCABULARY

conserving—using a resource carefully so that some is left
geothermal energy—power that comes from heat inside Earth

Summarizing

Summarizing Data

When you summarize, you make a short statement that includes the main ideas you have learned. For example, study this pie chart. (It is the pie chart from page 96.) To summarize the data, start by naming the topic and listing the data. Then make a short statement that includes the main ideas about it.

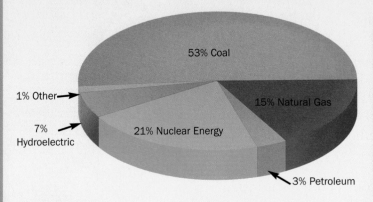

53% Coal

1% Other

7% Hydroelectric

21% Nuclear Energy

15% Natural Gas

3% Petroleum

Resources Used for Electricity in the United States in 2003
Coal - 53%
Nuclear energy - 21%
Natural gas - 15%
Hydroelectric - 7%
Petroleum - 3%
Other - 1%

Now think of how to make a short statement about fossil fuel energy resources. Look at the data for coal, natural gas, and petroleum. What percent of the resources are fossil fuels? You could write a summary like this.

In 2003, the United States made 71 percent of its electricity from fossil fuels. It made 29 percent of its electricity from other resources.

Practice Summarizing

1. Tell Look again at the pie chart on page 91. Then, with your partner or group, summarize the data in that pie chart in your own words.

2. Write Look again at the pie chart above. Copy the data in a way that tells you what percent of electricity in the United States came from renewable resources. Then summarize your data in a short paragraph. Words from the Word Bank can help you.

Word Bank

renewable
nonrenewable
more
less

energy
fuel

compare
use

Activities

Grammar Spotlight

Using *more* and *fewer* The words *more* and *fewer* tell that you are writing about an amount. You can use them to compare amounts. Use *more* for plural count nouns and for noncount nouns. Use *fewer* only for plural count nouns. First, use one of the words before a noun. Then, use the word *than* right after the noun.

To Talk About	Use	Example
A larger amount	more than	*I found* more *gold* than *you did.*
A smaller amount	fewer than	*Some countries have* fewer *resources* than *other countries have.*

Write two sentences about renewable resources that use the word *more* or *fewer*. Write the sentences in your notebook.

Oral Language

Using Math to Organize Data Talk in your group about the following data. These are energy sources in a town called Conserve: 40% hydroelectric, 30% solar, 30% coal. How would you make a pie chart of these data?

Hands On

Collecting Energy On a sunny day, put a dish of cold water next to a window at the beginning of class. At the end of class, feel the water. Is it warmer? How would you explain what happened? Tell what kind of energy was used and whether it was renewable or nonrenewable.

Partner Practice

Plan to Conserve First make a list of 3 resources you use at school. Then make a list of things you can do at school to conserve these resources. Trade your list with a partner. Talk about the ideas you have that are alike and the ideas you have that are different. Share your lists with the class. Try to decide on "5 Ways to Conserve."

How People Affect Earth

Here you'll learn about the many ways that people change Earth. You'll also learn how to infer from evidence and practice explaining an inference.

Building Background

▲ My aunt has a garden, too, even though she lives in the middle of a city.

- **Where do you think this garden is?**
- **How are these people changing Earth?**
- **What things do you do that change Earth?**

People do things every day that change the land, water, and air. Some of these things are helpful, but others are harmful.

1 Wherever people live, they change the environment.

Pollution caused by people can affect the global climate. **2**

3 People can help Earth in many ways.

Key Concepts

environment   global   habitat

Global Environment

Habitat

Habitat

Your **environment** is everything that surrounds you. All people on Earth share the same **global** environment. It includes everything on the planet.

Your **habitat** is the place where you and your family live. Every living thing has a habitat where it can live most easily. Your habitat may be a city. A frog's habitat may be a swamp. The global environment includes many habitats.

One Farm's Effect

People affect Earth when they grow crops.

Tilling

Watering

Tilling, or digging, loosens and mixes the soil. Roots, worms, and water move easily through loose soil.

Watering crops adds water to the soil and helps plants stay alive.

Infer from Evidence

When you infer, you reach a conclusion. Your conclusion is based on a combination of evidence and what you already know. To infer, follow these steps.

1. Collect evidence about your topic. For example, make some observations.

2. Consider what you already know about the topic and think about what the evidence means.

3. Decide what conclusion comes from your evidence.

Topic: Conservation in my town

Observations	Inference
• The town turned some empty land into a park. • The town started recycling services. • The newspaper says the town has more birds this year.	I conclude that my town's conservation efforts have not harmed the town's habitat for birds.

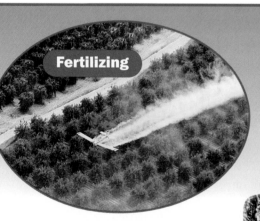

Fertilizing

Fertilizer, or plant food, is good for plants. However, too much fertilizer can pollute land and water.

Harvesting

Harvesting the crops leaves the soil exposed to wind and erosion.

How People Affect Earth

People affect Earth in both helpful and harmful ways. Where people choose to live and the pollution people create affect Earth and the global climate. People can help Earth by protecting habitats and conserving resources.

Where People Live

People live in many different **environments.** In each place, people affect Earth and the global environment.

HABITAT

All living things try to live where they can get energy and live well and **comfortably.** The place where this happens is called the living thing's **habitat.**

In the past, people's habitats depended on how they got their food. Some people followed the animals they hunted. Other people traveled to find good plants to eat. Later, people began farming. After farming began, people stopped moving and lived near their **crops** and near water.

Most people live near water and in **temperate** climates. However, people can make almost any habitat comfortable. Pipes carry water to **desert** habitats and oil and gas to cold habitats. Airplanes, trucks, and boats carry food and other resources to cities and other places where people live.

▲ People swim in a pool near the Dead Sea in Israel.

Language Notes

Confusing Word Pairs
These words are easily mixed up.

- affect: a verb that means to make a change. Breathing dirty air can affect your health.

- effect: a noun that means the result of doing something. Coughing is one possible effect of breathing dirty air.

VOCABULARY

environments—living and nonliving surroundings
comfortably—having all needs met
habitat—the place where a plant or animal lives and produces seeds or babies
crops—plants that people grow for a purpose, such as to eat or to make clothing
temperate—not very hot or very cold
desert—a very dry area on Earth

THE HUMAN POPULATION

In 1950, 2,555,360,972 people lived on Earth. In 2003, more than 6,300,000,000 people lived on Earth. Scientists predict Earth's human **population** will reach at least 9,000,000,000 by the year 2050.

Many cities have more than a million people living in them. In crowded cities, people live closely together. They live in cities because cities have jobs, schools, and places to live.

Look at the map below. Today, most people live where you can see purple and orange, and some live where you can see yellow. Wherever people live, they have an effect on the land, air, and water.

(TALK AND SHARE) **With your partner, talk about what your habitat is like.**

Some areas of Earth have a lot of people (purple and orange areas). How are these areas different from areas where fewer people live? ▼

Global Population 2004

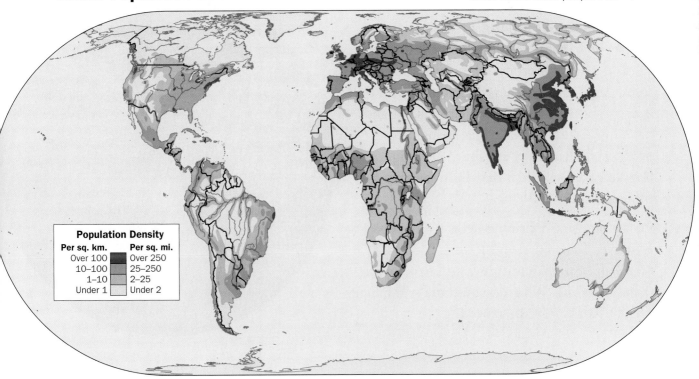

Population Density

Per sq. km.	Per sq. mi.
Over 100	Over 250
10–100	25–250
1–10	2–25
Under 1	Under 2

▲ On average, each person in the United States throws away over 4 pounds of garbage per day.

Pollution

Sometimes people affect Earth in harmful ways. **Pollution** happens when something harmful mixes with soil, water, or air. When land, water, or air is dirty, it is polluted.

POLLUTING THE LAND

Humans throw billions of tons of **garbage** into **dumps** every year. Food scraps will rot away, but plastic and rubber will not. Cans with leftover paint or cleaning materials can **poison** the soil. Many waste materials contain **germs.** They can pollute the soil around a dump.

Pesticides help farmers grow healthy, bug-free crops. When farmers use too many pesticides, however, the pesticides poison the soil, humans, and other animals.

Science, Technology, and Society

Slash-and-Burn Farming

Farmers in some tropical areas cut down trees to make fields for crops. They burn the cut trees. After several years, the crops use up the energy in the soil. Then the farmers cut and burn more trees to make new fields. This process is called slash-and-burn farming. People have used slash-and-burn farming for thousands of years.

Slash-and-burn farming helps feed people. However, it also destroys forests. More than half of the kinds of life on Earth live in tropical forests. What do you think will happen if these habitats are destroyed?

VOCABULARY

pollution—dirty air, water, or land
garbage—unwanted waste materials
dumps—places where many people put their garbage
poison—harm; make unsafe

germs—very small living things that can cause sickness
pesticides—substances used to kill living things that eat crops

POLLUTING THE WATER

Rain washes salt, pesticides, and **fertilizer** into rivers and lakes. Large amounts of these **chemicals** can kill the plants and animals that use the polluted water.

Factories sometimes put waste material into water. Some of the material may contain harmful chemicals.

Metal cans filled with **poisons** get rusty in a dump. The poisons leak out. They **seep** through the soil and into the **groundwater.** The groundwater around the dump stays polluted for a long time.

▲ A worker cleans up oil that spilled from a large ship. When oil spills into water, it can kill birds and fish.

POLLUTING THE AIR

Most air pollution comes from cars and other motor vehicles. Cars burn gasoline when their engines run. Burning gasoline adds **gases** to the air. The gases can make the air dirty.

Acid rain can kill trees. ▼

People burn **fossil fuels** when they use electricity and gas to heat their homes. This adds harmful gases to the air. When people burn wood, small bits of ash enter the air.

Some factories put gases into the air. When these gases mix with **precipitation,** they make **acid rain.** Over time, acid rain kills fish, damages plants, and eats away at buildings.

(TALK AND SHARE) **Talk with your partner about how land, air, and water can become polluted.**

VOCABULARY

fertilizer—food added to soil to help plants grow
chemicals—materials found in Earth
poisons—harmful substances
seep—drip down slowly
groundwater—water beneath Earth's surface that fills wells and springs

gases—substances that are invisible like air
fossil fuels—energy resources such as oil, coal, and natural gas
precipitation—water in the form of fog, rain, sleet, or snow
acid rain—polluted precipitation

Global Climate Change

Solar **radiation** is heat and light energy from the sun. The **atmosphere** protects life on Earth from harmful solar radiation. Earth's atmosphere **reflects,** or bends back, much of the radiation into space.

Look at the diagram. Land and water **absorb** most of the solar radiation that reaches Earth.

What Happens to Solar Radiation

Much is reflected by the atmosphere.

Some is absorbed by the atmosphere.

Solar radiation

A little is reflected by land.

Most is absorbed by land and water.

Earth's atmosphere

Hole in ozone lets in more heat.

Increased gases trap more heat.

Earth's surface

Gases such as water vapor, methane, and carbon dioxide in the atmosphere are called **greenhouse gases.** They stop some of Earth's heat from going back out into space. Greenhouse gases help keep Earth warm. The **global climate** is warmer when more energy from the sun stays within Earth's atmosphere.

When fossil fuels burn, they add extra greenhouse gases to the air. More gases trap more heat. That means the global climate could get warmer. Habitats would change all over Earth.

If the global climate gets much warmer, it could affect living things. For example, glaciers in many parts of the world are melting. If a lot of the ice melts, **sea levels** around the world would rise. Then habitats near coastlines could be flooded.

(**TALK AND SHARE**) **With your partner, talk about how greenhouse gases can raise global temperatures.**

VOCABULARY
radiation—energy that travels through space
atmosphere—the layer of air that surrounds Earth
reflects—bends or turns back
absorb—take in or soak up
greenhouse gases—substances in the air that help keep Earth warm
global climate—the long-term pattern of temperature and precipitation for all of Earth
sea levels—the heights of ocean water where it meets the land

Helping Earth

People can affect Earth in helpful ways. They can **protect** habitats by setting aside land and water for parks. Parks help **preserve** habitats.

People can **restore** land and water by removing pollution. Farmers can choose to use fewer pesticides and fertilizers. Factories that don't pollute can replace factories that do.

Gardeners can plant flowers and bushes that would normally grow in their area. For example, cacti and prairie flowers need less water and fertilizer than a grassy lawn does.

People can also **conserve** natural resources. One easy way is by **recycling** paper, glass, plastic, and metal. People can conserve water by taking shorter showers. They can turn off the water while washing dishes or brushing their teeth.

Countries can work together to increase the amount of renewable resources (like sun and wind) they use. This will help conserve the nonrenewable resources on Earth.

(TALK AND SHARE) **Talk with your partner about some things you can do to affect Earth in a helpful way.**

▲ This team of people is restoring land near a highway by removing garbage.

Summary

Humans affect Earth wherever they live. Sometimes the effect is harmful, such as with pollution and global climate change. Humans can affect Earth in helpful ways by conserving resources and protecting habitats.

VOCABULARY

protect—keep from being damaged or harmed
preserve—keep whole and safe

restore—put back or make as good as new
conserve—use carefully so that some is left
recycling—using a material again

Explaining

Explaining an Inference

When you explain, you make something clear. You can explain an inference by clearly describing the evidence you used to make the inference. Look at the Web. Notice how the evidence supports the inference.

Web

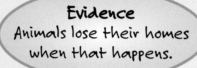

Evidence
Animals lose their homes when that happens.

Evidence
The people who live in the homes throw away garbage every day.

Evidence
Sometimes people cut down trees when they build homes.

My Inference:
When people build houses, they affect the environment and animal habitats.

Practice Explaining

1. Draw Make a Web like the one above. Look for evidence at home that shows how you affect Earth. Draw or talk about evidence to put in the small circles. After you look at the evidence, make an inference about your effect on Earth. Draw or explain your inference in the large circle.

2. Write Think about how your school affects Earth. Collect evidence and put it in a Web like the one above. Make an inference using your evidence. Then write a paragraph that explains your inference. Clearly describe the evidence you found. Include details that helped you make your inference. Use the Check Your Writing checklist when you are done.

Check Your Writing

Make sure you
- Use complete sentences.
- Use a period at the end of each sentence.
- Spell all the words correctly.

Grammar Spotlight

Statements Using *was/were* *Was* and *were* are the past tense forms of the verb *be*.

Rule	Example
Use *was* when the subject is one person or thing.	*Last year, corn* was *the only crop.*
Use *were* when the subject is two or more people or things.	*This spring, corn and beans* were *the crops we planted.*
Add *not* after *was* or *were* if you want to make your statement negative.	*The air* was not *clean.* *The crops* were not *ready to pick.*

Make one sentence about habitats using *were* and one sentence using *were not*.

Oral Language

Habitat Walk With a partner or a group, talk about what your habitat is like. Then take a walk around your habitat. Describe 3 or 4 things that make it comfortable for you, such as how easy it is to find food, water, and a place to live.

Hands On

Population Maps Think about the state where you live. Make a quick drawing of its shape. Then color the areas where you think most of the people live. Trade drawings with a partner and talk about any ways your maps are alike and different.

Partner Practice

Infer from Evidence With a partner, collect evidence about what happens to garbage at your school. List a few of the main things in the garbage every day. Using your evidence and what you already know, make an inference about how the school garbage might affect the neighborhood habitat.

Exploring
Ecology

Here you'll learn about how living things interact with each other and the environment. You'll also learn how to think about systems and practice explaining cause and effect.

Building Background

▲ Last year my neighbors went to Alaska and saw snow—even in summer!

- **What do you know about this place by looking at the pictures?**

- **Have you ever been to a place like this?**

- **What do you think there is to eat in this place?**

1 In an ecosystem, living things interact with each other to live and reproduce.

Cooperate

Hunt

Pollinate

Compete

2 Living things get energy and nutrients from the food they eat.

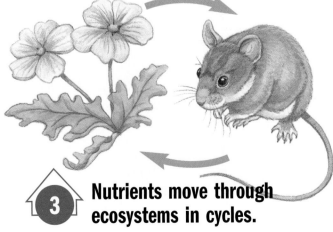

3 Nutrients move through ecosystems in cycles.

Key Concepts

ecology   interact   ecosystem

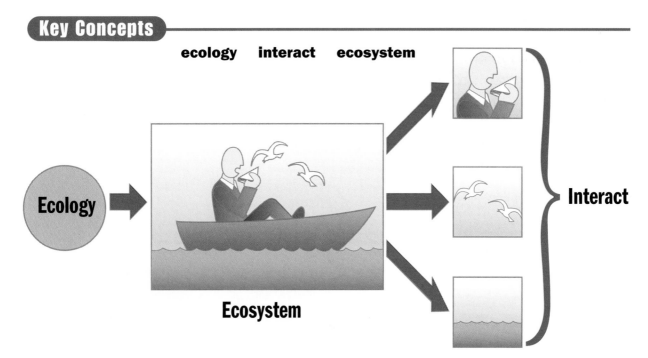

Ecology

Ecosystem

Interact

Ecology is the science of how living things and their environments **interact,** or affect one another.

Living things and the environment in which they live make up an **ecosystem.**

Biomes

A biome is a large area where certain kinds of plants and animals live together. The kinds of plants that can grow in a biome depend on its climate.

Forest

Grassland

Marine

Tall, sturdy plants grow in the forest biome.

Grasses, with their tiny flowers, grow in the grassland biome.

Oceans are marine biomes.

Think About Systems

A system is a set of parts that work together as one. For example, like all systems, an animal's digestive system has many parts that work together. All the parts of the digestive system help the animal get energy from food. When you think about systems, ask yourself these questions.

1. What parts make up this system?

2. What job does the system have?

3. What happens if one of the parts is missing or doesn't work?

Look at the Web. It shows how living and nonliving things work together in an ecosystem.

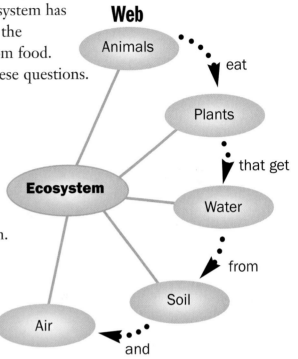

Web

Plants like water lilies grow in freshwater biomes.

In the desert biome, desert plants have thick skins to store water.

Plants in the tundra biome grow close to the ground because of the cold.

Exploring Ecology

In an ecosystem, all living things interact with each other and the environment. Through nutrient cycles, living things get the energy they need to stay alive.

Ecosystems

An **ecosystem** is made up of an environment and everything that lives in it. Think about a desert. Many **individual** desert plants and animals live there. Each is a member of its own **species,** which is a group of similar living things that can **reproduce.** Desert species can survive in the hot, dry climate. The **populations** of each species in a single environment make up a **community.**

| Ecosystem |
| Community |
| Population |
| Individual |

Parts of a Desert Ecosystem

Living Things	Nonliving Things
Cactus plants	Sunshine
Snakes	Air
Flies	Sand

A desert biome contains many separate and different desert ecosystems. Each ecosystem includes both living and nonliving things.

(TALK AND SHARE) With your partner, list 3 living things and 3 nonliving things in your ecosystem.

VOCABULARY
ecosystem—an environment and everything that lives in it
individual—single
species—a group of similar living things that can reproduce
reproduce—make a copy
populations—groups of the same kind of living things
community—populations of different species living together in the same environment

Energy Powers an Ecosystem

Energy makes things move and grow. Ecosystems depend on the sun for energy. Sunlight, like other nonliving things, makes life in an ecosystem possible. Both living and nonliving parts of an ecosystem keep energy moving through the ecosystem.

Everything on Earth is made of **matter,** even the things you can't see or touch, like air. Matter is made up of tiny **atoms.** Some atoms combine into **nutrients,** which provide energy and help living things survive and grow.

Nutrients are in air, water, and soil. Nutrients move from the environment to living things and then back again.

(TALK AND SHARE) **Describe to your partner how energy and nutrients can help living things.**

(Science, Technology, and Society)

Endangered Species

Some species of plants and animals die out, or become **extinct.** That means there are no more living members of their species. This often happens because of changes in their environment. Sometimes, people cause these changes.

The peregrine falcon was at one time in danger of becoming extinct. Poisons in its habitat destroyed most of the falcon population. Scientists, with the help of volunteers, saved this **endangered species.** They stopped people from using poisons that were killing the falcons. Then the falcons were able to return to their habitat, and the falcon population grew.

▲ Peregrine falcon

VOCABULARY

energy—the power to make something change
matter—anything that has mass and takes up space
atoms—the smallest parts of everything on Earth
nutrients—substances that living things need to survive and grow
extinct—gone from Earth
endangered species—a group of living things that could become extinct

Nutrient Cycles

Earth's ecosystems include oxygen, carbon, and nitrogen. Each of these nutrients moves in a **cycle** from living things to nonliving things and back again.

THE CARBON DIOXIDE–OXYGEN CYCLE

To stay alive, living things depend on the movement of **oxygen** and **carbon dioxide** in an ecosystem. During the day, plants take in carbon dioxide from the air and give back oxygen. Living things in the oceans take in carbon dioxide from the air and **release** oxygen. Humans and other animals breathe in oxygen and breathe out carbon dioxide. The life-supporting nutrients never get used up because they go back and forth in the carbon dioxide–oxygen cycle.

The Carbon Dioxide-Oxygen Cycle

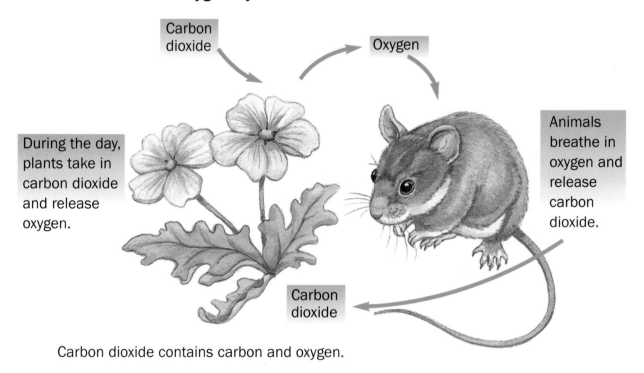

Carbon dioxide

Oxygen

During the day, plants take in carbon dioxide and release oxygen.

Animals breathe in oxygen and release carbon dioxide.

Carbon dioxide

Carbon dioxide contains carbon and oxygen.

VOCABULARY

cycle—a regularly repeating set of events
oxygen—a nutrient, symbol O, that most living things need to survive
carbon dioxide—a nutrient made of one carbon atom and two oxygen atoms, symbol CO_2
release—set free

The Carbon Cycle

The plant takes in carbon dioxide and uses the carbon to make sugars.

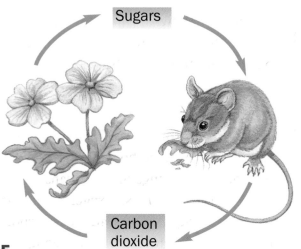

Sugars

Carbon dioxide

The animal eats the carbon in the plant and releases carbon dioxide.

THE CARBON CYCLE

The bodies of all living things contain **carbon** atoms. The air, rocks, and soil also contain carbon atoms. In ecosystems, carbon gets used over and over again. Much carbon comes from carbon dioxide.

Plants take in carbon from the carbon dioxide in the air. They use it to make **sugars.** When animals eat plants, they take in carbon. When animals breathe out, they release carbon dioxide back into the air.

THE NITROGEN CYCLE

Living things also need **nitrogen** to grow. Plants take in nitrogen through their roots. When animals eat plants, they take in the nitrogen. Animal wastes and dead animals and plants return nitrogen to the soil.

Bacteria in the soil also take part in the nitrogen cycle. Some bacteria turn nitrogen from air into a form plants can use. Others add nitrogen to the air.

◀ Plants can get nitrogen from the soil.

(TALK AND SHARE) **With your partner, take turns explaining what happens during the carbon dioxide–oxygen cycle, the carbon cycle, and the nitrogen cycle.**

VOCABULARY

carbon—a nutrient, symbol C, that is part of many living and nonliving things on Earth
sugars—foods made of carbon, oxygen, and hydrogen atoms
nitrogen—a nutrient, symbol N, that helps living things grow
bacteria—living things made of just one cell

Energy and Food

All living things take in nutrients to stay alive. The energy in food makes it possible for animals and plants to grow. Earth's energy comes from sunlight. Plants change the energy of sunlight into food that all members of the community can eat.

PRODUCERS

Plants are the first food-makers, or **producers,** in an ecosystem. They use sunlight to make different kinds of sugar. When they need energy to grow, they use their stored sugar.

CONSUMERS

Animals cannot make food from sunlight. They need to get food from plants, which makes animals **consumers.** Animals like deer and rabbits only eat plants. They are called **primary** consumers. Animals like wolves and lions eat plant-eating animals. This makes them **secondary** consumers.

DECOMPOSERS

Plants and animals store energy in their bodies. When they die, this energy stays in the ecosystem. **Decomposers** turn dead plants and animals into their own food energy, so they keep nutrients moving through the ecosystem.

Slugs, snails, worms, mushrooms, and bacteria are all decomposers. They break down rotting wood, leaves, and stems.

▲ You are a consumer in your habitat.

Energy Pyramid

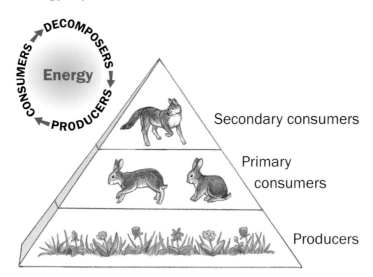

Secondary consumers

Primary consumers

Producers

FOOD CHAINS

A **food chain** is a **model** of how energy moves from producer plants to consumer animals. A food chain is all about eating and being eaten. A single ecosystem can have many food chains. For example, in a midwestern farm field, food chains might include:

- Corn → mouse → owl
- Corn → blackbird → cat
- Corn → caterpillar → crow

FOOD WEBS

When a member of one food chain eats a member of another food chain, the chains connect. Then scientists draw bigger models called **food webs.** They show how food chains interact.

Each ecosystem contains many food chains and food webs. In this way, all living things depend on each other. Every individual in the ecosystem helps all the others live and survive.

(TALK AND SHARE) **Talk with your partner about examples of producers and consumers interacting in a food chain.**

Food Chain

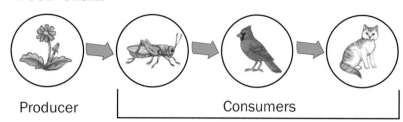

Producer   Consumers

Food Web

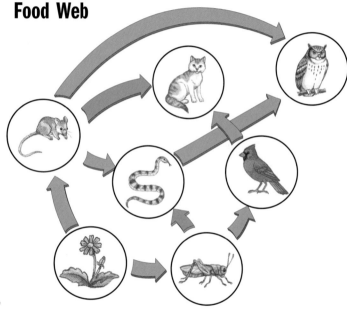

Summary

In ecosystems, living things interact with each other and the environment. Energy powers every living thing. Each individual needs nutrients and energy to stay alive.

VOCABULARY

food chain—a model of how energy moves from producers to consumers
model—a copy of an object or system
food webs—models showing how food chains interact

Explaining

Explaining Cause and Effect

When you explain cause and effect, you clearly say what happened and why it happened. Scientists who study ecology ask cause-effect questions. For example: What causes bees to land on flowers? What will the effect be if a garden doesn't get enough water? Look at this Web about a garden ecosystem. A scientist would try to explain what would happen if one of the parts disappeared.

Web

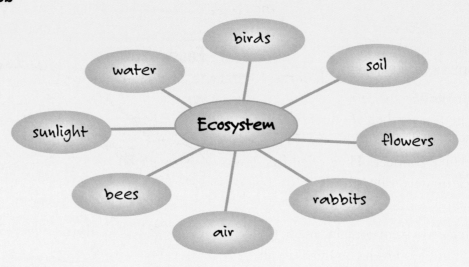

Practice Explaining

1. Tell With a partner, think about the Web above but with one part missing. Talk about how the garden ecosystem would be different without that part.

2. Write Look again at the Web above. Think about how the ecosystem would change—the *effect*—if one part were removed—the *cause*. Write a short paragraph to explain what might happen. Use the Check Your Writing checklist to review your work.

Check Your Writing

Make sure you
- ☐ Use complete sentences.
- ☐ Use a period at the end of each sentence.
- ☐ Spell all the words correctly.

Grammar Spotlight

Verbs Plus Prepositions You can use a preposition such as *to*, *on*, or *with* after a verb to show a relationship between two things. Scientists use verb-preposition combinations to describe life in an ecosystem.

Verb	Plus Preposition	Example
relates	to	*The amount of rain relates to climate.*
depends	on	*The panda depends on bamboo trees.*
interacts	with	*The bee interacts with the flower.*

Make a sentence for each of these verbs and prepositions: *relates to*, *depends on*, and *interacts with*.

Partner Practice

Comic Strip With your partner, choose one animal or plant in your ecosystem. Together, make a comic strip that explains the ecosystem from the animal's or plant's point of view. What does it need to live? Where does it get food? Share your comic strip with the class.

Oral Language

Think About Systems Think about how you are a consumer in your ecosystem. Talk with your partner about the food you consumed today. Then think about your whole ecosystem. Explain which living things were the producers of the food you ate.

Hands On

Count a Population Every ecosystem contains many populations. Each population is a group of the same kind of living things. Work with a partner to count a single population near your school. You can count people. You could also count flies, maple trees, or mushrooms. Be sure to count only the same kind of living thing. Record your counts. Then repeat the process exactly and compare your first and second totals. Are they the same or different? Talk about how you could make sure that someone else's total will be the same as yours.

Life's Diversity

Here you'll learn about the major groups of living things. You'll also learn how to make observations and practice classifying living things.

Building Background

▲ What a cool plant! I've never seen anything like it!

- **How many living things can you see here?**
- **What do you think they are doing?**
- **What does this remind you of?**

Big Idea

All living things share basic characteristics. Scientists classify living things by the characteristics they share, such as the kind of cells they have. You can see these characteristics in the living things you observe.

You can sort living things into 6 big groups called kingdoms.

1 Archaebacteria

2 Eubacteria

3 Protists

4 Fungi

5 Plants

6 Animals

Key Concepts

Diversity	Characteristics	Classify	Categories

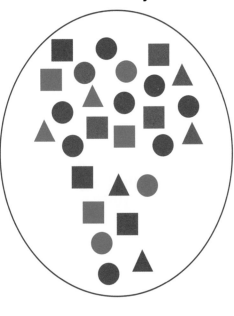

Diversity means differences. Differences are **characteristics** you can observe. You can **classify** characteristics into **categories.**

circle category

red category

green category

It Is Alive If ...

Cells

It is made of one or more cells.

Energy

It takes in and uses energy.

Make Observations

When you observe, you use your senses—sight, hearing, taste, smell, and touch. To observe something as a scientist, follow these steps.

1. Carefully pay attention to how it looks, sounds, and behaves.

2. Record your observations.

This chart includes characteristics you might observe about the living thing in this picture.

Characteristic	Observation
where it lives	a grassy place
its color(s)	gray
unicellular or multicellular?	multicellular
how it gets energy	eating

Response

It can keep a constant inside environment. It responds to the outside environment.

Reproduction

It reproduces.

Life's Diversity

Scientists classify living things based on their characteristics, such as the number and kind of cells they have. Scientists place living things into 6 kingdoms based on characteristics they share.

Classifying and Naming

People have observed at least 1.5 million kinds of living things and estimate that there may be over 3 million more! Living things come in so many **varieties** that people look for ways to group them. The most common system for classifying living things puts them into categories based on their similar **characteristics**. The category that includes all of the other categories is the kingdom.

Kingdom similar phyla (plural of *phylum*)

Phylum similar classes

Class similar orders

Order similar families

Family similar genera (plural of *genus*)

Genus similar species

Species can **reproduce.**

Scientists give each kind of living thing its own **scientific name,** made up of its genus name and its species name. Human beings have the name *Homo sapiens.*

(TALK AND SHARE) **What is your scientific name and what does it tell about you? Talk about it with your partner.**

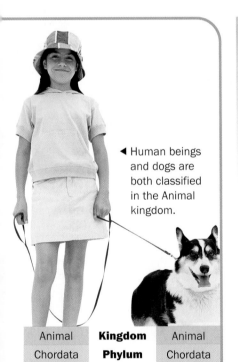

◀ Human beings and dogs are both classified in the Animal kingdom.

Animal	**Kingdom**	Animal
Chordata	**Phylum**	Chordata
Mammalia	**Class**	Mammalia
Primates	**Order**	**Carnivora**
Homonidae	**Family**	**Canidae**
Homo	**Genus**	*Canis*
sapiens	**Species**	*familiaris*

VOCABULARY
varieties—different kinds
characteristics—differences you can observe
reproduce—make a copy
scientific name—genus name and species name

Starting with Cells

One of the main ways to begin classifying a living thing is to observe its **cells,** the basic units of life. The tiniest living things on Earth **consist of** just one cell. They are **unicellular.**

UNICELLULAR LIVING THINGS

Most unicellular living things are **prokaryotic.** This means that their cells do not have a **nucleus,** a part that contains the information needed to reproduce.

Unicellular

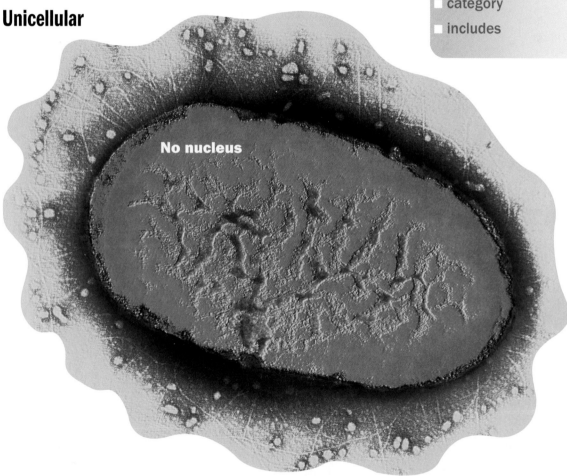

No nucleus

▲ This cell is prokaryotic because it has no nucleus.

VOCABULARY

cells—basic units of life
consist of—have, are made up of
unicellular—having one cell
prokaryotic—without a nucleus
nucleus—the cell part that contains information needed to reproduce

MULTICELLULAR LIVING THINGS

All other living things are **multicellular.** This means that they have two or more cells. The cells of all multicellular living things, and of some unicellular living things, are **eukaryotic.** This means the cells do have a nucleus.

Multicellular living things have cells that work together. The cells are **specialized.** This means they do specific jobs in the body. In a plant, for example, some cells are specialized to take in energy from the sun and others are specialized to turn this energy into food.

(TALK AND SHARE) **What are some multicellular things you can see from your desk? Talk about it with your partner.**

Multicellular

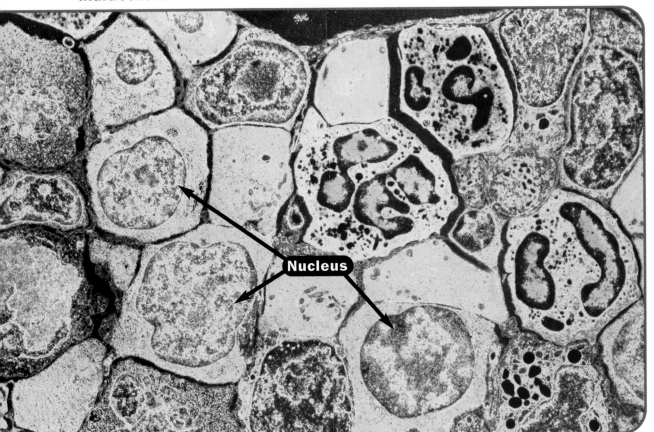

Nucleus

▲ These cells are eukaryotic because each one has a nucleus.

VOCABULARY
multicellular—having two or more cells
eukaryotic—having a nucleus
specialized—having one particular job

The Six Kingdoms

When biologists classify living things, they depend on what they can observe. Long ago, they classified everything they observed as either a plant or an animal. Today, using laboratory tools to study cells, biologists classify **organisms** into 6 kingdoms.

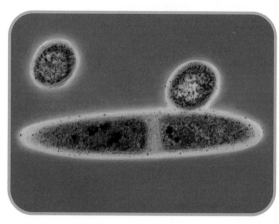

▲ Archaebacteria

ARCHAEBACTERIA

- Unicellular
- Prokaryotic cells

Archaebacteria used to be classified with eubacteria because the two kinds of organisms look alike. Both reproduce by splitting in half, but the two kingdoms of **bacteria** have very different cell activities. Many archaebacteria can live in places where all other organisms would die. Some examples are hot deep-sea vents and salty places like the Great Salt Lake.

EUBACTERIA

- Unicellular
- Prokaryotic cells

Eubacteria live nearly every place on Earth. Many live inside other organisms and help them break down food to get energy. They come in three shapes—spheres (balls), rods (sticks), and spirals (corkscrews). Some make **poisons** that can cause sickness in other living things.

Eubacteria ▼

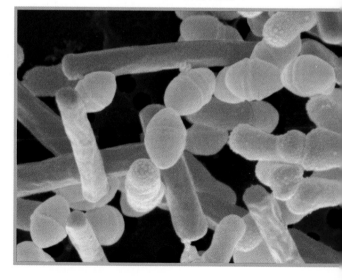

VOCABULARY

organisms—living things
bacteria—all prokaryotic living things (also called *prokaryotes*)
poisons—harmful substances that cause illness or death

PROTISTS

- Unicellular and multicellular
- Eukaryotic cells
  There are 3 groups of protists. Plant-like protists are **producers** in ecosystems. Animal-like protists are **consumers.** Fungus-like protists are **decomposers.**

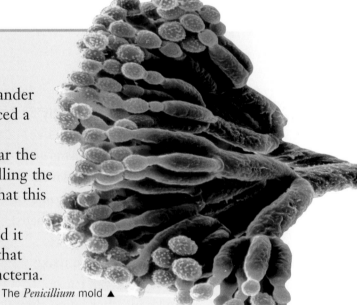

▲ An amoeba is an animal-like protist.

FUNGI

- Multicellular (except for yeast)
- Eukaryotic cells
  Fungi, such as mushrooms, are decomposers. Mushrooms are made of cells that are specialized to reproduce. The mold you might see growing on an orange is also the reproducing part of a fungus. The bodies of fungi grow into their food source.

▲ Mushrooms are fungi.

Science, Technology, and Society

Penicillin

Penicillium is a mold from the kingdom Fungi. It often grows on fruit. In 1928, Alexander Fleming was studying bacteria when he noticed a mold growing in a laboratory dish. When he looked closely, he could see dead bacteria near the mold. Fleming thought that the mold was killing the bacteria. Through experiments, he showed that this was true. Soon scientists found the bacteria-killing chemical inside the mold. They named it *penicillin*. Penicillin is a powerful **antibiotic** that medical doctors use to kill disease-causing bacteria.

The *Penicillium* mold ▲

VOCABULARY
producers—organisms that make their own food
consumers—organisms that eat other living things for food
decomposers—organisms that break down dead material for food
antibiotic—a drug that can kill disease-causing organisms

PLANTS

- Multicellular
- Eukaryotic cells

Plants are all producers. They cannot move from place to place, but they can respond to light, touch, and **gravity.** Mosses are plants that need to live in watery places. Their simple bodies cannot move water from one part to another. Other plants have specialized cells to carry water and can live in dryer places.

▲ Ferns are plants.

ANIMALS

- Multicellular
- Eukaryotic cells

Animals are all consumers—they get energy from eating other living things. All animals can move from place to place, sometimes very quickly! Two main groups of animals are those with backbones and those without. Most animals have no backbones. These include worms and **arthropods,** such as insects, spiders, and shrimp. There are more arthropods on Earth than any other kind of animal. Fish, **amphibians, reptiles,** birds, and **mammals** (including humans) all have backbones.

▲ Spiders and people are animals.

(TALK AND SHARE) **With your partner, talk about what makes all plants different from all animals.**

Summary

You can classify living things based on their characteristics. Living things can be grouped by the kind of cells they have. Today, scientists put living things in 6 kingdoms.

VOCABULARY

gravity—the force that pulls things together
arthropods—insects, spiders, and crustaceans
amphibians—frogs, toads, and salamanders

reptiles—snakes, lizards, turtles, alligators, and crocodiles
mammals—animals with fur or hair

Classifying

Classifying Living Things

You can classify a living thing by observing its characteristics. A Classification Organizer can help you keep track of the characteristics. For instance, this organizer shows how you can list characteristics and then classify the living thing shown in the picture below.

Classification Organizer

Characteristic	Observation
where it lives	in a sandy spot, probably a desert
its color(s)	green, brown, red, yellow
unicellular or multicellular?	multicellular
how it gets energy	from the sun and from the soil
Classification	Plant kingdom

Practice Classifying

1. Draw With a partner, practice classifying a living thing. Choose a living thing to observe. Draw a picture of it. Then talk about how to classify this living thing.

2. Write Choose a living thing to classify. Fill out a Classification Organizer like the one above. Use the organizer to write a paragraph about your classification. Words from the Word Bank can help you.

Word Bank

see
classify
can
wonder

specialized
like
several

color
energy

Activities

Grammar Spotlight

Using *can* The word *can* is a verb you might put in front of another verb. *Can* adds to the meaning of the verb that follows. One of its meanings is "have the ability to."

Example	What It Means
I *can* see the plant.	I am able to see the plant.
Can you classify this plant?	Are you able to classify the plant?
If I *can* find a nucleus, I'll know it's eukaryotic.	If I am able to find a nucleus, I will know it is eukaryotic.

Use *can* in a sentence about making observations.

Oral Language

Cell Rap Read this rap aloud with a partner.

> *I am a nucleus.*
> *I take the biggest spot.*
> *I'm in some cells,*
> *and in others I'm not.*
> *"Eu" means true.*
> *"Pro" means no.*
> *Sing this song and you'll know where I go.*

Hands On

Kingdom Sort Have everyone in your class write the name of one kingdom on a card. Have one person take all the cards and mix them up. Hand out the cards and tell everyone to keep his or her kingdom secret. Then ask each other questions until you can sort one another into kingdoms.

Partner Practice

Make Observations Talk with a partner about something each of you ate today. Make observations about the food's color, taste, smell, and feel. From your partner's observations, draw a picture of what your partner ate today.

Cell
Structure

Here you'll learn about what happens inside cells. You'll also learn how to visualize cells and practice comparing and contrasting the parts of a cell.

Building Background

▲ I wonder what these things are doing!

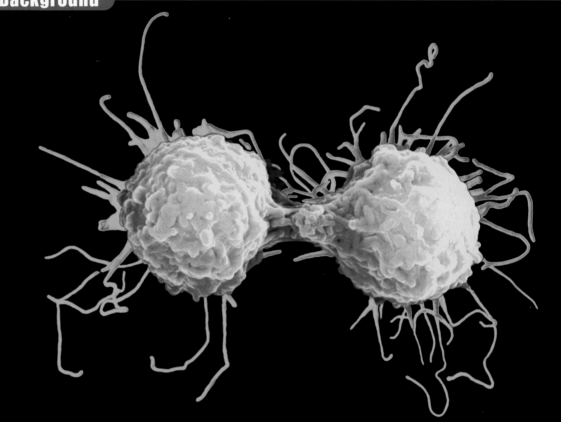

■ **What is happening here?**

■ **What changes are taking place?**

■ **Where could something like this be happening inside you?**

Cells have special parts called organelles. Each part has a job to do. All cells can make exact copies of themselves through cell division.

1 **Parts of a Cell** Animal and plant cells have many similar parts. Both have mitochondria, but only plant cells have chloroplasts.

Animal Cell   **Plant Cell**

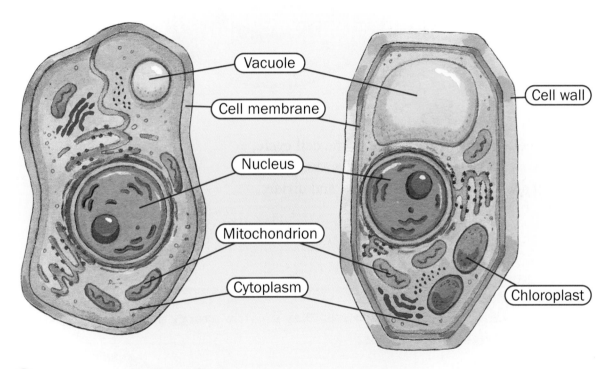

Vacuole

Cell membrane

Cell wall

Nucleus

Mitochondrion

Cytoplasm

Chloroplast

2 **Cell Division** All cells have a life cycle. During cell division, a cell divides into two new cells.

Key Concepts

cell   cell cycle   cell division

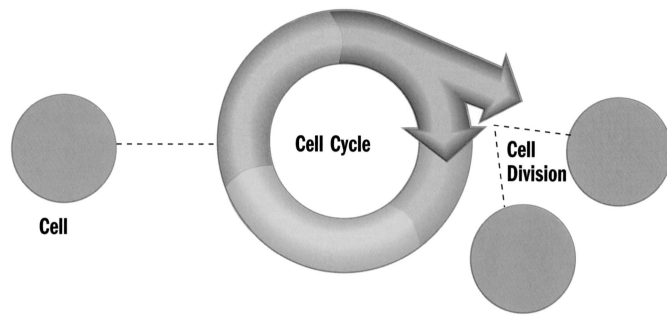

Cell Cycle

Cell Division

Cell

A **cell** is a tiny part of your body. Every cell does work.

In the **cell cycle**, a cell works, grows, rests, and divides.

Cell division produces two cells from one cell.

Jobs of a Cell

Cells do the work that keeps you alive. They provide energy and help you grow, reproduce, and fight off sickness.

Providing energy

Cells take in nutrients that carry energy.

Growing

Cells multiply and help you grow.

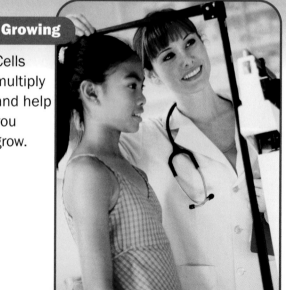

Visualize

When you visualize something, you make a picture of it in your mind. This can help you remember it. You can use tools to build the picture in your mind. Here are some tools for visualizing very small things.

- Drawings

- Models

- Animations

For example, cells are so tiny that you can only see them with a microscope. This means that to learn about cells, you need to visualize what they look like and what they do. Cell animations, drawings, and models help you visualize cells.

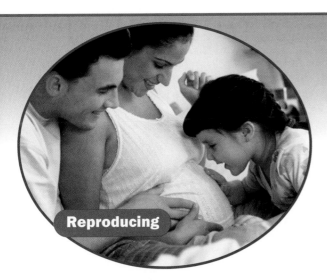

Reproducing

Cells make copies of themselves. Every living thing reproduces through its cells.

Fighting infection

Most of your cells have special jobs. One job is to stop sickness by attacking germs.

Cell Structure

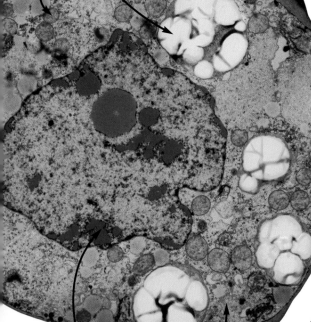

Organelles   Cell wall

Nucleus   Cytoplasm

▲ This picture of a plant cell shows the cell wall, the cytoplasm, the nucleus, and some other organelles.

Cells contain special parts. Each part, such as the organelles and the cell membrane, plays a role in helping the cell take in matter and energy. This allows the cell to grow and divide.

Parts of a Cell

The working parts inside **eukaryotic** cells are called **organelles.** The **nucleus** tells the other organelles what to do. The cell is full of **cytoplasm,** a jelly-like fluid. Organelles float in this fluid.

Every cell is surrounded by its **cell membrane.** The membrane controls what gets into the cell and what stays out. Things the cell needs can enter. The membrane keeps dangerous things outside.

A cell membrane is very thin but very strong. It keeps the cytoplasm and organelles inside the cell. If the membrane breaks, it quickly repairs itself.

Plant cells have added protection. They have a **cell wall** around the membrane. The tough wall gives the plant its shape.

TALK AND SHARE **Talk with your partner about the job a cell membrane does. List examples of other things, such as fences, that do a similar job.**

Language Notes

Homophones
These words sound alike, but they have different spellings and meanings.

- ☐ **cell:** the basic unit of life

- ☐ **sell:** give or exchange something for money

VOCABULARY
eukaryotic—having a nucleus
organelles—parts inside a eukaryotic cell with special jobs
nucleus—the organelle that contains the chemicals needed to reproduce and that tells the other organelles what to do
cytoplasm—the jelly-like fluid that fills a cell
cell membrane—the covering that controls what enters the cell and what leaves the cell
cell wall—the tough outer case of a plant cell

Organelles

The nucleus is just one organelle in eukaryotic cells. Both animal and plant cells also have **mitochondria.** Only plant cells have **chloroplasts.**

MITOCHONDRIA

The mitochondria supply energy to the cell. They make energy from food. The cell uses the energy to move, grow, and divide.

CHLOROPLASTS

In plant cells, chloroplasts **capture** energy from sunlight. These organelles turn sunlight into food through a process called **photosynthesis.**

Animal cells do not have chloroplasts. Humans and other animals depend on plants for food.

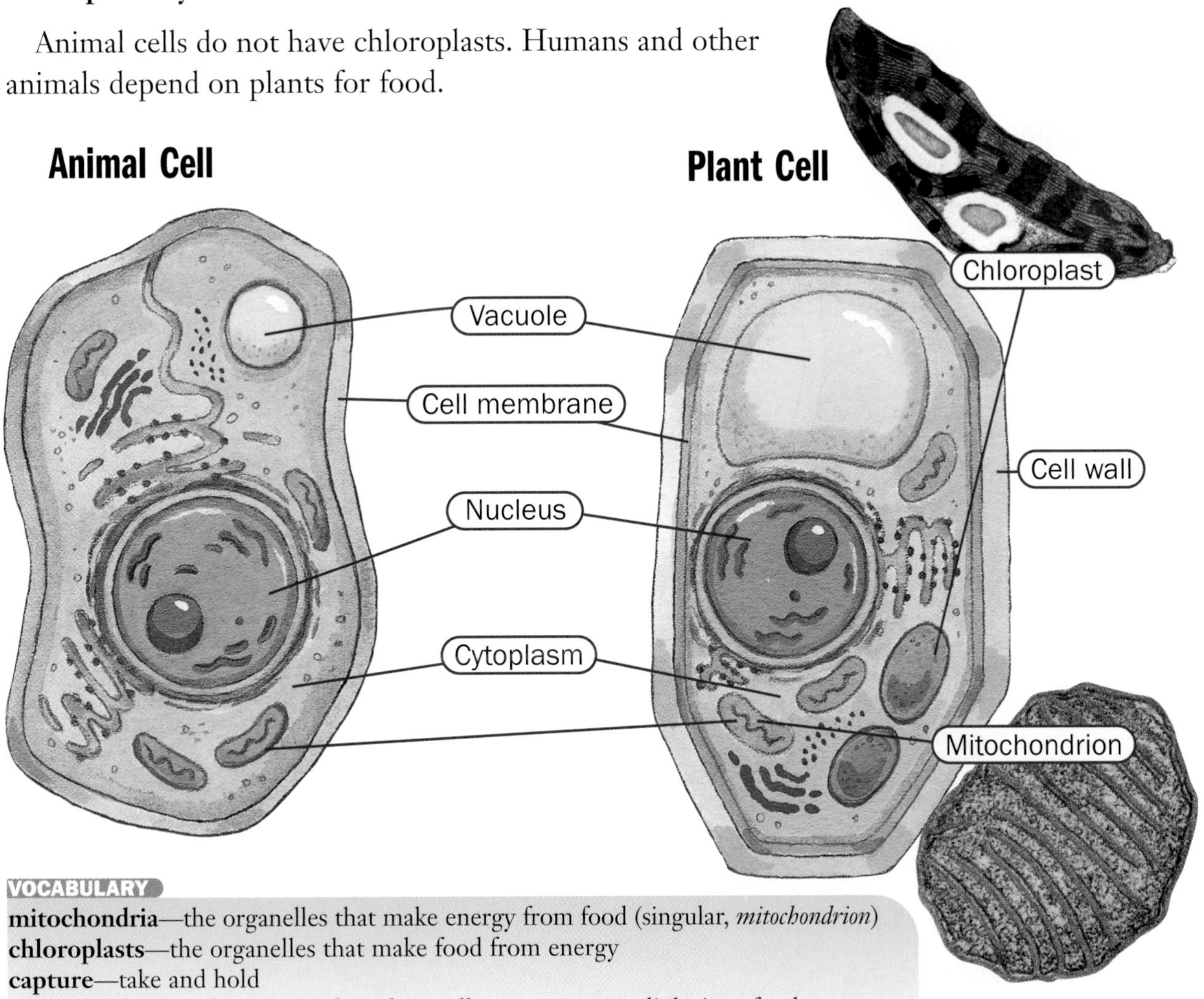

Animal Cell　　　　　　　　　　**Plant Cell**

Vacuole

Cell membrane

Nucleus

Cytoplasm

Chloroplast

Cell wall

Mitochondrion

VOCABULARY
mitochondria—the organelles that make energy from food (singular, *mitochondrion*)
chloroplasts—the organelles that make food from energy
capture—take and hold
photosynthesis—the process that plant cells use to turn sunlight into food

OTHER ORGANELLES

A eukaryotic cell also contains other **specialized** parts. Look at the chart below. What job does each organelle do to keep the cell alive?

Organelle	Job
Nucleus	Directs the activities of other organelles and controls reproduction
Mitochondrion	Turns food into energy
Chloroplast	Uses energy from the sun to make food
Golgi body	Holds and moves materials the cell makes
Lysosome	Digests (breaks down) materials no longer needed
Vacuole	Stores materials
Ribosome	Makes proteins

Organelles

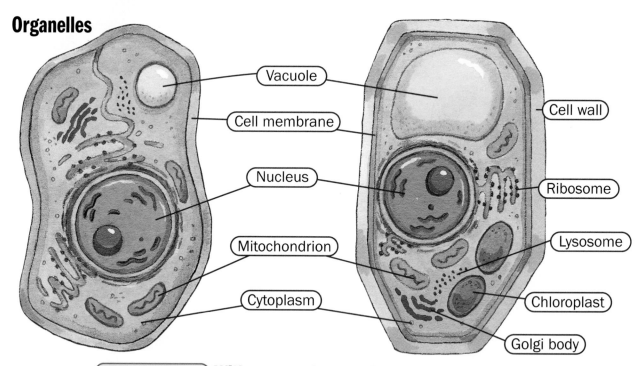

TALK AND SHARE With your partner, make note cards for the terms *mitochondria*, *chloroplasts*, and *nucleus*. Write the terms on one side of the card. Write or draw a description of each term on the other side.

VOCABULARY
specialized—having one particular job

Making New Cells

Every day your cells make new cells—billions of them! Whenever the body needs new cells, a **parent cell** divides itself into two, making an exact copy of itself. The new cells are called **daughter cells.** Each daughter cell can become a parent cell.

THE CELL CYCLE AND THE NUCLEUS

Cells have a **cycle.** They are born, live, and work as a single cell. Sometimes they rest. At the end of their cycle they divide. Some cells divide once a day. Others divide much less often. The nucleus tells the cell when to start and when to stop dividing.

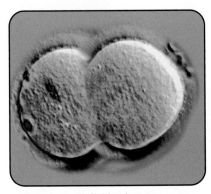

▲ A parent cell divides into two daughter cells.

A cell's nucleus contains its **chromosomes.** These structures hold all the information the cell needs. This information must be passed on to the daughter cells. As the cell divides in two, the chromosomes make copies of themselves. There are then two sets of chromosomes. One set goes into each new cell.

Imagine you are a **liver** cell inside your own body. What would your life cycle look like? Look at the illustration. A liver cell completes its **cell cycle** in 22 hours.

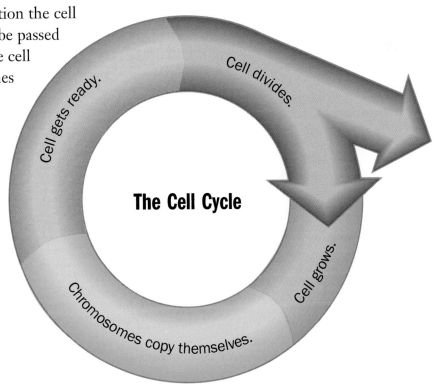

Cell gets ready.

Cell divides.

The Cell Cycle

Cell grows.

Chromosomes copy themselves.

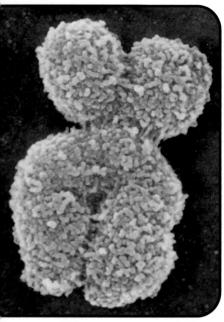

▲ A human chromosome during Stage 3 of cell division

CELL DIVISION

During its cycle, a parent cell grows. Before it divides, it must make copies of its organelles. It also copies the chromosomes in its nucleus. Daughter cells are the same size as parent cells. Each daughter cell has organelles, cytoplasm, and a membrane, just like the parent cell.

You, like all living things, grow because your cells constantly divide. New cells replace old cells that have died. New cells also help you grow bigger and taller. **Cell division** helps you grow and stay healthy.

Look at the picture of cell division on the next page. Cells divide in a series of steps, or stages. The cell nucleus divides along with the cell. People call the stages of nucleus division **mitosis.**

Science, Technology, and Society

Cancer

Some cells can go out of control. They suddenly start dividing over and over again. Nothing tells them to stop. These are **cancer** cells. Their wild growth causes a **tumor** to form.

Scientists and doctors look at cancer cells with microscopes. They watch the cells and think of possible ways to stop out-of-control cell division. They test their ideas to find ways to **cure** cancer.

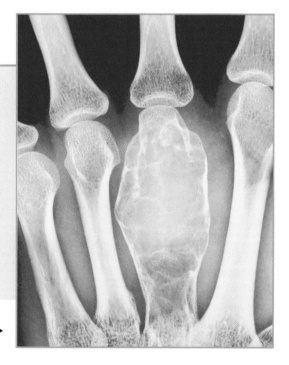

A colored X ray shows a tumor growing in the bone of one finger. This person has bone cancer. ▶

VOCABULARY

cell division—the process by which cells make copies of themselves and increase in number
mitosis—the set of stages in division of the cell nucleus
cancer—a disease caused by out-of-control cell division
tumor—a group of cells that may contain cancer cells
cure—stop a disease

Mitosis

Stage 1:

The parent cell gets ready to divide when each chromosome in the nucleus makes an exact copy of itself.

Stage 2:

The nucleus gets ready to divide.

Stage 3:

The two chromosome copies line up in the center of the cell.

Stage 4:

The chromosome copies separate. Each set goes to one side of the cell.

Stage 5:

The cytoplasm pinches together in the middle of the cell. The parent cell divides, making two new daughter cells.

(TALK AND SHARE) **With your partner, explain how cells divide.**

Summary

Cells have different parts, such as a nucleus and other organelles. These parts of cells do different jobs. In its life cycle, every cell copies its organelles and divides. Cell division makes new cells. It also helps living things grow and stay healthy.

Comparing and Contrasting

Comparing and Contrasting Parts of a Cell

When you compare, you show how things are alike. When you contrast, you show how things are different.

You know that each part of the cell has a special job. You can visualize how the parts work together. Study this Venn Diagram to compare and contrast the cell membrane and the cell wall.

Venn Diagram

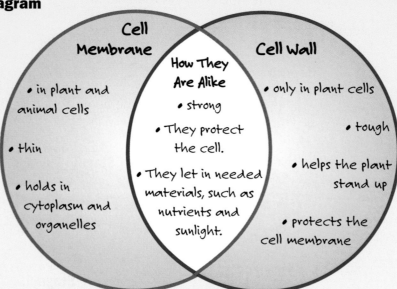

Cell Membrane
- in plant and animal cells
- thin
- holds in cytoplasm and organelles

How They Are Alike
- strong
- They protect the cell.
- They let in needed materials, such as nutrients and sunlight.

Cell Wall
- only in plant cells
- tough
- helps the plant stand up
- protects the cell membrane

Practice Comparing and Contrasting

1. Draw With a partner, talk about mitochondria and chloroplasts. Make a Venn Diagram like the one above to show how they are alike and how they are different.

2. Write Write a paragraph that compares an animal cell and a plant cell. Tell how an animal cell is different from a plant cell. Then tell how the two kinds of cells are alike. Words from the Word Bank can help you.

Word Bank

energy
food
membrane
wall

capture
release

green
invisible

Grammar Spotlight

Using *one of the* You can use the phrase *one of the* to draw attention to a single part of a process or a single member of a group. When you use this phrase, the verb is always singular.

Example	What It Means
The nucleus is one of the parts of a plant cell.	The plant cell has many parts. You are calling attention to the nucleus.
One of the jobs of the nucleus is to tell the cell when to start dividing.	The nucleus does many jobs. You are calling attention to one of these jobs.

Write a sentence about the cell cycle using the phrase *one of the*.

Oral Language

Explore Contrasting In a small group, contrast a cell membrane and the door to a room. Talk about how the door is different from a cell membrane and how other things in the room are different from organelles.

Hands On

Visualize With a partner, make a model of a cell using things you can find in your classroom or at home. For example, you can use clay or even different colors of paper. Make sure to include some organelles. Write labels for the main parts.

Partner Practice

Nice to Meet You Pretend to be an animal and have your partner pretend to be a plant. Introduce yourselves to each other and describe your cells. Ask and answer questions to find out what you have in common and how you are different. You may want to refer to page 141. If you wish, you and your partner can draw a Venn Diagram to help you visualize the cells.

Cells to
Organisms

Here you'll learn about how organisms are made of cells. You'll also learn how to organize data by size and practice describing body parts of different sizes.

Building Background

▲ My friends and I sometimes play basketball after school.

- **What is going on here?**
- **What kinds of work do your cells do?**
- **How are cells working here?**

Every living thing has parts that work together. From cells to organs, each part of the body has a job. The parts are called *structures,* and the kinds of work they do are called *functions.*

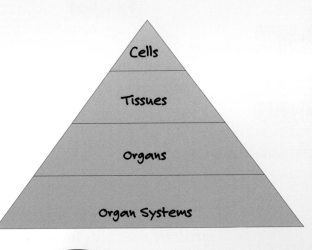

Cells

Tissues

Organs

Organ Systems

1 The cell is the basic unit of life.

2 Different cells work together in tissues.

3 Different tissues work together in organs.

4 Organs work together in organ systems.

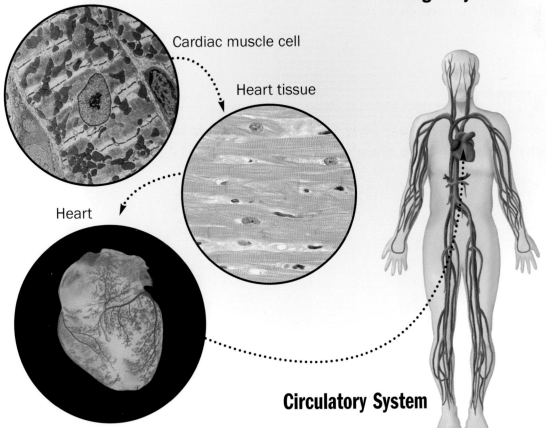

Cardiac muscle cell

Heart tissue

Heart

Circulatory System

Key Concepts

structure   function

Structure

Leaves
take in sunlight to make food.

Stems
move nutrients and water.

Roots
take in nutrients and water.

Function

A **structure** is a part or anything made out of parts. Add energy, and the parts do work.

The kind of work a structure does is its **function**.

Healing a Wound

You can see how the parts of your body work when your skin is cut or scraped. Your circulatory system delivers blood cells that repair it.

Blood cells

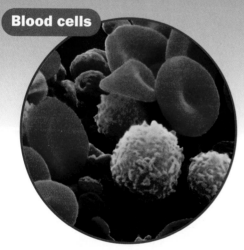

Blood carries nutrients to body cells.

Blood vessels

When you get a cut, blood travels to the wound through blood vessels.

Organize Data

When you work as a scientist, some of your data will include observations. Scientists look at things of different sizes and put the parts in order. This helps them study how the parts interact.

To organize data by size, follow these steps.

1. Put the smallest things at the top or on the left.

2. Put the next smallest thing underneath or to the right.

3. Continue the process until you have put the largest thing on the bottom or on the right.

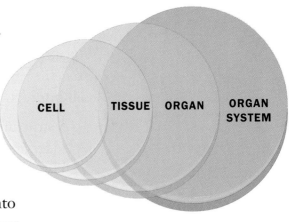

CELL   TISSUE ORGAN ORGAN SYSTEM

For example, your body has billions of very tiny cells. When many cells work together, they form tissues. Different kinds of tissue combine into organs, such as the heart and stomach. To keep your body running, organs work together in larger organ systems.

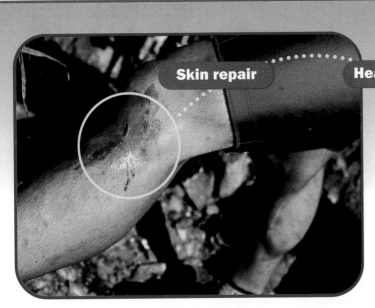

Skin repair   Healing body

White blood cells attack germs and infections.

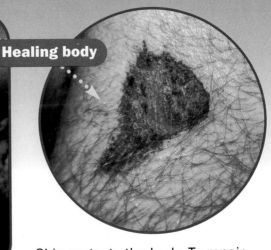

Skin protects the body. To repair broken skin, blood forms a scab to seal the wound.

Cells to Organisms

From cell to organ to organ system, each part of your body is made to do a job. The structure of each part is tied to its job, or function.

How the Body Works

Your body is like a well-organized machine. It depends on an enormous number of **structures.** All of them work together in 10 main **systems.** The structures in these systems all **interact.**

A structure is something made of parts. A cell, a house, and a ladder are all structures. A **function** is a job. The job of a cell is to stay alive. The job of a house is to give shelter. The job of a ladder is to help a person climb.

Structure and function are related. For example, the structure of your hand relates to how you hold a pencil, catch a ball, or use a computer.

▲ Your body is a structure that makes you able to move in many ways. ▶

STRUCTURE AND FUNCTION IN CELLS

Your body depends on many kinds of cells. Inside they have the same parts. Their sizes, shapes, and colors relate to their functions.

Cell Examples

Cells	Shape	Function
Cheek	Flat and oval	Form a **protective** layer inside your mouth
Red blood	Like a disc	Carry oxygen around your body
Skin	Flat and like scales	Protect the surface of your body

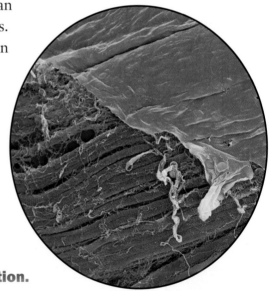

▲ Blood cells

TISSUE STRUCTURE AND FUNCTION

Most cells in your body combine into **tissues.** In a tissue, different cells work together to do a job. A **muscle** is an example of a tissue. No other cells are like muscle cells. They are long, thin **fibers.** The fibers work together in **bundles.** Your **brain** tells all your muscles what to do.

There are three kinds of muscle tissue. Each kind has a different structure and function. When you run and jump, your skeletal muscles are at work. They attach to your bones and make your body move. Cardiac muscles keep your heart beating. When you digest food, smooth muscles in the stomach help break the food into small pieces.

(TALK AND SHARE) **Ask your partner to give you an example of a structure in your body and its function.**

▲ Bundle of skeletal muscle fibers

VOCABULARY
protective—able to keep from danger
tissues—groups of cells that work together to do a job
muscle—a tissue that makes a body part move
fibers—long, thread-like structures
bundles—groups of things held together
brain—the control center of an animal body

How Organ Systems Work

Your body works because it runs on an organized set of systems. Systems let you breathe, eat, stand up, and move. They control your body's activities and get rid of things you don't need. Each system begins with small cells.

CELLS, TISSUES, AND ORGANS

Let's look at what happens to food you eat. It goes into your mouth, which is the beginning of your **digestive system.** This system makes it possible for you to eat and get **nutrients** from food. Many kinds of cells and tissues make up the **organs** of your digestive system.

Some digestive cells group together to form **epithelial** tissue. This tissue covers the inside of your stomach and protects it. Cells in other tissues make chemicals that help break down food. Muscle cells also form tissue in your stomach. Layers of muscle run along and across the stomach. They help twist and crush your food. Their action breaks down food for nutrients.

All of the tissues in your stomach give it a unique structure and function. Each organ in your body has its own structure and function.

Building an Organ

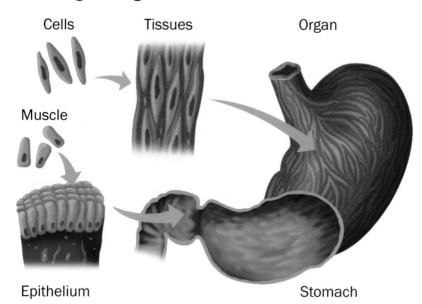

Cells   Tissues   Organ

Muscle

Epithelium   Stomach

VOCABULARY

digestive system—a body system that breaks down food
nutrients—substances a living thing needs for health and growth
organs—structures made of specialized tissues that do particular jobs
epithelial—relating to cells and tissues that cover the outside of the body and line the inside of the body

ORGAN SYSTEMS AND ORGANISMS

Organs work together in **organ systems.** For example, your digestive system includes your stomach. It also includes such organs as your intestines and liver. All these organs work together as part of the digestive system.

Different organ systems work together, or interact. Your **circulatory system** brings oxygen to every cell. Without oxygen, cells in the digestive system could not do their jobs. Look at the chart of human organ systems below. Think about how their functions are connected.

Human Organ Systems

System	Function
Skeletal system	Supports the body
Endocrine system	Controls body activities through **hormones**
Excretory system	Removes wastes
Immune system	Protects the body from infection and fights disease
Reproductive system	Allows individuals to reproduce
Muscular system	Makes the body move
Circulatory system	Carries oxygen and carbon dioxide through the body
Respiratory system	Takes in oxygen from air and sends out carbon dioxide
Nervous system	Controls body activities through the brain, spine, and nerves
Digestive system	Breaks down food and takes in nutrients

(TALK AND SHARE) **With your partner, talk about the difference between a cell and an organ system.**

VOCABULARY

organ systems—groups of organs that work together in the body
circulatory system—the body system that carries blood with carbon dioxide and oxygen in it
hormones—substances made by one tissue and carried to another tissue

▲ A plant's vascular system carries water and nutrients from its roots to its leaves.

Same Function, Similar Structures

Have you ever forgotten to water a plant? It doesn't take long for it to die without water. Many plants have a **transport system** that keeps water moving in their cells and tissues. Humans also need a transport system to move water and nutrients.

ORGANISMS AND SYSTEMS

All **organisms** move materials in their cells. Nutrients such as oxygen and nitrogen need to travel throughout the body.

Some plants have a **vascular system** to carry water and nutrients from their roots to their leaves. This system also sends food from the leaves into buds and roots. Animals and humans have a circulatory system that does similar jobs (see the drawing on page 149). In humans, another name for the circulatory system is the **cardiovascular system.**

Science, Technology, and Society

Radioisotopes

In people, blood moves through the body in the circulatory system. Doctors can use materials called **radioisotopes** to take pictures of the circulatory system. The radioisotope travels through the circulatory system and gives off safe levels of radiation. With an X ray, doctors can see areas where there might be problems. Doctors can then study how the heart is working, how much blood is going to the brain, and where the system is blocked.

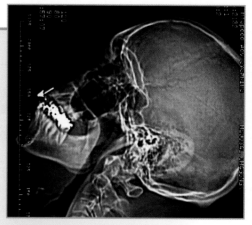

▲ This picture of the skull was made using radioisotopes.

VOCABULARY

transport system—an organized way of carrying material from one place to another
organisms—individual living things
vascular system—a system for moving food and water
cardiovascular system—another name for the human circulatory system
radioisotopes—atoms whose nuclei send out particles

ORGANS, TISSUES, AND CELLS

The human circulatory system is powered by the **heart,** an organ. The heart pumps blood through the lungs and around the body in less than a minute.

The human circulatory system is built with lots of **blood vessels. Arteries** carry blood away from the heart. **Veins** carry blood back to the heart. Tiny **capillaries** connect arteries and veins. Capillary walls are just one cell thick. Capillaries give food and oxygen to nearby cells and take away wastes.

The plant vascular system moves water and food. It also keeps the plant from falling over.

Plants have two kinds of **vascular tissue.** Phloem moves food. Xylem carries water and nutrients from the roots, up the stem, and out to the leaves. Usually, the two kinds of vascular tissue are in bundles.

(TALK AND SHARE) **With your partner, talk about how transport systems in plants and animals are alike.**

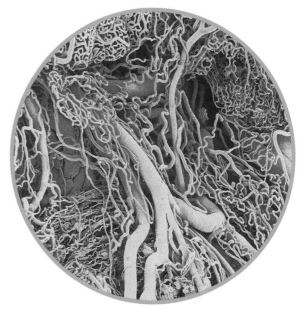

▲ Blood vessels

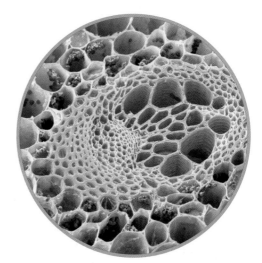

▲ Plant vascular bundle

Summary

To stay alive, the body has different structures that perform functions, or jobs. Each cell, tissue, and organ has a specific job in its organ system.

VOCABULARY

heart—the animal organ that sends blood through the body
blood vessels—tubes that carry blood
arteries—blood vessels that carry blood away from the heart
veins—blood vessels that carry blood to the heart
capillaries—small blood vessels that connect arteries and veins
vascular tissue—a group of cells that work together to move food and water

Describing

Describing Parts of Different Sizes

In the human body, each part relates to every other part. Each part has a job. Other parts rely on those jobs getting done. In science, you will have to describe how parts of systems work. For example, think about the circulatory system. Make a Size Organizer to list its parts from small to large. Then describe how each part relates to the next largest one.

Size Organizer

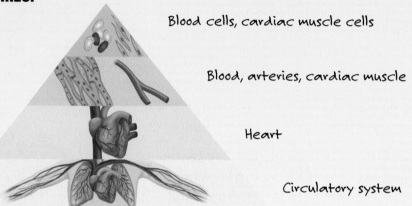

Blood cells, cardiac muscle cells

Blood, arteries, cardiac muscle

Heart

Circulatory system

Blood cells make up blood tissue. Cardiac muscle tissue makes up the heart. The heart pumps blood. The heart is the main organ in the circulatory system.

Practice Describing

1. Draw With a partner, study the organizer above. Then make a simple drawing of a human body. Together, put the heart and arteries where you think they should go. Take turns describing your drawing to each other.

2. Write Think about the following parts of the human body: stomach muscle cells, stomach muscle tissues, stomach, and digestive system. Make a Size Organizer that puts the parts in order. Describe how each part relates to the other parts. Words from the Word Bank can help you.

Word Bank

squeeze
break apart
make up

food
structure
function
nutrient

Activities

Adding *er* to Adjectives   You can add *er* to many adjectives when you want to compare two things. After you add *er*, use the word *than* to connect the things you want to relate.

What You Are Comparing	Using *er* and *than*
The sizes of two kinds of blood vessels	*Capillaries are smaller than veins.*
The shapes of two kinds of cells	*Skin cells are flatter than blood cells.*
The strengths of two kinds of body parts	*A tissue is stronger than a cell.*

Write a sentence that uses *er* and relates tissues and organs.

Oral Language

Structures and Functions   In a small group, make a set of 6 cards. Make 3 with these structures: hand, eye, and knee. Make 3 with these functions: see, bend, and hold. Have someone mix up all the cards and hand them out. Talk to each other to match each structure card with its function card. Take turns describing each structure and each function.

Hands On

Organize Data   Work in a small group to make a chart that shows the following things from smallest to largest: nutrient, cell, tissue, organ, organ system, and organism. Draw a picture to go with each word. Then have your group display its poster and explain it to the other groups.

Partner Practice

Quiz Cards   With your partner, create study cards for these terms: *cells, tissues, organs, function, arteries, veins, capillaries,* and *system*. Write the term on one side of a file card and the meaning on the other. Then quiz each other on the terms until you know them.

Energy and
Nutrients

Here you'll learn about how living things get and use energy. You'll also learn how to use math and practice interpreting numbers.

▲ My favorite food is Chinese, especially the spicy dishes!

■ **Why are these people eating?**

■ **Where do you get your energy?**

■ **How do you use it up?**

Producers use energy to make food. The nutrients in food give living things energy. All living things can turn food back into energy.

1 Turning Energy into Food

IN
- Sun energy
- Carbon dioxide
- Water

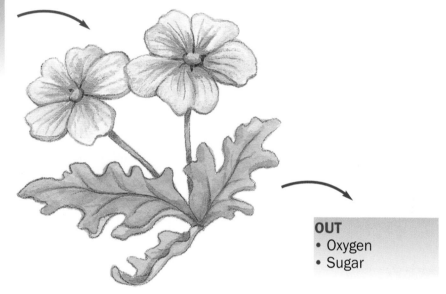

OUT
- Oxygen
- Sugar

2 Turning Food into Energy

IN
- Oxygen
- Sugar

OUT
- Energy
- Carbon dioxide

Key Concepts

energy   **nutrients**   **calorie**   **Calories**

All living things need **energy** to live. A lot of the energy comes from **nutrients,** such as those found in food.

A **calorie** (with a small *c*) is a small unit of energy. People need thousands of calories each day. Most food is labeled with **Calories** (with a big *C*). One Calorie is 1,000 calories. This is also called a kilocalorie.

Food Groups

Your body needs different nutrients for energy.

Bread, Cereal, Rice, Pasta Group

6–11 servings

Fruit Group

2–4 servings

Vegetable Group

3–5 servings

Use Math

How can you make sure you are fueling your body with the right nutrients and enough energy? You can use math to find out.

The number of Calories you need depends on your age, weight, and height. Girls entering their teens need about 2,200 Calories per day. Teenage boys need around 2,800 Calories.

Nutrient	Percent of Daily Calories Needed
Carbohydrates	60
Fats	30
Proteins	10
Total	100

Look at the chart above. At most, only 30 percent of your daily Calories should be from fat. To find out the most fat Calories you should eat each day, use these steps.

Multiply your total recommended Calories by 30 percent (30 percent is 0.30).

Teen girl: 2,200 x 0.30 = 660 Calories from fat, at most

Teen boy: 2,800 x 0.30 = 840 Calories from fat, at most

Eating the right amount from each food group will give your body what it needs.

Milk, Yogurt, Cheese Group
2–3 servings

Meat, Poultry, Fish Group
2–3 servings

Fats, Oils, Sweets Group
Zero or few servings

Energy and Nutrients

Plants make food using light energy. Food contains nutrients. All living things can turn nutrients into energy.

▲ Corn is one of many
▼ plants that people eat.

Turning Energy into Food

In a process called **photosynthesis,** plants use energy from the sun to make food. Photosynthesis also sends **oxygen** into the air.

WHAT IS NEEDED FOR PHOTOSYNTHESIS?

You already know that plants need sunlight to make photosynthesis happen. They also use other **ingredients.**

Plants need carbon dioxide (CO_2) from the air. Most carbon dioxide enters the plant through its green parts. Plants also need water (H_2O). Water travels from the roots of the plant up to the leaves. Plants then break down carbon dioxide and water to make food.

Here's a **chemical equation** for the ingredients of photosynthesis.

$$CO_2 \quad + \quad H_2O \quad + \quad \text{Energy from sunlight} \longrightarrow$$

Carbon   Water
dioxide

VOCABULARY

photosynthesis—the process in which plants use water, carbon dioxide, and energy from the sun to make food
oxygen—a colorless gas. Plants send oxygen into the air during photosynthesis.
ingredients—the materials that make up something
chemical equation—a sentence, made of symbols and words, that tells what happens when atoms combine

HOW DO PLANTS MAKE FOOD?

Plants make food in their leaf cells. **Chloroplasts** in the cells **capture** energy from the sun. Then they use this energy to break apart water and carbon dioxide.

During photosynthesis, plants **rearrange** these ingredients. They make **sugar** molecules. Sugar is a **nutrient** that mixes with water and travels to other parts of the plant, where the sugar is used as food. As the plant makes food, it also sends oxygen (O_2) out into the air.

Here is the chemical equation for photosynthesis.

$$CO_2 + H_2O + \text{Energy from sunlight} \longrightarrow O_2 + \text{Sugar}$$

Carbon   Water   Oxygen
dioxide

(**TALK AND SHARE**) **With your partner, talk about the ways photosynthesis affects your daily life.**

The chloroplasts in leaves absorb sunlight. ▶

▲ A single chloroplast

Language Notes

Multiple Meanings
These words have more than one meaning.

◻ plants
1. a noun that means living things that use energy to make food
2. a noun that means factories
3. a verb that means puts in the soil so it will grow
4. a verb that means sets down firmly

◻ leaves
1. a noun that means parts of a plant growing from the stem
2. a verb that means goes away

VOCABULARY

chloroplasts—the organelles in plant cells that make food from energy
capture—take and hold
rearrange—put in a new order
sugar—a nutrient that usually has a sweet taste
nutrient—a substance in food that an organism can break down and use for growth and health

How to Turn Food into Energy

The sugar that plants make during photosynthesis can be used as **fuel** for cell activities. Living things need a way to turn this fuel into energy.

Cells turn food into energy through a process called **cellular respiration.** This process uses the materials made by photosynthesis.

The cell needs sugar for cellular respiration. It also needs oxygen. These ingredients come from nutrients and from the air.

Within the cell, **mitochondria** use the oxygen to break up the sugar. Then they make carbon dioxide and water along with energy. When respiration is finished, the cell has both water and energy to use.

Here is the chemical equation for cellular respiration.

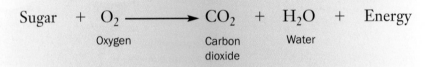

$$\text{Sugar} \quad + \quad \underset{\text{Oxygen}}{O_2} \quad \longrightarrow \quad \underset{\substack{\text{Carbon} \\ \text{dioxide}}}{CO_2} \quad + \quad \underset{\text{Water}}{H_2O} \quad + \quad \text{Energy}$$

Eukaryotes have mitochondria inside their cells that turn energy into food. ▼

TALK AND SHARE Ask your partner to explain cellular respiration and how it is different from photosynthesis.

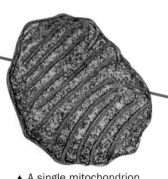

▲ A single mitochondrion

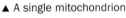

VOCABULARY
fuel—an energy resource
cellular respiration—the process by which cells break down food to make energy
mitochondria—the organelles in cells that make energy from food (singular, *mitochondrion*)

What Are Nutrients?

Food gives you energy. It also has nutrients that help your body grow. There are 4 main categories of nutrients: carbohydrates, fats, proteins, and vitamins and minerals. The food pyramid shows you how many servings you need each day to get these nutrients.

CARBOHYDRATES AND FATS

Carbohydrates come in foods made from grains and cereal—like bread, rice, and pasta—and from fruit. These foods contain sugar and **starch,** which plants use to store energy. Cells break down carbohydrates and give off energy. Some simple sugars, such as those in fruits, give you quick energy. **Complex carbohydrates,** like bread, give out energy more slowly.

We also get energy from **fats,** such as butter. Fats provide about twice the energy of carbohydrates. Our bodies need some fat to work, but not too much.

Fats, oils, sweets	zero or few servings
Meat, poultry, fish	2–3 servings
Milk, yogurt, cheese	2–3 servings
Fruit	2–4 servings
Vegetables	3–5 servings
Bread, cereal, rice, pasta	6–11 servings

What nutrients do you see here? ▼

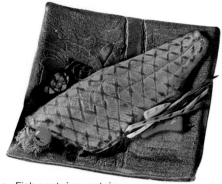

▲ Fish contains protein.

Milk contains calcium and phosphorus. ▶

Spinach contains calcium. ▶

PROTEINS

Proteins have many jobs in the body. Your body uses protein to repair itself. Your muscles and organs are mostly protein. Protein also helps your body fight diseases.

When you eat meat, fish, eggs, beans, nuts, seeds, and dairy products, protein enters your body. Most foods have some protein.

VITAMINS AND MINERALS

Vitamins are nutrients that help cells do their work. You need vitamins every day, but in small amounts. Your body can't make vitamins. You have to get them from the food you eat. For example, vitamin C helps your body **assemble** tissues and helps prevent diseases. Good sources of vitamin C are fruits and vegetables.

Minerals are nutrients you get from food, salt, and drinking water. You need minerals in small amounts each day. One mineral nutrient is **phosphorus,** which helps form teeth and bones and helps cells release energy. Teens and older adults need a lot of the mineral **calcium** to build bones.

Science, Technology, and Society

Sodium

People need the mineral sodium for good health. We get most of our sodium from table salt. Most people get more sodium than they need. Packaged foods and fast foods often contain large amounts of sodium. When too much sodium enters the body, there are health risks. Think about the amount of table salt you use each day. Check food labels for sodium levels.

VOCABULARY

proteins—body-building nutrients made of carbon, hydrogen, oxygen, and nitrogen
vitamins—carbon-containing molecules that help cells do work
assemble—put together
minerals—nutrients from food that help support structures in the body
phosphorus—a mineral that humans need for energy and to form teeth and bones
calcium—a mineral found in dairy products, such as milk and cheese, that helps build bones

MEETING YOUR ENERGY NEEDS

What did you eat for breakfast today? That food gave you the nutrients and energy to last until lunch time. Look at the Breakfast Choices chart below. Think about what you might like to eat from this set of foods.

Breakfast Choices

Food	Total Calories	Carbohydrate Calories	Protein Calories	Fat Calories
Yogurt, 6 oz.	150	44	34	72
Oatmeal, 1 c.	150	96	36	18
Bacon, 2 slices	105.5	0.50	24	81
Orange juice, 1 c.	111.5	104	7	0.50
Plain bagel	153	120	24	9
2% milk, 1 c.	125	48	32	45

A **Calorie** is a unit of energy. A teenager usually needs between 2,200 and 2,800 Calories each day. Use math to decide how many of your daily Calories you should have at breakfast.

TALK AND SHARE **Talk with your partner about your breakfast. Tell what nutrients it included and which foods they came from.**

Summary

Plants make food through photosynthesis. Living things can turn food into energy. Food contains nutrients, such as fats, carbohydrates, and proteins.

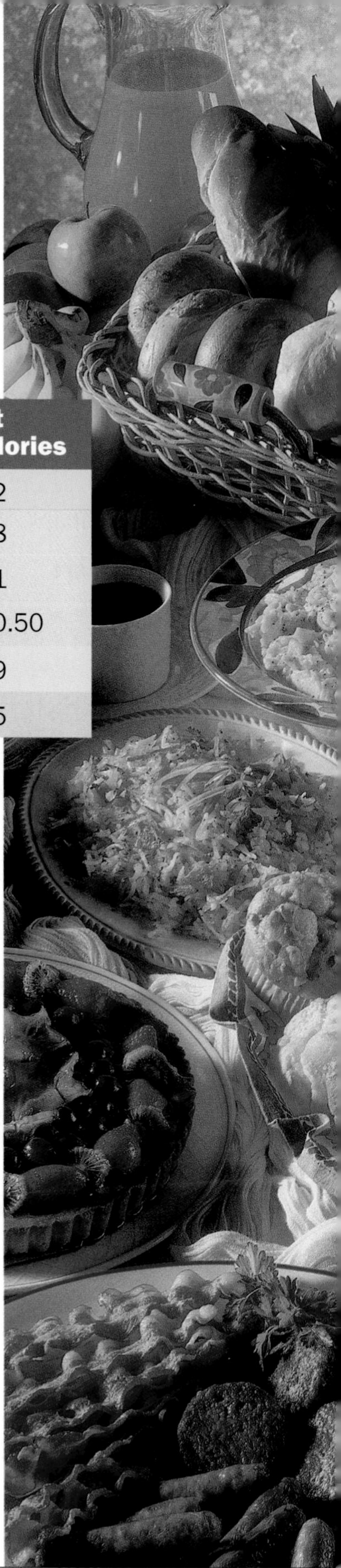

A variety of breakfast foods will give you energy. ▶

VOCABULARY

Calorie—a unit of energy supplied by food

Interpreting

Interpreting Numbers

When you interpret, you decide what something means. You can interpret numbers on a food label to make choices. For example, think about snack foods. How can you choose one that is good for your body? The food label tells you how much of each nutrient is contained in the food. It has information about the size of the serving. For carbohydrates and fats, the label also lists the percent of daily Calorie needs the food meets.

Use the chart to interpret how much fat and carbohydrates each food contains. Which do you think is better for your body?

Chart

Nutrient	Percent of Daily Calories Needed	Daily Percent in Snack A	Daily Percent in Snack B
Carbohydrates	60	6	10
Fats	30	9	20

Practice Interpreting

1. Draw Draw a picture of the foods you could eat in one day to get the right percentage of carbohydrates, fats, and proteins. (See the chart on page 163.) Trade drawings with your partner. Take turns interpreting each other's pictures.

2. Write Write a note or letter to a friend in which you recommend either Snack A or Snack B from the Chart above. Explain why you think this food is a good choice. Use details that show how you interpreted the numbers on the food label. Words from the Word Bank can help you.

Word Bank

Calorie
percent
total
vitamin
sugar
need
provide

Grammar Spotlight

Using Subject Pronouns with *am*, *is*, and *are* Subject pronouns in English are either singular or plural. Singular forms are *I*, *you*, *he*, *she*, and *it*. Plural subject pronouns are *we*, *you*, and *they*. Look at the chart.

Subject Pronoun	Verb (be)	Example
I	am	*I am a healthy eater.*
he she it	is	*She is a healthy eater.*
we you they	are	*You are a healthy eater.*

Make a sentence about photosynthesis. Use the words *it* and *is* in your sentence.

Oral Language

Compare Foods Bring the "nutrition facts" label from a food package to class. In your group, compare the amounts of fat and carbohydrate on each label. Then discuss which food would be the best to eat for health.

Hands On

Make a Model In your group, draw a model using pictures and symbols to show how an animal uses sugar from plants. Remember to draw the ingredients for photosynthesis and cellular respiration. Use pages 164–166 for help.

Partner Practice

Use Math Imagine that you have a friend who wants to take in 2,500 Calories each day. With a partner, use math and the information on page 163 to find out how many Calories should come from each kind of nutrient.

Responding to
the Environment

Here you'll learn about how living things respond to their environments. You'll also learn how to use the science process and practice predicting a response.

▲ My sister takes karate and sometimes she shows me her new moves.

- **What is happening inside these people?**
- **How are they responding to their environment?**
- **How does your body respond to the world around you?**

Responding to the Outside and Inside Environments

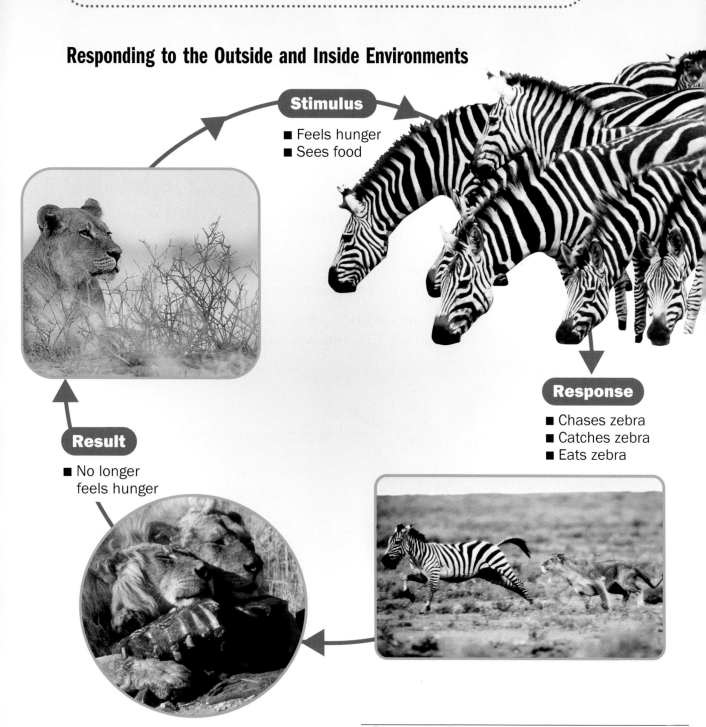

Stimulus
- Feels hunger
- Sees food

Response
- Chases zebra
- Catches zebra
- Eats zebra

Result
- No longer feels hunger

Key Concepts

maintain equilibrium   **senses**   **stimulus**   **response**

All living things work to **maintain equilibrium.** This means they work to keep everything in balance.

When a living thing receives new information from its **senses,** it receives a **stimulus.** For example, a loud noise is a stimulus.

To maintain equilibrium, the living thing reacts to the stimulus. The reaction is called a **response.** Covering your ears might be a response to a loud noise.

Maintaining Equilibrium

To survive, every organism maintains equilibrium. For example, pores, or openings, in leaves open and close to balance water levels in a plant.

Open Pore

Plenty of water

Water and nutrients enter and leave.

in H_2O, CO_2

out H_2O, O_2

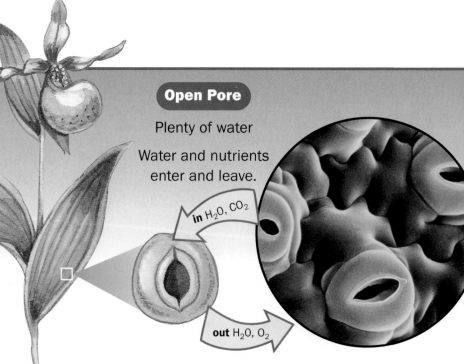

Use the Science Process

When you use the science process, you make predictions based on your hypotheses. To make a prediction, follow these steps.

1. Start with a question.

2. Make a hypothesis about the answer.

3. Turn the hypothesis into a prediction you can test.

Prediction Organizer

Stimulus *If*	Predicted Response *Then*
If its stomach growls with hunger,	then the animal will find something to eat.
If an animal is thirsty,	then it will find water to drink.
If a fly lands inside a Venus's-flytrap,	then the leaves will close and trap the fly.

For example, for every stimulus that reaches a living thing, you can predict what the response will be. You can state the prediction by saying, "If the stimulus happens, then the response will happen." Look at the Prediction Organizer. As you read, think about predictions you can make to connect a stimulus and a response.

Closed Pore

Not much water

Less water is lost to the air.

Responding to the Environment

Living things receive stimuli from inside their bodies and from the environment outside their bodies. When a living thing receives a stimulus, it responds.

Responding to the Inside Environment

Organisms keep a steady **internal** environment. This steadiness is called **equilibrium.** It keeps the body healthy.

When equilibrium is **disturbed,** a **stimulus** will alert the body. The body **responds** to bring itself back to equilibrium. The body is always checking and changing its internal environment to stay balanced.

BALANCING TEMPERATURE

One way an organism stays balanced is by controlling its body **temperature.** To keep your internal temperature steady, you break down food to stay warm. When you get too hot, the sweat on your skin helps you cool off. Some animals grow thick fur or feathers to stay warm in cold weather. They lose fur and feathers during the hot summer.

Japanese snow monkeys and many other mammals grow a heavier coat in cold weather. ▶

VOCABULARY
internal—inside
equilibrium—a state of being in balance
disturbed—upset, unsettled, put out of order
stimulus—something an organism can sense (plural, *stimuli*)
responds—reacts to a stimulus. The reaction is called a *response*.
temperature—the amount of thermal energy. You can measure temperature with a thermometer.

BALANCING FLUID LEVELS

Organisms respond to changes in the amount of **fluid** in their bodies. Plants pull in water through their roots. Animals respond to thirst by getting a drink.

BALANCING ENERGY

All organisms need energy. When your energy level gets too low, you find food to eat. Many organisms store energy in their bodies to use when they need it. For example, plants like potatoes store starch.

BALANCING CHEMICAL LEVELS

Your body contains millions of atoms and **molecules** that help cells do work. The body works to keep levels of all these **chemicals** in balance.

Imagine you suddenly see a bear. The stimulus of fear causes some **glands** to send out chemicals called **hormones** that help you take action. This disturbs your body's chemical equilibrium. When you are safely out of danger, different glands send out chemicals to **restore** equilibrium.

(TALK AND SHARE) **With your partner, discuss how your body responds when its internal environment signals hunger.**

Language Notes

Verb Phrases
These phrases have special meanings.

- **break down:** divide into parts
- **cool off:** remove heat or make cool

▲ People drink water to replace fluids lost during exercise.

How the Body Balances

Bringing In	Moving Out
Energy	Chemicals
Nutrients	Waste
Air	Heat
Water	Water

VOCABULARY

fluid—any liquid that flows, such as water
molecules—pairs or groups of atoms
chemicals—atoms and molecules
glands—the body parts that make chemicals and send them somewhere else in the body, where they are used
hormones—chemicals, sent out by glands in animals, that affect body function
restore—put back in place

▲ When this animal senses danger, it responds very quickly.

▲ Plants bend toward sunlight.

Responding to the Outside Environment

The outside world always changes. Animals **perceive** the **external** environment through their **senses.** Senses, such as sight and hearing, receive stimuli. Your body responds to stimuli to maintain equilibrium.

Most animals have a **nervous system** to help them do this. A nervous system receives information from senses. It sends signals to different parts of your body to tell it how to respond.

ORGANISMS AND LIGHT

Plants respond to light stimulus. If you put a houseplant near a window, cells in the leaves and stems will grow so that the plant bends toward the sunlight. If you turn the plant away from the light, soon you will see it turn back. The plant's response to light is controlled by plant hormones.

Sunlight attracts animals, too. Heat from the sun can make you feel warm and comfortable. However, the stimulus of sun shining in your eyes will cause you to **squint.** Your eyes start to close so that less light will come in. Too much light can harm your eyes, and squinting protects them.

VOCABULARY

perceive—notice, become aware of
external—outside
senses—sight, hearing, taste, smell, and touch
nervous system—the body system by which sensations are received. It is made up of the brain, spinal cord, and nerves.
squint—close the eyes partway

REFLEXES

Reflexes are **automatic** responses. They happen too fast to think about. Reflexes are great for emergencies. If you touch a hot plate, you will quickly move your hand. This protects you from burns. If something touches the back of your throat, you will gag. This keeps you from choking. There is a reflex that makes your foot and leg jump when something hits your knee.

HOW THE NERVOUS SYSTEM WORKS

Three main groupings of cells make up the human nervous system.

1. Brain
2. Spinal cord
3. Nerves

Nerve cells stretch throughout the body like branches on a tree.

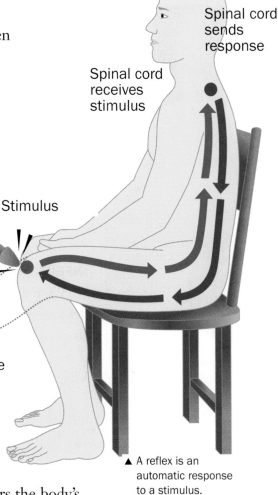

Spinal cord sends response

Spinal cord receives stimulus

Stimulus

Response

▲ A reflex is an automatic response to a stimulus.

A stimulus from the external environment enters the body's sense **organs,** such as the skin. Sense organs are part of the nervous system. The signal quickly travels along nerve cells to the spinal cord and brain. The brain sends instructions for response back through the spinal cord and along the nerve cells. Muscles, organs, glands, and other parts of the body carry out the responses needed to maintain equilibrium.

(TALK AND SHARE) **With your partner, list some ways the nervous system can protect you from getting hurt.**

VOCABULARY
reflexes—automatic responses to a stimulus
automatic—happens without thinking. For example, bright lights make your eyes close automatically.
organs—parts of the body that perform special functions. The eyes, stomach, heart, and skin are all organs.

Defending the Body

Every second of the day your body **defends** itself. Your **immune system** protects you from attacks by **germs.** It also responds to harmful nonliving substances. Your immune system knows which substances entering your body are safe and which ones must be stopped and destroyed.

THE FIRST DEFENSE

Your skin is like a protective wall. It is your first defense against germs. Your nose and throat catch germs in sticky **mucus.** Chemicals in your stomach kill germs you swallow. Even the tiny hairs in your nose help stop germs.

INFECTIONS

When a dangerous organism breaks through your first defense system, it can reproduce and cause **infection. Viruses** also cause infections, but they are not alive. A virus is a particle that enters healthy cells and uses the cells to reproduce. Viruses cause such infections as chicken pox and colds.

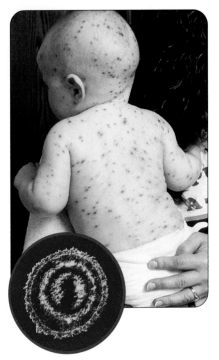

▲ The chicken pox virus often infects young children.

Science, Technology, and Society

Vaccinations

Vaccinations help protect you against dangerous diseases. A shot for a disease like measles contains dead measles viruses. White blood cells make chemicals that attack the viruses. Any time those viruses enter your body, your immune system can quickly make them harmless.

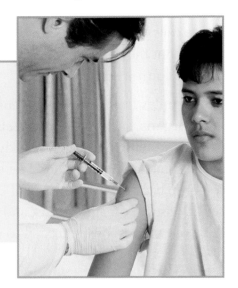

VOCABULARY

defends—protects from danger
immune system—a body system that can tell what is unsafe and responds to destroy it
germs—tiny organisms that cause infection
mucus—a liquid protective material in the body
infection—a sickness that spreads from one organism to another
viruses—nonliving particles that reproduce in living cells

THE SECOND DEFENSE

Your immune system's **white blood cells** fight infections. When a white blood cell meets a germ or virus, the blood cell wraps around the germ or virus and destroys it.

Some white blood cells make **proteins** called **antibodies.** Antibodies can **recognize** and destroy bacteria and viruses.

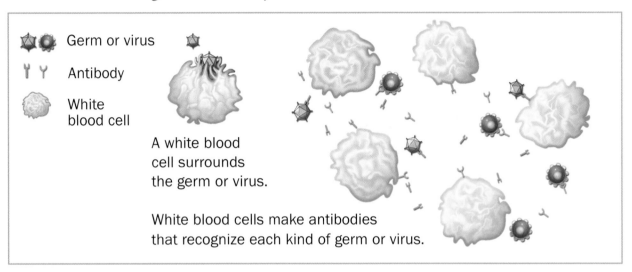

Germ or virus

Antibody

White blood cell

A white blood cell surrounds the germ or virus.

White blood cells make antibodies that recognize each kind of germ or virus.

After white blood cells stop an infection, they remember how to make the antibodies that destroyed the germ or virus. The next time the same germ or virus gets into your body, your antibodies will attack it before it can make you sick.

(TALK AND SHARE) **Talk with your partner about how your immune system protects you from infection.**

Summary

Living things respond to stimuli from the internal and external environments. Some responses help the organism get what it needs to live. Other responses help it fight germs and viruses. When body systems respond, they maintain equilibrium.

VOCABULARY
white blood cells—body cells that destroy germs
proteins—chemicals the body uses for growth and repair
antibodies—blood proteins that recognize certain germs or viruses
recognize—realize or identify something that was known before

Predicting

Predicting a Response

When you predict, you make an *If . . . then* statement about a hypothesis. This is a kind of statement you can test.

For example, you know that plants need light to grow. You might make the following prediction: *If I put my plants in a dark closet, then they will stop growing*. Look at the Prediction Organizer for other examples.

Prediction Organizer

If	Then
If a germ enters the body,	then the immune system will send white blood cells to attack it.
If the temperature is hot,	then runners will sweat and need to drink a lot of water to replace fluids.

Practice Predicting

1. Draw Make a picture of the environment inside your classroom. Then circle at least 3 stimuli in this environment that can affect your body. Think about things like light, heat, sound, water, food, and germs. Draw how you think you will respond to each of the stimuli.

2. Write Prepare a Prediction Organizer like the one above. Then write a prediction sentence for each of the following stimuli. That means deciding what the outcome will be *if* the stimulus happens. Words from the Word Bank can help you.

Word Bank

shiver
move
itch
bleed
scratch
feel hungry
eat

Stimulus

■ A window breaks during lunch and lets in cold air.

■ You get a mosquito bite.

■ You smell someone cooking good food.

Grammar Spotlight

Using *if* to Talk About the Future   When you make a prediction, you tell what you think will happen in the future. You state the first part of your prediction using the word *if*. The second part of the prediction often begins with *then*. Use the simple present tense of the verb in the *if* clause and the future tense in the *then* clause.

If Plus Present Tense	*Then* Plus Future Tense
If her stomach growls,	then my cousin will find food.
If dogs bark,	then the cat will hide.
If I hurry,	then I will arrive first.

Make a sentence about the future using the word *if* and the verb *cough*.

Oral Language

Animal Observations   With your group, choose an animal you like. For example, you might choose a dog, snake, or polar bear. Talk about how the animal acts when it is hungry. Then talk about what the animal does when it is cold. As you talk, name each stimulus and how the animal responds to it.

Partner Practice

Use the Science Process   Choose a stimulus from the list below. Have your partner choose another one. Take turns predicting what you think your body will do in response to the stimulus you choose.

    hunger   cold weather   a baseball pitch

    a loud siren   a karate kick   drinking very hot milk

Hands On

Balancing Act   Try placing different objects on a laboratory balance. Add or subtract objects until both sides of the measuring device are balanced. Talk to your group about what it means to be in balance.

Reproduction
and Inheritance

Here you'll learn about how living things reproduce. You'll also learn how to look for patterns and practice describing patterns of inheritance.

▲ Last summer my grandparents and my great-grandmother came to visit us in our new home.

- **What makes these family members look alike?**
- **How are you different from your parents?**
- **What makes people different from each other?**

When living things reproduce, their offspring inherit genes. Genes determine traits. Different gene combinations result in individuals with different traits, called *genetic variation*.

1 Living things reproduce.

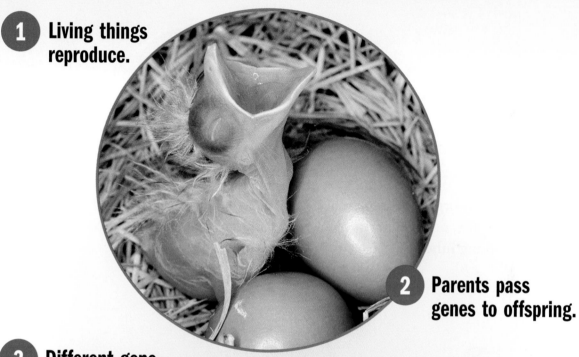

2 Parents pass genes to offspring.

3 Different gene combinations create genetic variation.

Key Concepts

reproduce   genes   traits   offspring   inherit

When organisms **reproduce,** they pass on **genes.** Genes determine the **traits,** or characteristics, of their children (also called **offspring**). The offspring **inherit** these traits from the parents.

Reproduction

Animal Reproduction

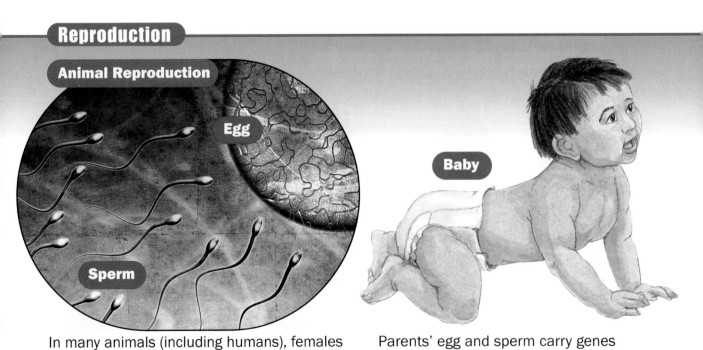

Egg

Baby

Sperm

In many animals (including humans), females produce eggs and males produce sperm.

Parents' egg and sperm carry genes that determine the baby's traits.

Look for Patterns

Patterns are repeating sets of events. Living things inherit genes in patterns. By observing traits, scientists can often find these patterns.

The picture shows a deer with white hair, called an *albino* deer. Its parents are brown. Scientists who first observed this pattern asked themselves how brown parents could have albino offspring. To find out, they studied the parents' genes and the different ways those genes could combine.

▲ Animals can be albino even if their parents are not.

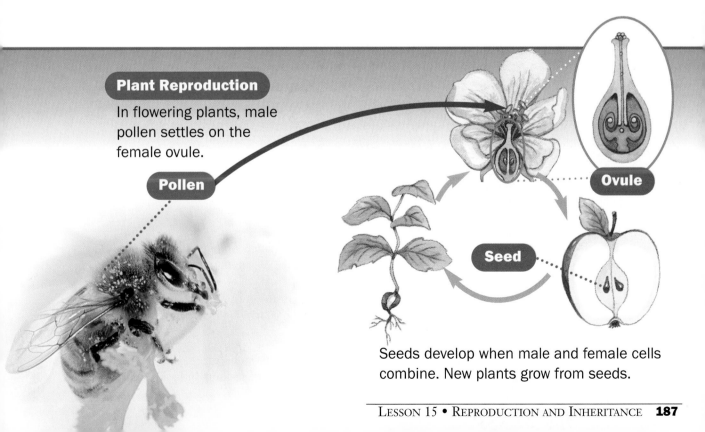

Plant Reproduction

In flowering plants, male pollen settles on the female ovule.

Pollen

Ovule

Seed

Seeds develop when male and female cells combine. New plants grow from seeds.

Reproduction and Inheritance

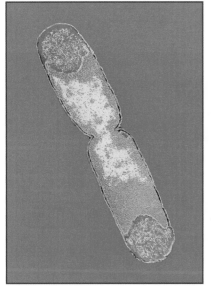

L iving things reproduce to create babies, or offspring. Traits pass from parents to offspring. Different genes combine and produce different traits. Variation can happen when genes combine in new ways.

Reproducing

Living things reproduce in many ways. Some individuals make exact copies of all their traits. The **offspring** are identical to the parent. In other cases, two parents combine their **traits.** The result is an individual that is different from its parents.

ASEXUAL REPRODUCTION

Some organisms need just one parent to reproduce. They produce without sex, or **asexually.** The offspring **inherits** all its traits from one parent. The offspring has exactly the same traits as its parent.

Bacteria reproduce asexually. They use a process called **binary fission.** A single bacterium divides in two, creating two bacteria just like it.

Some plants and animals also reproduce asexually. For example, tulips and onions have underground bulbs that divide to form new plants. Some sea star offspring form from *buds* that grow on the parent's body.

▲ Some sea stars can reproduce asexually. This sea star has bumps called *buds* on its arms. The buds will grow into new sea stars.

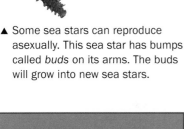

◄ Bacteria reproduce asexually through binary fission.

VOCABULARY

offspring—an organism or organisms born of a parent
traits—characteristics that can be controlled by genes, such as eye color, hair color, and height
asexually—by one parent
inherits—receives a set of traits from one or more parents
binary fission—the bacterial process of dividing in half to reproduce

SEXUAL REPRODUCTION

Sexual reproduction always takes two parents. Each parent makes **sex cells.** When sex cells from each parent come together, a new offspring develops.

In animals, the male's **sperm** unites with the female's **egg** to create a cell called a **zygote.** This cell will develop into a baby. In many plants, the sperm cell found in **pollen** settles on the egg cell in a structure called the **ovule.** Then seeds develop and grow into new plants.

An offspring from sexual reproduction is different from its parents. It inherits half its traits from its mother and half from its father. This mix of traits creates a one-of-a-kind **individual.**

The offspring of sexual reproduction have new combinations of traits. Even if they look alike, each one is different.

TALK AND SHARE With your partner, talk about how some offspring can have traits that are different from their parents' traits.

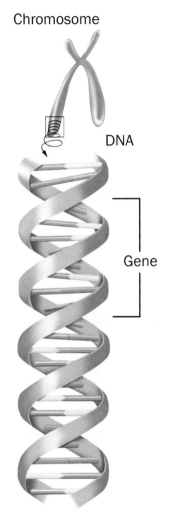

Chromosome

DNA

Gene

▲ A gene is a section of DNA. Every chromosome is made of DNA and proteins.

A fruit fly has 8 chromosomes. ▼

Genes

Why are your eyes different from your neighbor's eyes? Why can your uncle wiggle his ears and you can't? These questions all have the same answer—genes! **Genes** are instruction books for our bodies.

Genes pass from parent to offspring in different combinations. Unless you are an identical twin, your combination of genes belongs only to you. Each gene controls a different trait, such as eye color or ear wiggling.

CHROMOSOMES

The **chromosomes** in cells are full of genes. Every species has a set number of chromosomes in each cell. Bacteria each have 1 chromosome. Fruit flies have 8. Humans have 46 in all cells except half that number (23) in sex cells. Your 46 chromosomes are arranged in 23 pairs. In each pair, one chromosome comes from your father. The other comes from your mother.

DNA

Genes are stored in **DNA** (deoxyribonucleic acid) molecules. DNA is the chemical **code** that gives all the instructions for growing a new life. Each cell in your body contains a complete set of DNA molecules.

DNA looks like a twisted ladder. Parts of this ladder contain your genes and their instructions for how you will grow, look, and act.

(TALK AND SHARE) **Ask your partner where genes are located. Then tell your partner what genes do.**

VOCABULARY
genes—sections of DNA from chromosomes that pass traits from parent to offspring
chromosomes—structures in the cell nucleus that carry genes
DNA—a chemical in the cell that stores genes
code—a system of rules or signals

Meiosis

In sexual reproduction, sex cells are made by a kind of cell division called **meiosis.** Instead of dividing once, into two identical cells, a cell divides twice. During this process, chromosomes may exchange genes. At the end of the process, the 4 new cells have only half of the number of chromosomes of the parent cell.

First, each chromosome in a regular cell makes a copy of itself. During this process, chromosomes may exchange genes.

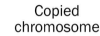
Copied chromosome

Single chromosome

The two daughter cells each have a complete set of chromosomes.

Next, the daughter cells divide without copying their chromosomes.

The result is 4 new sex cells. Each sex cell has only half the usual number of chromosomes.

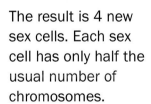

(TALK AND SHARE) **Ask your partner how the daughter cells of meiosis are different from the parent cell.**

VOCABULARY
meiosis—cell division that produces 4 sex cells, each with half the number of chromosomes of the parent cell

Variation

Imagine you have a friend with blond hair. Her mother and father both have dark brown hair. How did she get her blond hair? The answer is that her parents each had a gene for blond hair and passed those genes on to her.

Your friend is an example of **genetic variation.** Variation can happen when genes combine in a new way. This occurs when chromosomes exchange genes in meiosis.

PUNNETT SQUARES

An offspring receives genes from both parents. Genes that control a trait like hair color come in pairs—one from the father and one from the mother. Scientists show the ways these genes might combine by using a **Punnett square.** Look at the Punnett square on page 193.

Science, Technology, and Society

The Danger of Monocultures

Variations help keep the world healthy. Some organisms do well in conditions that would harm others. If every organism were exactly the same, a single disease could destroy an entire species or population. That's what happened during the Irish potato famine in the 1840s.

At that time, the potato was Ireland's main source of food. A small potato garden could feed a family for an entire year! But the potatoes were planted as a **monoculture.** They had little genetic variation. When a fungus infected the potatoes, it destroyed most of Ireland's crop. As a result, more than one million people starved to death.

VOCABULARY

genetic variation—the different traits that come from new combinations of genes

Punnett square—a way of showing possible gene combinations

monoculture—the growing of a single crop in an area

DOMINANT AND RECESSIVE

You can see in the Punnett square below that 3 possible combinations of Bb and Bb also have a capital B. The capital B represents the **dominant gene** for brown hair. This means the chance of the children having brown hair is 3 out of 4. The dominant gene is always **expressed** when it is present. Anyone with a B will have brown hair.

One square in the diagram has bb. There is no B for brown hair. The b stands for a **recessive gene.** This gene will only be expressed when there is no dominant gene for the same trait. Although the parents had brown hair, both of them carried a gene for blond hair. That is why your friend is blond.

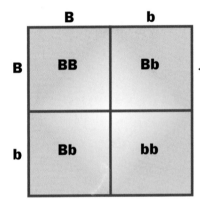

◄ The hair color genes, Bb, from the mother are on the top. The hair color genes from the father, also Bb, are on the left side. The possible combinations of hair color genes in the children are in the squares. The blond child is bb. B = brown and b = blond.

(TALK AND SHARE) **With your partner, discuss how recessive genes can explain variations in hair color.**

Summary

All living things reproduce. Offspring inherit genes from their parents. Individuals have different traits because they have different combinations of genes. When genes combine in a new way, genetic variation happens.

VOCABULARY

dominant gene—a gene greater in power. A dominant gene will "win" and the offspring will have the trait it carries.

expressed—in science, turned into a trait by a gene

recessive gene—a gene having less power. A recessive gene can only produce a trait when there is no dominant gene for the same trait.

Describing

Describing Patterns of Inheritance

When you describe something, you tell about it. To describe a pattern of inheritance, you tell about events that you observe more than once.

You know that hair color is an inherited trait. Another inherited trait is whether hair is curly or straight. Curly hair is dominant. Look at the Punnett square below on the left. One parent has curly hair. The other has straight hair. All of their children have curly hair.

Now look at the Punnett square below on the right. One child from the first Punnett square has married someone else with curly hair. One of their children has straight hair. You can describe this pattern of inheritance. You can tell how the gene for straight hair was expressed in the child whose parents had curly hair.

Punnett Squares

	C	C
s	Cs	Cs
s	Cs	Cs

	C	s
C	CC	Cs
s	Cs	ss

Practice Describing

1. Draw Choose one of the Punnett squares above. Draw it. Then in each square draw a picture of a child. Show what kind of hair that child would have. Tell your partner how you knew what to draw.

2. Write In a paragraph, describe a pattern of inheritance in your family. Choose either hair color or whether hair is curly or straight. Then trade paragraphs with a partner and check each other's writing.

Check Your Writing

Make sure you
- Use complete sentences.
- Use a period at the end of each sentence.
- Spell all the words correctly.

Activities

Grammar Spotlight

Be + Adjective   An adjective is a word that helps describe a noun. You can use a form of the verb *be* followed by an adjective to describe a person, place, or thing. For example: *They are blond.* The adjective stays the same whether the noun is singular or plural.

The present-tense forms of the verb *be* include *am*, *is*, and *are*. See the chart below.

Noun	Form of *be* (verb)	Adjective
I	am	blue-eyed.
The dog	is	small.
They	are	tall.

Make a sentence using *am*, *is*, or *are* and an adjective to describe a person.

Oral Language

Talk About Patterns   In your group, pick a kind of animal you can all describe, such as a dog, an elephant, or a fish. Find a picture of an adult animal with its babies. Talk about how the babies look like their parents. Then talk about how the babies are different from their parents. For example, do the babies and parents have the same color fur, scales, or skin? Try to find at least two patterns and two differences.

Hands On

Brown and Blond   Draw a Punnett square with the parent genes Bb and bb—a brown-haired parent and a blond parent. If these parents have four children, how many children will have the recessive gene for blond hair? Answer the question with a partner.

Partner Practice

Is It Inherited?   Make a list of 5 traits you think are carried by genes. Trade your list with your partner. Compare your lists and talk about any differences.

Change
over Time

Here you'll learn about how species change over many generations. You'll also learn how to identify evidence and practice summarizing evidence.

▲ I wonder what this thing is! It looks like a dinosaur that's trying to fly!

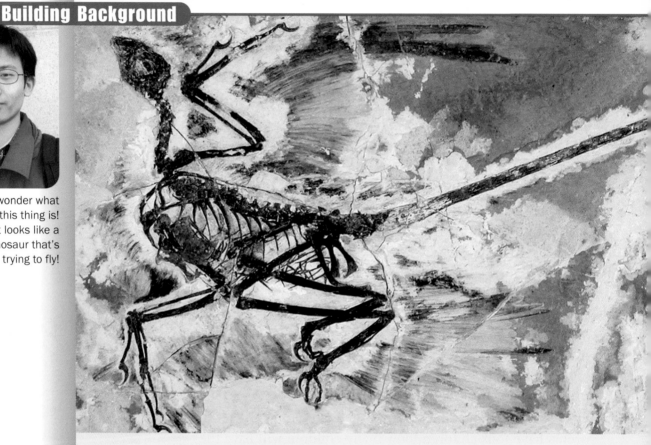

■ **What do you think this animal is?**

■ **How old do you think it is?**

■ **What have you seen that looks something like this?**

Living things have traits that help them survive and reproduce in their habitats. As habitats change over time, so do the traits needed to help species survive.

1 Traits and Adaptations

Some individuals have traits that help them survive in a changing habitat. These individuals are better adapted to the habitat, so they live longer.

Bugs that are not killed by a poison survive and reproduce.

2 Natural Selection

Populations that survive and reproduce successfully may become new species through the process of natural selection.

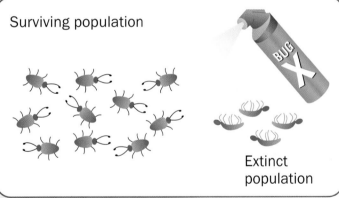

Surviving population

Extinct population

3 Evidence

We study how species have changed by studying evidence such as fossils.

Key Concepts

adaptation   advantage   natural selection

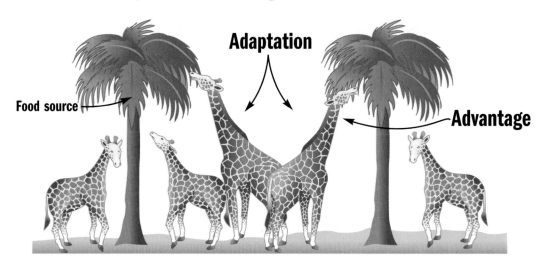

Adaptation

Food source

Advantage

An **adaptation** is a change that helps an organism survive in its habitat.

Sometimes an adaptation gives an organism an **advantage** over other organisms in the habitat. An organism with an advantage will live longer and have more offspring than the others. Over time, organisms with the adaptation will outnumber organisms without it. This is called **natural selection**.

Fossil Formation

Fossils form in many ways. This is one example.

Remains

An animal's body is buried in mud.

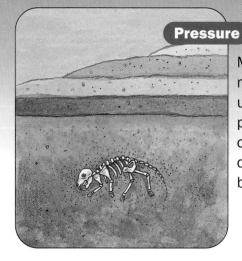

Pressure

More mud piles up and presses on the decaying bone.

Identify Evidence

Evidence is information and facts you can use to support a hypothesis. When you identify evidence in science, you find information that relates to a hypothesis. Here's how to identify evidence.

1. Look at information used to describe something.

2. Decide whether or not the evidence relates to your hypothesis.

Now study the chart. Find the hypothesis about finches. What does the evidence tell you? How does this evidence support the hypothesis?

Hypothesis

Different finches have adapted to the food sources in their habitats.

Evidence

Insect-eating finches have sharp beaks that are good for pulling insects out of tree bark.

Evidence

Fruit-eating finches have wide strong beaks that are good for grinding fruit skins.

Warbler finch

Large ground finch

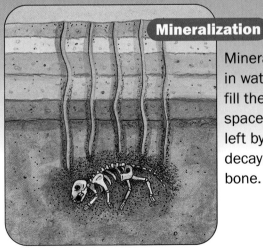

Mineralization

Minerals in water fill the spaces left by the decaying bone.

Fossil

The water disappears. The minerals form a fossil that looks like the bone.

Change over Time

Species have traits that help them in their habitats. Over time, habitats change. Adaptations help a species survive in the changed habitat. Fossils are evidence of changes over time.

Traits and Adaptations

Adaptation happens very slowly. Some organisms have **traits** that help them **adapt** to a changing environment. Over a long time, organisms with such traits live longer and produce more offspring. Over time, the whole **population** changes. Sometimes the whole **species** changes. Members of a species may also have **behaviors** that **increase** their chances of staying alive and reproducing.

▲ This toad blends into its environment. How might this trait help it survive?

▲ Many species of birds migrate when seasons change. This adaptation helps the species survive.

VOCABULARY

adaptation—a change or changes that help an organism survive and reproduce in its habitat
traits—characteristics that are controlled by genes
adapt—fit a situation
population—a group of individuals of a single species
species—a group of similar organisms that can reproduce
behaviors—ways of acting
increase—make larger or raise in number

CHANGING TRAITS

Consider an example. Long ago, a species of insect struggled to survive. Its **predator,** a bird, ate most of the insect population. The species slowly developed an adaptation that changed the way its body looked. Over many **generations,** it began to look more like a twig and less like an insect. Birds don't eat twigs, so this species increased its chances of survival. It gained an **advantage** over insects that did not look like twigs.

CHANGING BEHAVIORS

Bears once faced **extinction** because of a change in their food supply. It became harder each winter to find enough food to eat. Over many generations, bears adapted by sleeping longer during the winter when food is **scarce.** The new eating and sleeping behaviors helped the species survive.

(TALK AND SHARE) **With your partner, think of at least 3 examples of ways species might adapt to changing food sources.**

▲ The walking stick insect blends into its environment.

◄ Bears sleep longer in the winter when it is hard to find food.

VOCABULARY
predator—an organism that hunts, catches, and eats another organism
generations—groups of individuals living during the same time and at the same stage of descent from an ancestor. Grandparents, parents, and children are 3 different generations.
advantage—a benefit, such as something that improves the chances of survival
extinction—disappearance from life
scarce—very hard to find

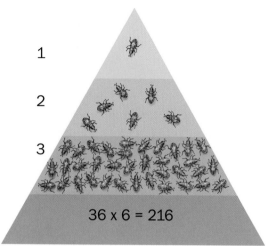

1

2

3

36 x 6 = 216

▲ If each successful individual can have 6 offspring with another parent, generation 2 has 6 offspring, or 6 individuals. Generation 3 has 36 individuals and so on.

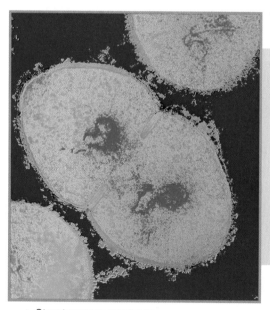

▲ *Streptococcus pyogenes,* an antibiotic-resistant strain of bacteria

Survival and Selection

Natural selection is how living things change over time. **Variations** in an organism's body structure or behavior may give it an advantage. It can live longer and reproduce more successfully. These variations grow slowly stronger with each new generation. Study the diagram on the left.

REQUIREMENTS FOR SURVIVAL

Living things depend on their habitats to meet their survival needs. Changes in the surroundings may threaten a species with extinction. Species adapt to changes in many different ways. Some **develop** longer, stronger legs. Others develop fins to swim. The process of natural selection helps a species adapt in ways that **ensure** its **survival.** Adaptation can take thousands of years.

Science, Technology, and Society

Antibiotic-Resistant Bacteria

Some bacteria can make you sick. Scientists make drugs called *antibiotics* that fight harmful bacteria. Sometimes a **strain** of bacteria becomes **resistant to** these antibiotics. This means that the bacteria are not killed and the drugs don't work. Scientists have to create new variations of antibiotic drugs to match the bacteria's adaptations.

VOCABULARY

natural selection—the process by which helpful traits pass on to new generations
variations—small differences among organisms of the same type
develop—form over time
ensure—make certain
survival—the ability to continue living
strain—a group within a species that has a special set of traits
resistant to—able to defend itself against

Two Examples of How Species Change

Species	Need	Threat	Variation
Lobe-finned fish lived millions of years ago.	They needed to live in water. 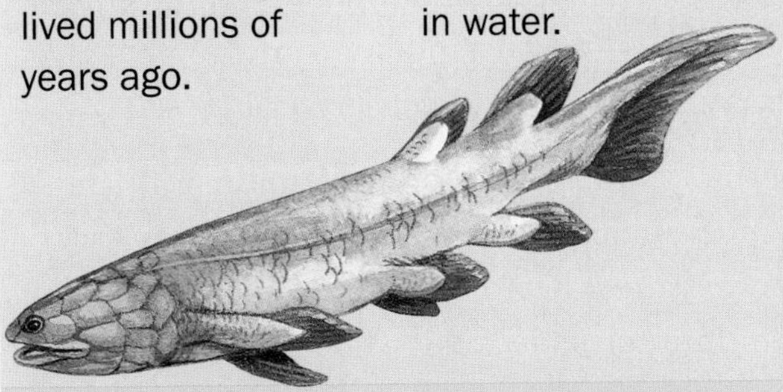	The streams in their habitat dried up slowly over thousands of years.	The fins of this species became legs. The gills disappeared and lungs developed. Later, the animals moved onto land as **amphibians.**
The first horses were only as big as large dogs.	Horses needed to escape predators. 	The predators became faster runners, which made them better hunters.	Horses that could run fast survived and had larger, faster-running offspring.

VARIATIONS

Most scientists think that all life on Earth **descended** from a common parent. If this is true, then why is one species so different from the others?

Over millions of years, different populations adapt in different ways. They develop variations that help them respond to change. The variations pass along to their offspring. In each new generation, more and more offspring have the variations that ensure survival.

This process of natural selection helps species become different from each other. Look at the chart above for examples of how two species changed over time.

(TALK AND SHARE) **Talk with your partner about some changes in an environment that could threaten the survival of the whole species.**

VOCABULARY

amphibians—animals that are born in water but can also live on land
descended—came down

Evidence of Change

The idea that species can change over time is a **theory.** What kind of evidence supports it? Scientists have identified two kinds of evidence—**fossils** and **anatomy.**

STUDYING FOSSILS

Fossils are the **ancient remains** of plants and animals. Most living things **decay,** or rot away, after they die. The soft parts, like skin and muscles, decay first. Harder parts, such as bones and teeth, decay more slowly. If the conditions are right, fossils form. A fossil is the preserved part of an organism that died long ago.

Fossils help scientists compare traits of extinct organisms with traits of organisms living today. When they do this, they can see the ways organisms have changed. In this way, fossils give us clues about how life on Earth has changed over millions and millions of years.

◄ The woolly mammoth (top) is extinct, but elephants today (bottom) have many of the same traits.

VOCABULARY

theory—an explanation with evidence to support it
fossils—the preserved parts of organisms that lived a long time ago
anatomy—the structure of a living thing
ancient—from a time long past
remains—dead bodies
decay—rot and break apart

OBSERVING ANATOMY

Scientists compare the anatomy, or structure, of different species. Sometimes they find evidence of **links.** A link between species usually means that they descended from the same ancient parent. The species share an **ancestor.**

Do you think whales and humans have much in common? Scientists found a link. The bones inside a whale flipper are similar to the bones inside your hand. This is evidence that whales and humans may have shared an ancestor.

Sometimes a species slowly loses a trait it no longer needs. You probably know that people need pelvis bones to stand up and walk. But some snakes have tiny pelvis bones, too. Snakes don't need these bones because snakes don't have legs.

Scientists think a snake's tiny pelvis is an example of a **disappearing trait.** It is evidence that snakes had an ancestor with legs. Over many generations, the snake's pelvis became smaller as the animal no longer used it.

(TALK AND SHARE) **Talk with your partner about how fossils show that species change over time.**

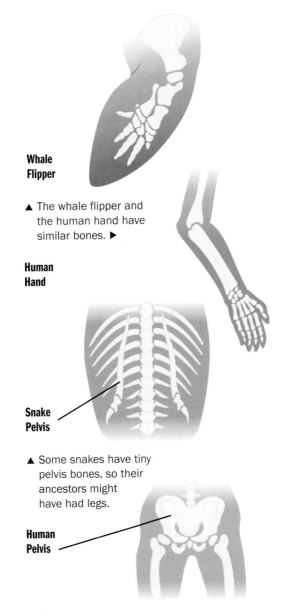

Whale Flipper

▲ The whale flipper and the human hand have similar bones. ▶

Human Hand

Snake Pelvis

▲ Some snakes have tiny pelvis bones, so their ancestors might have had legs.

Human Pelvis

Summary

Species adapt slowly as their habitats change. The more successful a species is at surviving, the more its traits will pass from generation to generation.

VOCABULARY

links—traits that are similar in two species
ancestor—an individual from whom one is descended. Parents, grandparents, and great-grandparents are all ancestors.
disappearing trait—a characteristic that is being lost over time

Summarizing

Summarizing Evidence

When you summarize, you make a short statement that includes only the most important information. You can summarize the evidence you have identified about how organisms adapt to their habitats. An Evidence Organizer can help you arrange your information and summarize it.

Evidence Organizer

Hypothesis
Different birds have adapted to the food sources in their habitats.

Evidence
A beak is good for grinding fruit.

Evidence
A beak is good for picking insects out of tree bark.

Evidence
A beak is good for eating small seeds.

Summary
Different beaks help the birds eat the food they find in their habitats.

Practice Summarizing

1. Draw With a partner, draw an Evidence Organizer for this hypothesis: "Cats have body parts that help them catch food." Think about traits like the cat's teeth, claws, tail, whiskers, and ears. Draw a trait in each evidence box. Talk about your choices.

2. Write Make an Evidence Organizer for this hypothesis: "People have traits that help them live in hot climates." Fill in evidence boxes with structures and behaviors that you know help people survive in the heat. Then write a summary box to tell how the evidence supports the hypothesis. Words from the Word Bank can help you.

Word Bank

temperature
humidity
heat

sweat
drink
cool
rest

Grammar Spotlight

Indefinite Pronouns You can use an indefinite pronoun when you are not talking about a specific person or thing. Singular indefinite pronouns include *somebody*, *everybody*, *nothing*, *anything*, and *each*. Plural indefinite pronouns include *many*, *both*, *few*, and *some*. Remember that singular indefinite pronouns take a singular verb and plural indefinite pronouns take a plural verb.

Singular Pronoun + Singular Verb	Plural Pronoun + Plural Verb
Nothing survives for long without food.	*Many study natural selection.*
Each needs a habitat.	*Some are now extinct.*

Write a sentence about change using the indefinite pronoun *anything*.

Hands On

Clay Impressions Some fossils look like leaves pressed into clay. Use soft clay and a leaf to make your own model of a fossil. As you work, think about how hard you have to press on the clay to make the leaf pattern show. Then talk with your partner about why you think many fossils are found underground.

Partner Practice

Pets and Adaptations With your partner, pick a pet you both like a lot. On a sheet of paper, list 5 things in the pet's habitat. On another sheet of paper, write an adaptation you think the pet has. Give at least one adaptation for each of the 5 habitat features you listed.

Oral Language

Adaptations and Advantages Here are some adaptations people have that make them different from many other animals. In your group, brainstorm about possible advantages of each adaptation.

People walk on 2 legs instead of 4.
People have thumbs and fingers instead of paws or hooves.
People breathe with lungs instead of with gills.

The Structure of
Matter

Here you'll learn about the smallest pieces of everything in the world. You'll also learn how to read a model and practice interpreting a model of an atom.

Building Background

▲ Sometimes I wonder what air is made of!

■ **What do air and water have in common?**

■ **What do soil and stars have in common?**

■ **What do you have in common with fire?**

Matter has mass and takes up space. It is made of very tiny particles called *atoms*. Atoms of different elements combine in a variety of ways to form molecules and compounds.

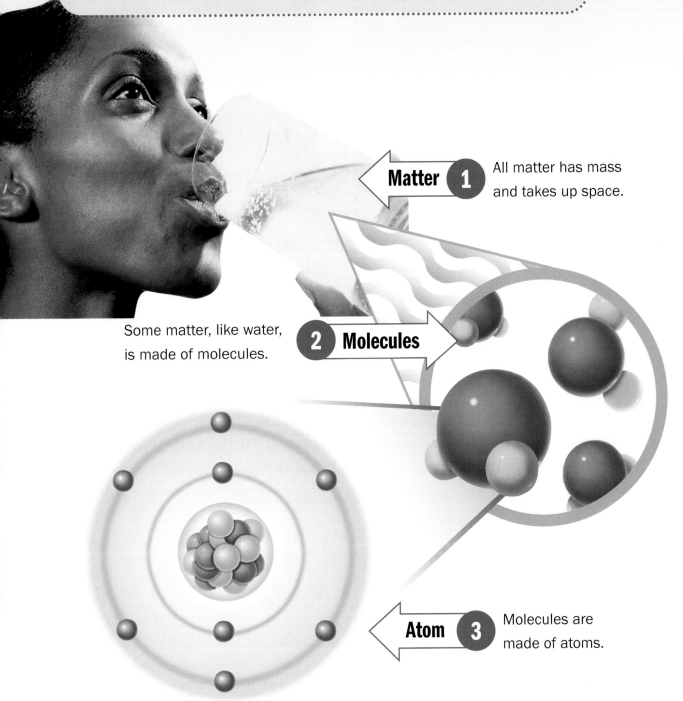

Matter **1** All matter has mass and takes up space.

Some matter, like water, is made of molecules.

2 **Molecules**

Atom **3** Molecules are made of atoms.

Key Concepts

matter   volume   mass   weight

Earth's gravity pulls on the astronaut.

The moon's gravity pulls less strongly on the astronaut.

The astronaut's volume and mass stay the same. The astronaut's weight changes.

Everything is made of **matter.** The total amount of space something takes up is its **volume.** The total amount of matter in something is its **mass.** Mass does not change unless you add matter or take away matter. Weight is different from mass. **Weight** is a measure of the force of gravity on an object's mass. Weight can change depending on the strength of the force of gravity.

Charge!

Sometimes matter has an electric charge. A charge can be positive (+) or negative (–). Opposite charges attract each other. Identical charges push each other away (repel each other).

Opposite charges attract.

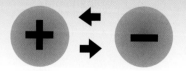

Like charges repel.

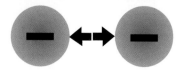

Negative charges may collect at the bottom of a storm cloud. Lightning strikes when the negative charges are attracted to positive charges on the ground.

Read a Model

A model is an image of something. You use a model to help explain an object or idea. The model can be a sculpture, diagram, drawing, or computer animation.

Reading a Model

1. Look at the title. It tells you what is being explained.

2. Look at the labels. They name the parts.

3. Look at how the parts are related. What is on the outside? What is on the inside?

4. Try thinking aloud. Talk softly to yourself and explain what the model shows.

Now, look at this model. It is a very simple drawing of an atom.

Model of an Atom

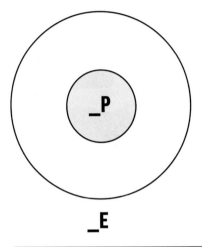

_E

_P	Number of protons
_E	Number of electrons

Electricity is the interaction of electric charges.

Electricity

Current electricity flows from the ball to the hand to the hair. Charged strands of hair repel each other.

The Structure of Matter

Anything that has mass and takes up space is matter. Matter is made of atoms of elements. Atoms can combine in many ways to form molecules and compounds.

Mass and Volume

Everything in the world has **matter.** Matter is anything that has **mass** and takes up space. A glass of water, a car, a tree, and your body all have mass and take up space. Even things you can't see have mass and take up space. For example, the air you breathe is matter.

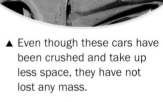

▲ Even though these cars have been crushed and take up less space, they have not lost any mass.

Imagine holding an empty soda can. You can feel its mass. Mass is the amount of matter in any object or substance. Scientists use a **balance** to measure mass in **grams.**

The soda can takes up space too. The amount of space something takes up is called its **volume.** People measure volume in **liters** or **cubic centimeters.**

(TALK AND SHARE) **Imagine jumping on a soda can to flatten it. Talk with your partner about this question: Does the can still have the same mass and volume?**

VOCABULARY

matter—anything that has mass and takes up space
mass—the amount of matter in something, measured in grams
balance—a measuring device in which a beam is brought to equilibrium when the masses on each end are the same
grams—units of mass
volume—the amount of space something takes up, measured in liters or cubic centimeters
liters—units of volume. One liter equals 1,000 cubic centimeters.
cubic—having 3 equal dimensions. If something is one cubic centimeter, its length, height, and width are each one centimeter.
centimeters—units of length

The Atom

You know that everything is made of matter. **Atoms** are the building blocks of matter. It is hard to imagine how tiny atoms are. It would take thousands of them to cross the width of a single human hair.

THE NUCLEUS OF AN ATOM

Atoms are tiny, but there are even smaller things than atoms. Atoms are made of smaller pieces, or **particles.** Some of these particles are called **protons, neutrons,** and **electrons.** Protons have a positive charge, and neutrons have no charge. The two kinds of particles form the atom's center, or **nucleus.** The protons and neutrons make up most of the atom's mass. The nucleus has a positive charge.

Language Notes

Verb Phrases
These phrases have special meanings.

☐ take up: fill or occupy

☐ make up: put together, compose, imagine

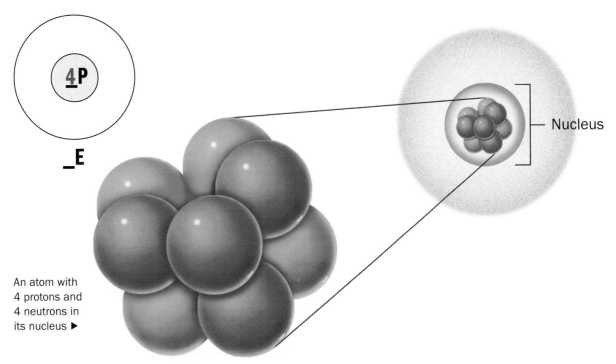

4P

_E

An atom with 4 protons and 4 neutrons in its nucleus ▶

Nucleus

VOCABULARY

atoms—the smallest parts of something that can be identified
particles—very small pieces of something
protons—the particles in the nucleus of an atom that have a positive charge
neutrons—the particles in the nucleus of an atom that have no charge
electrons—particles that move around the nucleus of an atom and have a negative charge
nucleus—the center of an atom (plural, *nuclei*)

Models of Atoms

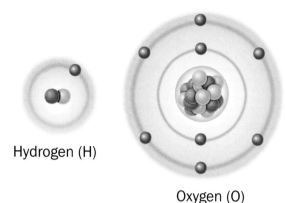

Hydrogen (H)

Oxygen (O)

In these atoms, the number of electrons equals the number of protons.

ELECTRONS

Atoms are mostly empty space. Electrons move around the nucleus in a cloud. Electrons have a negative charge. Because of this negative charge, the electrons are **attracted** to the positively charged nucleus. An atom usually has the same number of protons and electrons. This makes the atom **neutral.**

DIFFERENCES AMONG ATOMS

Scientists identify each kind of atom by the number of protons in its nucleus. For example, hydrogen, the simplest atom, has 1 proton. Oxygen has 8 protons. Iron has 26 protons.

(TALK AND SHARE) **Work with your partner to draw a model of an atom of iron. How many electrons would it have? Where would the electrons be?**

(Science, Technology, and Society)

Radiation

Most atoms stay the same. However, some substances have atoms that are **unstable.** Particles shoot out of the nucleus and travel at a high speed. The particles give off energy called **radiation. Rays** of these particles are called *alpha*, *beta*, and *gamma rays*. Radiation can be very dangerous to living things, but it can also be useful. For example, doctors use radiation to kill cancer cells.

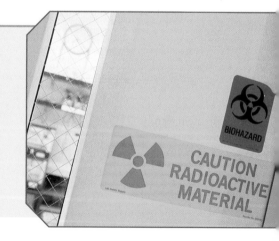

VOCABULARY

attracted—pulled toward
neutral—having an equal number of positive and negative charges
unstable—ready to fall apart
radiation—the energy made by particles shooting out of the nuclei of atoms
rays—streams of particles shooting out of the nuclei of atoms

Elements and Molecules

The universe is made of matter. Different atoms make different kinds of matter. What makes a piece of gold different from a drop of water?

ELEMENTS

Imagine having a piece of gold. Now think of cutting it into pieces. If you could keep cutting it into smaller and smaller pieces, you would eventually have atoms of gold. Gold is made only of gold atoms. A **substance** that is made of only one kind of atom is called an **element.**

Scientists have identified more than 100 different elements. Each element has a set of characteristics called **properties.** Scientists use letter symbols for the names of elements. For example, the symbol for gold is Au. The symbol for hydrogen is H and the symbol for oxygen is O. Each element has atoms with a **unique** number of protons in the nucleus.

▲ The element gold has 79 protons.

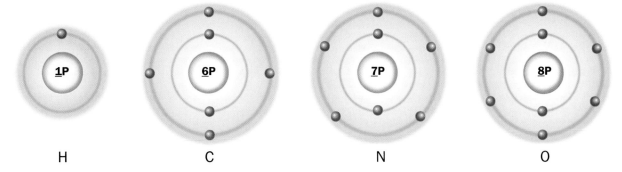

▲ Each element has a particular number of protons in its nucleus.

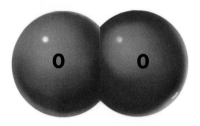

Molecule (oxygen)

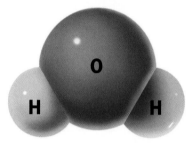

Molecule (water)

MOLECULES

When two or more atoms combine, they form a **molecule.** The simplest molecules contain only two atoms. For example, when two oxygen atoms join, they create a molecule of oxygen.

Most molecules form from two or more different kinds of atoms. A molecule of water consists of two atoms of hydrogen and one atom of oxygen. A molecule of water is the smallest part of water that has the properties of water. The separate atoms of H and O do not have the properties of water.

Scientists use different kinds of models to show molecules. Look at the models of the water molecule below.

Models of a Water Molecule

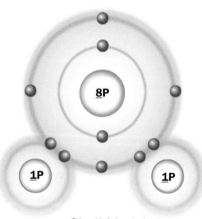

Shell Model

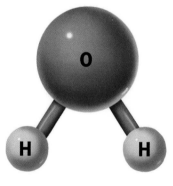

Ball-and-stick Model

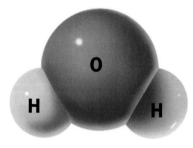

Space-filling Model

(TALK AND SHARE) **With your partner, talk about these questions: Can you break up water? If you boil it or freeze it, is it still water?**

VOCABULARY

molecule—any substance made of two or more atoms

Compounds and Mixtures

Atoms and molecules can combine. Many things you see are combinations called **compounds.** A compound has properties that are different from the elements that make it up. Water is a compound. Other compounds you might know include sugar, salt, gasoline, and chalk.

In compounds, atoms or molecules combine in a **chemical reaction.** When compounds form, the atoms gain, share, or lose electrons in the process.

You cannot separate the elements in a compound **physically.** For example, in a water molecule, you can't separate the hydrogen atoms from the oxygen atom by pouring water through a **filter.**

A **mixture** forms when two or more substances combine without a chemical reaction. If you put sand in water, you make a mixture. You can remove the sand from the water with a strainer. Other familiar mixtures include air, saltwater, milk, and blood.

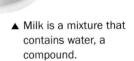
▲ Milk is a mixture that contains water, a compound.

(TALK AND SHARE) **With your partner, list some examples of compounds and mixtures you can find in a kitchen.**

Summary

Matter has mass and takes up space. Atoms are small particles of matter that can combine in many ways. Atoms of the elements combine in molecules and compounds.

VOCABULARY

compounds—matter made by two or more elements that cannot be separated physically
chemical reaction—a process in which atoms gain, lose, or share electrons
physically—using the body or tools
filter—a tool used to strain and separate substances from a liquid or a gas
mixture—a combination of two or more substances that can be separated physically

Interpreting

Interpreting a Model of an Atom

When you interpret something, you decide what it means. Look at the model of an atom below. Count its protons and electrons. What do the numbers mean? When you interpret a model of an atom, these numbers help you interpret the kind of atom you see.

Model of an Atom

Neon Atom

10P

_____ P
_____ E

Practice Interpreting

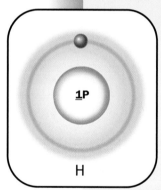

1P

H

1. Draw On the left is a model of a hydrogen (H) atom, which has one proton. If you add one more proton, you will have a helium atom (He). Draw a model of the helium atom with all its parts. Explain your drawing to your partner.

2. Write Below is the nucleus of a beryllium (Be) atom. Interpret the model. Write a paragraph of 3 or 4 sentences explaining what this model shows. Be sure to explain how many electrons this atom has. Words from the Word Bank can help you.

Word Bank

protons
electrons
neutrons

positive
negative
neutral

Activities

Grammar Spotlight

Using Numbers with Nouns   There are two types of nouns: count nouns and noncount nouns. Count nouns are things you can count. *Molecule* is a count noun because you can say *1 molecule, 2 molecules,* or *10 molecules.* Count nouns have singular and plural forms: *1 molecule, 10 molecules.*

Noncount nouns are things that you cannot count. *Water* is a noncount noun because you don't say *3 waters* or *14 waters.* Noncount nouns are neither singular nor plural. People often use the word *some* with them.

Count Noun Singular	Count Noun Plural	Noncount Noun
a boy	9 boys	some water
1 atom	2 atoms	a lot of homework
1 child	4 children	enough corn

Write two sentences to describe water molecules. Use one count noun and one noncount noun.

Oral Language

Push and Pull   Talk in your group about how charges work. Give an example of charges that attract each other. Then give an example of charges that repel each other.

Hands On

Making Models   In one dish, stir together some sugar and water. In another dish, stir together some salt and pepper. Let the dishes sit for 10 minutes and then look at them. Interpret the results with your partner. Tell whether you have made two mixtures, two compounds, or one of each.

Partner Practice

Mass   With your partner, use a lab balance to measure the mass of a piece of chalk. Then measure the mass of a chalk eraser. Compare the two measurements you get. Talk about what makes the masses different in these different materials.

States of Matter

Here you'll learn about solids, liquids, and gases. You'll also learn how to visualize changes in the states of matter and practice describing changes of state.

▲ Water and fire are amazing! We use them for everything.

- **What do you see here that is a solid, liquid, or gas?**
- **How does fire change matter?**
- **What other solids, liquids, and gases can you name?**

Solids, liquids, and gases are 3 states of matter. They are physical properties. You can see examples of the states of matter and visualize the changes that cause them.

1 **Solid, Liquid, and Gas**

A solid has a definite volume and shape.

A liquid has a definite volume but not shape.

A gas has no definite volume or shape.

2 **A change in energy can make a state change.**

3 **Physical properties include color, shape, and size.**

Key Concepts

energy   **motion**   **thermal energy**   **temperature**   **heat**

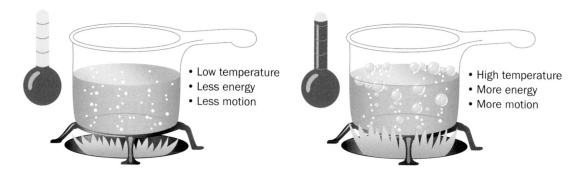

- Low temperature
- Less energy
- Less motion

- High temperature
- More energy
- More motion

Energy is the ability to do work, which means making something change. **Motion** is a change in position. Energy can affect motion, even in tiny atoms. One kind of energy is **thermal energy,** which is the energy of moving atoms.

Temperature is a measure of thermal energy, or how fast atoms move. You measure temperature with a thermometer. **Heat** is the transfer, or movement, of thermal energy between things of different temperatures.

Measuring Temperature

The United States uses the Fahrenheit scale in thermometers.

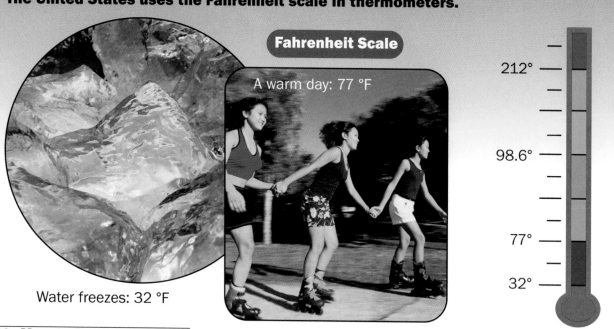

Fahrenheit Scale

A warm day: 77 °F

212°

98.6°

77°

32°

Water freezes: 32 °F

Visualize

When you visualize something, you form a picture in your mind. The picture is an image, like a model. It is useful to learn how to visualize things you cannot see, such as atoms and tiny particles.

Solid   **Liquid**   **Gas**

Look at the images here. They will help you visualize particles of matter in solids, liquids, and gases. As you read about states of matter,

- Make a picture of an object in your mind.
- Make changes in the picture as you learn about states of matter.

Scientists around the world use the Celsius scale in thermometers.

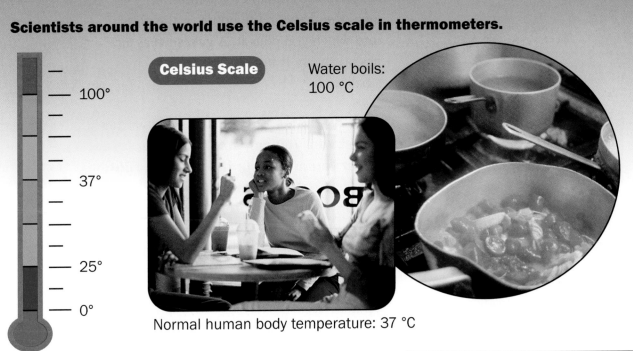

Celsius Scale

100°

37°

25°

0°

Water boils: 100 °C

Normal human body temperature: 37 °C

▲ This steaming soup contains all 3 states of matter.

States of Matter

On Earth, matter can be solid, liquid, or gas. These are physical properties. A change in energy may cause matter to change from one state to another.

Three Main States of Matter

Think about the different parts of hot vegetable soup. The vegetables keep their shape. The broth takes the shape of the bowl. If you spill the broth, it takes another shape. Steam rises from the soup and spreads through the air.

Solids, liquids, and gases are the 3 most familiar **states** of matter. In the soup, you see all 3 states of matter at once. The vegetables are solids, the broth is a liquid, and the steam is a gas.

A **solid** has its own shape. Imagine a sugar cube or a stick of butter, both of which are solids. A **liquid** takes the shape of the container it is in. Milk takes the shape of the bottle or the glass into which you pour it. A **gas,** such as air, has no shape. It fills its container, such as a balloon.

▲ In soda, gas bubbles in the liquid rise to the top of the liquid.

(TALK AND SHARE) **Talk with your partner about why you can smell hot soup even when you are not in the kitchen. Hint: Think about the shape of a gas.**

VOCABULARY

states—the physical forms of something. Solid, liquid, and gas are 3 states of matter.
solid—a state of matter with a definite shape and volume
liquid—a state of matter with a definite volume but no definite shape
gas—a state of matter with no definite shape or volume

Energy and States

Matter is made of atoms and molecules. These particles are all affected by **energy.** The amount of energy in a substance determines how fast its particles move.

MATTER IN MOTION

You can't feel it, but the particles in matter are always moving. In solids, the atoms are locked together and only **vibrate.** In liquids, the atoms and molecules are more loosely packed. They can move past each other. In gases, the atoms and molecules are free to move all over. Scientists call the motion of these particles **kinetic energy.**

HEAT AND TEMPERATURE

Temperature is a measure of how fast particles are moving. Each particle moves at its own speed. Temperature measures the average kinetic energy in all the particles of a substance.

Temperature and heat are different. Temperature is a measure, but **heat** is a movement. Heat is the **transfer** of **thermal energy** between things of different temperatures. Heat always moves from a warmer object to a cooler object.

Imagine that someone feels your forehead when you are sick and have a fever. The thermal energy from your forehead will make the person's hand feel warm. The transfer of thermal energy from your forehead to the person's hand will make you feel cooler.

(TALK AND SHARE) **With your partner, compare how fast the particles move in the 3 states of matter.**

Solid

▲ Atoms in a solid vibrate.

Liquid

▲ Atoms in a liquid move past each other.

Gas

▲ Atoms in a gas will move until they hit the wall of a container.

(VOCABULARY)
energy—the ability to do work
vibrate—move back and forth very quickly
kinetic energy—the energy something has because it is moving
temperature—a measure of the average kinetic energy of a substance
heat—the movement of energy between things of different temperatures
transfer—movement
thermal energy—the energy of moving atoms

Changing States

You know that water is a solid when it is ice. It can be a liquid you can drink. It can be a gas you can feel in a steamy room. What makes water change from one state to another?

ENERGY, MOTION, AND TEMPERATURE

Energy causes changes in state. If you add energy to something, its molecules move faster and farther apart. If the molecules move fast enough, they break away from each other and the substance changes states.

Whenever you heat or cool something enough, it will change states. When matter changes states, the change is a **physical change.** The substance does not turn into something else. Water, ice, and steam (water vapor) are all made of the same molecules of hydrogen and oxygen atoms—H_2O.

When you add energy, you **increase** the speed of particles. This raises the temperature. When you take away energy, the particles slow down. This means you **decrease** their speed and lower the temperature.

Glass can be heated, shaped, and cooled. These are physical changes because the glass doesn't change into something else. ▲

How Matter Changes States

Temperature (thermal energy)

SOLID

Melting

Freezing

LIQUID

Boiling and evaporating

Condensing and precipitating

GAS

VOCABULARY

physical change—a change that does not result in new substances
increase—make larger or raise the number
decrease—make smaller or lower the number

FIVE WAYS TO CHANGE

Matter can change state in 5 ways. Refer to the diagram on page 226 as you read.

▲ Ice cream melts from a solid to a liquid.

1. **Solid to liquid** If you leave ice cream in the sun, it melts. Thermal energy from the sun makes the particles in the solid ice cream move faster and farther apart. The particles move fast enough to **overcome** the attraction that locks them together. The temperature at which a solid turns to liquid is called the **melting point.**

2. **Liquid to solid** The **reverse** of melting is freezing. As a liquid cools, the particles slow down. They lock back together. The temperature at which a liquid turns to solid is the **freezing point.**

3. **Liquid to gas** If you add enough thermal energy to a liquid, it begins to boil. The particles get enough energy to move very fast. They separate and turn into a gas. An example is the steam coming from boiling water. The temperature at which a liquid turns to a gas is the **boiling point.**

4. **Gas to liquid** When you cool a gas, thermal energy goes out of it. If you take away enough thermal energy, the gas **condenses.** That means the particles come back together to form liquid. This is what happens when water vapor forms rain.

5. **Solid to gas** Sometimes a solid changes right to a gas. Substances such as moth balls or dry ice go directly from a solid into a gas. This process is called **sublimation.**

(**TALK AND SHARE**) **Think about your kitchen. Tell your partner how changes in state occur in the kitchen.**

Language Notes

Multiple Meanings
This word has more than one meaning.

☐ **state**
1. a noun that means a condition or situation, such as the solid state of matter
2. a noun that means part of a country, as in the state of Florida
3. a verb that means to say something

▲ Dry ice turns directly into a gas from the solid state. This change is called *sublimation*.

VOCABULARY
overcome—break
melting point—the temperature at which a solid changes to a liquid
reverse—the opposite
freezing point—the temperature at which a liquid changes to a solid. Water changes to ice at 0 °Celsius.
boiling point—the temperature at which a liquid changes to a gas. Water boils at 100 °Celsius.
condenses—turns from a gas to a liquid
sublimation—the process of changing from a solid directly to a gas

Physical Properties

Physical properties are characteristics you can use to describe a substance. For example, you can describe something's color, shape, and size. The states of matter are physical properties, too. A substance can be a solid, a liquid, or a gas.

DENSITY

Density is a physical property. Density is a measurement of how much matter, or **mass,** is in a certain **volume** of a substance. For example, in a one-liter container, a gas like helium is usually less dense—or has fewer particles per liter—than a liquid or a solid. Examine the different densities in the diagram below.

Mass = 1 g

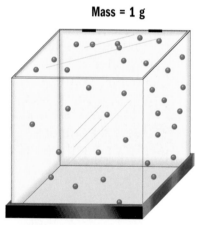

Density = 0.5 g/mL

▲ As more mass fills the same volume, density increases.

Mass = 3 g

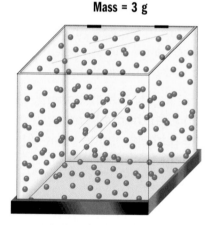

Density = 1.5 g/mL

Mass = 5 g

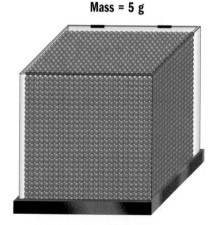

Density = 2.5 g/mL

A bowling ball and a basketball have almost the same volume, but the bowling ball has more mass and, therefore, greater density. ▶

VOCABULARY

physical properties—characteristics of matter that you can observe without changing the matter

density—mass per unit volume (D = m/v)

mass—the amount of matter in something

volume—the amount of space a substance takes up

ELEMENTS AND PROPERTIES

The density, mass, and **weight** of an object are physical properties. So are melting point, freezing point, and boiling point.

Each **element,** or kind of substance, has **distinctive** physical properties. For example, each element has its own freezing and melting points. Scientists **classify** elements by their properties because it gives them a way to describe the elements.

(TALK AND SHARE) **Talk with your partner about the different properties of 6 objects in your classroom. Make lists of their properties and then sort the objects by their properties.**

> ### Summary
>
> You can find matter in the solid state, the liquid state, and the gas state. Atoms in matter are always in motion. A change in motion may cause a change in state. Each element changes state according to its physical properties.

Science, Technology, and Society

Plasma

Plasma is known as the fourth state of matter. More than 99.9 percent of all visible mass exists in this form. That's because most stars are composed of plasma. The extremely high temperature of stars makes particles move so fast that the electrons separate from their atoms. Neon lights, fluorescent bulbs, and plasma television screens have some material in the plasma state.

VOCABULARY

weight—the measure of the force of gravity on an object's mass
element—a substance that cannot be split into simpler substances
distinctive—having qualities that set one thing apart from others
classify—sort or organize by characteristics
plasma—a state of matter, common in stars, in which particles have broken apart

Describing

Describing Changes of State

When you describe something, you tell about its characteristics. You make a mental picture. Then you can describe that picture with words. To describe changes in state, tell what properties go with each state. A Classification Organizer can help you.

Classification Organizer

Solid	Liquid	Gas
It keeps its shape.	It takes the shape of the container.	It fills its container.
Particles move slowly.	Particles move faster.	Particles move very fast.
Particles stay close together.	Particles begin to move apart.	Particles move farther apart.

Practice Describing

1. Draw Visualize a glass of cold water on a hot day. Drops of water form on the outside of the glass. These water drops come from the air. Draw a picture of what happens to water molecules when water vapor (gas) turns to liquid. Use your picture to tell your group what happens. Use the word *condenses*.

2. Write Look at the Classification Organizer above to see the characteristics of liquids and gases. Write a paragraph that describes what happens to water when it boils in a pan and produces steam. Decide how the water particles change. Describe the changes in 3 steps. Words from the Word Bank can help you.

Word Bank

particles
temperature
energy

farther
dense

move
speed up

Activities

Grammar Spotlight

Present Progressive Tense You use the present progressive tense to talk about something you are doing right now. The present progressive tense is different from the simple present tense.

Simple Present Tense	**Noun + Verb**
The action is true all of the time. It happens many times.	*The clouds are in the sky.*
	They form rain.
	The rain falls.

Present Progressive Tense	**Noun + Verb (be) + Verb (add ing)**
The action is happening now. It has two parts: a form of the verb *be* and the *ing* form of the verb.	*I am drinking water.*
	She is making ice cubes.
	They are driving their cars.

Make a sentence about adding heat to a substance using the present progressive tense.

Oral Language

Visualize Density Compare the densities of 3 different things you see every day. For example, compare a gallon of water, a textbook, and a basketball. Visualize the density of each one. Which is the most dense? Which is the least dense? Talk about it in small groups.

Hands On

Heating and Cooling Put a small dish of water on a windowsill or in a freezer. Leave it there for a day. Observe it after one day and describe any changes you see. Think about whether the water grew warmer or cooler during the day it sat in the window or in the freezer. With your partner, explain any change of state that happened.

Properties and the
Periodic Table

Here you'll learn about how scientists organize elements. You'll also learn how to ask questions and practice classifying elements.

▲ My cousin makes statues out of metal.

- **What is this person doing?**
- **Why do people make things out of metal?**
- **How does heat make metal easier to bend?**

Big Idea

Each element has its own set of properties. These properties make it different from every other element. The periodic table is a chart based on the properties of each element.

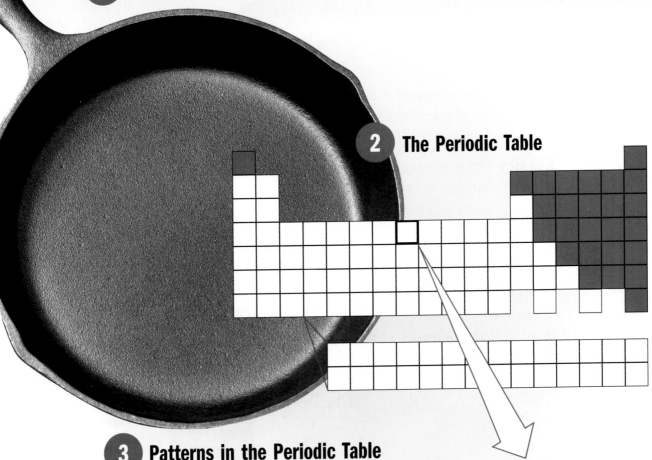

1 **Properties of Elements**

2 **The Periodic Table**

3 **Patterns in the Periodic Table**

Metal

Metalloid

Nonmetal

26 protons —→ 26
Chemical symbol —→ **Fe**
for iron   Iron

Key Concepts

chemical property   physical property

Chemical Property

Iron combines with oxygen and forms rust.

Physical Properties

Black
Heavy
Shiny
Smooth
Orange and black
Heavy
Dull
Flaky

A **chemical property** is a characteristic of matter that involves change. It is the ability of one substance to change into a new substance by combining with other substances. The new substance has new properties.

A **physical property** is a characteristic of matter that you can observe without changing the matter.

Metal, Metalloid, Nonmetal

All atoms can be classified into 1 of 3 groups: metals, metalloids, and nonmetals. The properties of substances from each group are different.

Metal

Properties
Shiny, bendable, conducts heat and electricity

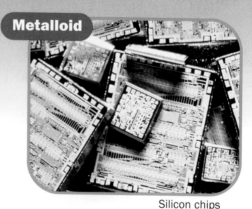

Metalloid

Silicon chips

Property
Conducts electricity under some conditions

Ask Questions

Asking questions is a skill. Scientists ask questions all the time. For example, you often need to ask questions about the properties of an object. The answers will help you identify which element or elements it contains. When you ask questions,

■ Decide what you want to know.

■ Think of a question you can ask to learn more. You might ask, "Is it shiny?" "Does it bend?" and "Is it easy to heat?"

For scientists, asking questions is a way to learn more about the world.

Sample Questions

Property	Question
Shiny	Is it shiny?
Bendable	Does it bend?
Conducts heat	Is it easy to heat?

Nonmetal

Neon lights

Graphite

Properties

Not shiny, easy to break, does not conduct heat or electricity

Properties and the Periodic Table

Each kind of element has properties that make it different from every other kind of element. The periodic table is a chart that organizes elements by their properties.

▲ Metal wires like these are good conductors. That is why people use them to carry electricity.

Properties

Every kind of substance, or **element**, has both physical and chemical properties. **Physical properties** are characteristics of matter you can observe without changing the matter. You can measure something, heat it, or freeze it, and it is still the same substance.

For example, **density** and mass are physical properties. So are the temperatures at which an element changes states. We call these temperatures the melting point, freezing point, and boiling point of the element. Each element has **distinctive** physical properties.

Chemical properties relate to how an element behaves with other elements. Each element also has distinctive chemical properties. Sometimes an element can combine with another element to form a new substance. The way each element does this is a distinctive chemical property of the element.

Examples of Properties

Physical
Color
Density
Taste
Melting point

Chemical
Ability to combine with oxygen
Ability to burn in air

VOCABULARY

element—a substance that cannot be split into simpler substances
physical properties—the characteristics of a substance you can observe without changing the substance
density—the mass per unit volume of a substance
distinctive—having qualities that set one thing apart from others
chemical properties—the ways an element behaves with other elements

PROTONS AND ELECTRONS

Scientists classify elements by observing their properties. What gives each element its properties?

Each **atom** of an element has a certain number of **protons** in its **nucleus.** The number of protons determines the number of **electrons** in an atom. The arrangement of electrons determines the properties that the element has.

ELECTRONS AND PROPERTIES

Scientists sometimes describe electrons as being in **shells** around the nucleus of the atom. Each shell can hold only a specific number of electrons. For example, the inside shell can hold 2 electrons. The next shell can hold 8 electrons.

An atom is most **stable** when its outer shell is full. Atoms that **react** often trade or share electrons so that their outer shells are full. The number of electrons an atom has determines whether it will react with another atom.

When you look at the table on the next two pages, you will see that each element has a different number of protons. This means that each element has its own number of electrons as well.

(TALK AND SHARE) **With your partner, list some physical properties you can observe in your classroom.**

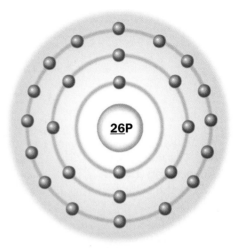

▲ Shell model of an iron atom

VOCABULARY

atom—the smallest part of an element that has the properties of that element
protons—the positively charged particles in the nucleus of an atom
nucleus—the center part of an atom, which contains protons and neutrons
electrons—the negatively charged particles that circle the nucleus of an atom
shells—imaginary paths around the nucleus of an atom in which electrons move
stable—balanced and not easy to change
react—change chemically

The Periodic Table

The **periodic table** of elements is a chart that organizes the elements according to their properties. It gives people a way to understand atoms and how they work together.

The modern periodic table lists more than 100 elements in order by the number of protons in each element's nucleus. The number of protons is the **atomic number** of an element. If you look at the table from left to right, you will see that the atomic number increases.

When you look at the table from left to right, you will see a pattern. The elements change as their atomic numbers increase. **Metals** are on the left. Most elements are metals. Many metals are strong, heavy, shiny, and easy to bend. They are good conductors. That means they allow electric current or heat to pass through easily.

The rows at the bottom are usually shown this way so the table will fit on a page.

Each box in the chart has information about an element. It includes the element's name, its **chemical symbol,** and its atomic number. Everywhere on Earth, scientists use the same chemical symbols to represent the elements.

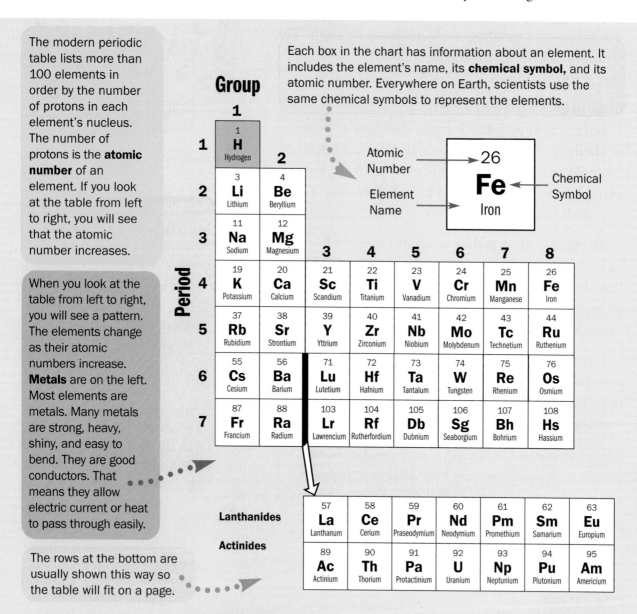

periodic table—a chart that organizes elements by their properties

atomic number—the number of protons in the nucleus of one atom of an element

chemical symbol—an abbreviation for an element, usually made of one or two letters from the beginning of its name. Sometimes the abbreviation comes from a Latin name, such as Fe for iron, which in Latin is *ferrum.*

TALK AND SHARE With your partner, find the element chlorine. Tell each other what you know about the properties of chlorine based on its position on the periodic table.

As you move from left to right on the table, the elements become poor **conductors**. **Metalloids** have some of the properties of both metals and **nonmetals.** Solid nonmetals are easy to break.

On the far right are the **noble gases.** They do not usually react with other elements.

				18
				2 **He** Helium

	13	14	15	16	17	
	5 **B** Boron	6 **C** Carbon	7 **N** Nitrogen	8 **O** Oxygen	9 **F** Fluorine	10 **Ne** Neon

9	10	11	12	13 **Al** Aluminum	14 **Si** Silicon	15 **P** Phosphorus	16 **S** Sulfur	17 **Cl** Chlorine	18 **Ar** Argon
27 **Co** Cobalt	28 **Ni** Nickel	29 **Cu** Copper	30 **Zn** Zinc	31 **Ga** Gallium	32 **Ge** Germanium	33 **As** Arsenic	34 **Se** Selenium	35 **Br** Bromine	36 **Kr** Krypton
45 **Rh** Rhodium	46 **Pd** Palladium	47 **Ag** Silver	48 **Cd** Cadmium	49 **In** Indium	50 **Sn** Tin	51 **Sb** Antimony	52 **Te** Tellurium	53 **I** Iodine	54 **Xe** Xenon
77 **Ir** Iridium	78 **Pt** Platinum	79 **Au** Gold	80 **Hg** Mercury	81 **Tl** Thallium	82 **Pb** Lead	83 **Bi** Bismuth	84 **Po** Polonium	85 **At** Astatine	86 **Rn** Radon
109 **Mt** Meitnerium	110 **Uun** Unununnilium	111 **Uuu** Unununium	112 **Uub** Ununbium		114 **Uuq** Ununquadium		116 **Uuh** Ununhexium		118 **Uuo** Ununoctium

Elements such as polonium (84), radon (86), and radium (88) are **radioactive.** All of the elements on the bottom row of the periodic table are also radioactive.

64 **Gd** Gadolinium	65 **Tb** Terbium	66 **Dy** Dysprosium	67 **Ho** Holmium	68 **Er** Erbium	69 **Tm** Thulium	70 **Yb** Ytterbium
96 **Cm** Curium	97 **Bk** Berkelium	98 **Cf** Californium	99 **Es** Einsteinium	100 **Fm** Fermium	101 **Md** Mendelevium	102 **No** Nobelium

VOCABULARY

conductors—materials that allow heat and electricity to pass through
radioactive—giving off high-energy particles

LESSON 19 • PROPERTIES AND THE PERIODIC TABLE   **239**

Materials

A **material** is any substance from which something can be made. For example, the plastic on your book cover protects the cover from tearing. Each material is used for a particular job.

Chemists use their knowledge of how elements react to create thousands of useful materials, such as plastics, steel, and computer chips. **Materials scientists** work in laboratories to learn about materials and find new ways to use them.

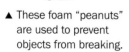

▲ These foam "peanuts" are used to prevent objects from breaking.

Patterns in the Periodic Table

In the periodic table, the elements are organized by increasing atomic number into columns and rows. Each column going down is called a **group.** Each row going across is called a **period.** There are **patterns** in each group and each period.

GROUPS

The outer electron shell of an atom determines its chemical properties. In each group, all of the elements have the same number of electrons in the outer shell. The elements in each group also have the same chemical properties.

The shell model helps us understand why the elements on the left side of the table are reactive. Their outside shells are not full. An atom of one of these elements can either lose or gain electrons by coming together with another atom in a **chemical change.**

Metals lose electrons more easily than nonmetals, because they have unfilled outer shells. That is why sodium and potassium (in Group 1), for example, are almost always found in combination with other elements.

Elements on the right side of the table are usually found by themselves. The noble gases (Group 18) have full outside electron shells. That is why they do not react with other elements.

VOCABULARY

group—a column in the periodic table
period—a row in the periodic table
patterns—events that happen over and over
chemical change—a change in matter that results in the formation of a new substance
material—any substance from which something can be made
materials scientists—people who find new ways to use elements and compounds

PERIODS

As you move across each period from left to right, the elements change from metals to metalloids to nonmetals. The number of protons and electrons increases by one with each element. However, the atoms actually get smaller. This is because with each new proton, the nucleus pulls harder on the electrons. The electrons spin closer to the nucleus, making the atom smaller.

Patterns Across a Period

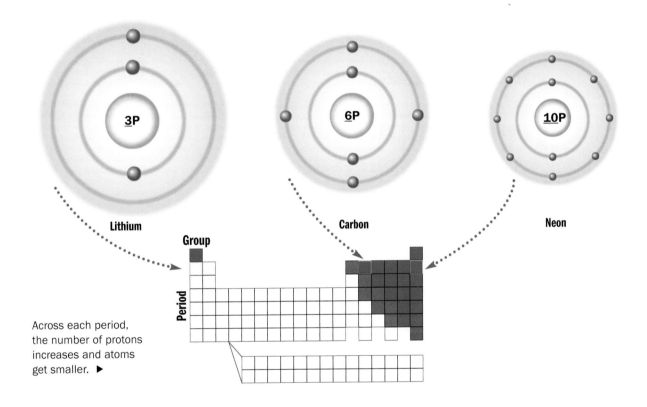

Lithium

Carbon

Neon

Group

Period

Across each period, the number of protons increases and atoms get smaller. ▶

(TALK AND SHARE) **With your partner, discuss what members of Group 17 have in common.**

Summary

The periodic table is a chart based on the properties of elements. The way electrons are organized in the atom of an element gives the element its properties. Each element has its own physical and chemical properties.

Classifying

Classifying Elements

You can classify an element as a metal, metalloid, or nonmetal by observing its physical properties. Start by deciding which questions to ask. Use the Classification Organizer to classify the element aluminum.

1. List properties you can observe.

2. Ask a question about each property.

3. Answer each question.

4. Based on your answers, classify aluminum.

Classification Organizer

Property	Question for Observation	Answer
appearance	What does it look like?	shiny, thin
bendable	Does it bend?	yes
conductor	Does it conduct heat?	yes
Classification: metal		

Practice Classifying

1. Create With a partner, make a Classification Organizer like the one above for copper. Ask questions about its properties, including whether it is shiny or dull, whether it bends or breaks, and whether it conducts heat. Decide together whether copper is a metal or a nonmetal.

2. Write Now describe in a paragraph the properties you see in copper. Tell why those properties help you classify copper as a metal or nonmetal. Use the Check Your Writing checklist after you have finished writing.

Check Your Writing

Make sure you

- Use complete sentences.

- Use a period at the end of each sentence.

- Spell all the words correctly.

Activities

Grammar Spotlight

Using *do* in Yes/No Questions Use *do* or *does* + a subject + the base form of the verb to ask a *yes* or *no* question.

Use **do** with **I, you, we,** or **they.**	*Do I* need gloves to touch this?
	Do you see the nucleus?
	Do we have enough?
	Do they pull like protons?
Use **does** with **he, she,** or **it.**	*Does he* have his textbook?
	Does she seem worried?
	Does it conduct heat?

Write one question with *do* and one question with *does*.

Oral Language

Precious Metals People use 3 metals from Group 11 of the periodic table—copper, silver, and gold—to make beautiful objects. Talk in your group about the physical properties of these metals. Explain why you think people have found these metals so beautiful for thousands of years. Give examples of how these metals can be used.

Hands On

Elements of Life Organisms need some elements to stay alive. They are H, C, N, O, P, and S. Find these elements on the periodic table and say their names. Draw their atoms to show the electrons in their shells. Use page 237 as a model. Talk about what these elements have in common and how they are different.

Partner Practice

Ask Questions With your partner, compare a penny and a nickel. The outside of the penny is made mostly of the element copper. The outside of the nickel is made mostly of the element nickel. Talk about the physical properties of the two coins. Write down some questions you could ask to find out more about their properties.

Bonds, Reactions, and Energy

Here you'll learn how atoms act with each other. You'll also learn how to infer from evidence and practice explaining a chemical reaction.

▲ Last year my cousin ran a marathon in New York.

- **What's happening here?**
- **What chemical reactions are happening to the runners?**
- **What kinds of chemical reactions are happening inside you now?**

Atoms can bond to each other with their electrons. Bonded atoms form molecules. When bonds form or when they break, a chemical reaction takes place. Energy and matter move in chemical reactions.

1 Forming Bonds

SODIUM

11P

17P

Sodium

Chlorine

2 Chemical Reactions

Bond

11P

17P

+ −

Molecule

One electron moves from sodium to chlorine.

Sodium chloride

3 Energy in Reactions

Sodium + Chlorine ⟶ Sodium chloride + Energy

Key Concepts

attraction   **chemical bond**   **react**

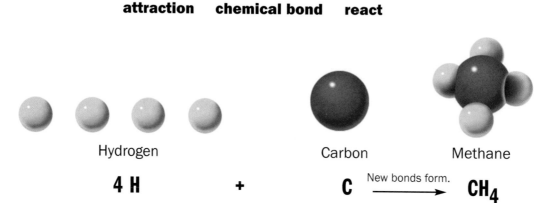

Hydrogen   Carbon   Methane

$$4\,H \quad + \quad C \xrightarrow{\text{New bonds form.}} CH_4$$

In science, an **attraction** means things come together. A **chemical bond** is a special kind of attraction. It is the attraction between atoms that holds them together in a molecule.

When substances **react,** the bonds between their atoms may break or new bonds may form between atoms.

Detecting a Chemical Change

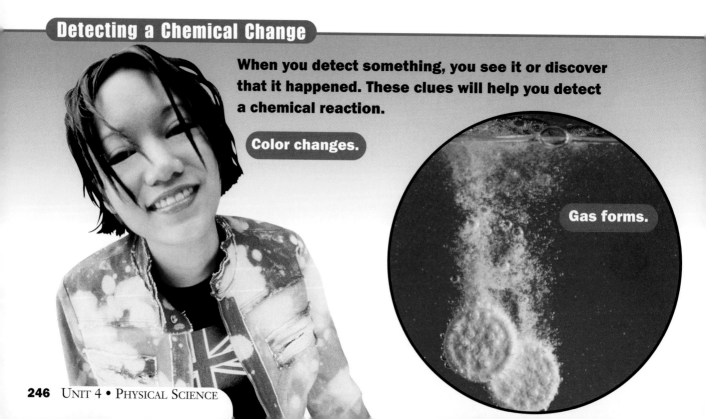

When you detect something, you see it or discover that it happened. These clues will help you detect a chemical reaction.

Color changes.

Gas forms.

Infer from Evidence

When you infer, you draw a conclusion based on facts. In science, to *infer* means to gather evidence, add it to what you already know, and decide what something means.

Making an Inference from Evidence

- Observe a change.

- Consider the evidence.

- Think about what you already know about the topic.

- Make an inference about what happened.

Imagine striking a kitchen match. What evidence would you observe about the change that occurs? You can probably see light, feel heat, smell smoke, and notice that the wood has a different color after it burns.

What would you infer from the facts you observe with a match?

Solids form in liquid.

Temperature changes.

Bonds, Reactions, and Energy

Atoms can bond to each other and make molecules. In chemical reactions, bonds form or break, and energy and matter move.

Forming Bonds

Atoms join together in all sorts of ways to make new substances. Molecules hold together because of an attraction called a **chemical bond.** Bonds form when atoms give away or share electrons.

COVALENT BONDS

Atoms will sometimes share electrons. **Covalent bonds** are bonds in which electrons are shared. For example, hydrogen (H) and oxygen (O) usually occur as two-atom molecules (H_2 and O_2). The atoms share their electrons. Water (H_2O) is a covalent substance.

▲ Every water molecule contains covalent bonds.

Covalent Bonds

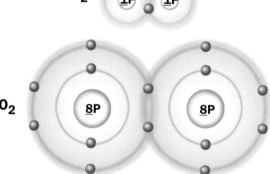

H_2 1P 1P

O_2 8P   8P

▲ Metals conduct heat due to their metallic bonds.

METALLIC BONDS

Sometimes many metal atoms share electrons. This is a **metallic bond.** Electrons in the outer shells of the atoms float loosely together in a "sea" of electrons. Heat or electricity flows through the metal as the electrons move. This explains why metals are good conductors.

> **VOCABULARY**
> **chemical bond**—an attraction that holds atoms together
> **covalent bonds**—the sharing of electrons between two atoms
> **metallic bond**—the sharing of electrons among many atoms

IONIC BONDS

Ionic bonds form when one atom takes an electron from another atom. For example, look at a sodium (Na) atom below. It has 11 electrons, with only 1 in its outer shell. It will give up that electron easily.

Now study the chlorine (Cl) atom. If it gets 1 more electron, it will have 8 in its outer shell. The chlorine atom takes the extra electron from sodium.

Ionic Bond

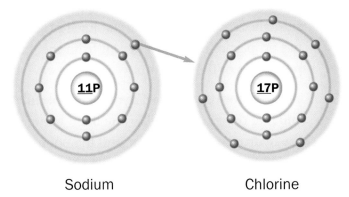

Sodium   Chlorine

▲ When the elements sodium and chlorine form an ionic bond, they form table salt.

Table salt (sodium chloride)

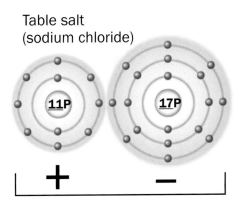

The sodium atom now has 11 protons and 10 electrons. This gives it a positive charge. The chlorine atom now has an extra electron and a negative charge. Atoms that have a charge are called **ions.** Atoms with opposite charges attract, so the sodium and chlorine ions stick together. The result is a new substance, **table salt.**

(**TALK AND SHARE**) **With your partner, make flash cards on the 3 kinds of chemical bonds. Practice learning them together.**

The salt flats of Utah ▼

When wood burns, the reactants include carbon and oxygen. ▼

Chemical Reactions

Chemical reactions happen around you all the time. Whenever you burn wood, you cause a chemical reaction. When you eat, chemical reactions in your body help digest your food.

REACTANTS AND PRODUCTS

A chemical reaction happens when substances break apart or combine. The starting substances are called **reactants.** The result is at least one new substance. New substances are called **products.** Each product has properties that are different from the properties of the reactants.

Water forms from two hydrogen molecules and one oxygen molecule. The bond between the hydrogen atoms breaks, and the bond between the oxygen atoms breaks. New bonds form to combine two hydrogen atoms with one oxygen atom. This happens two times, and you get two molecules of water.

The Formation of Two Water Molecules

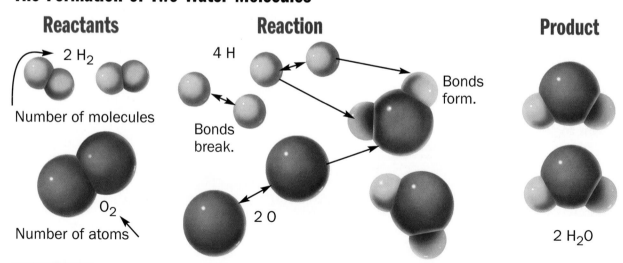

Reactants

$2 H_2$

Number of molecules

O_2

Number of atoms

Reaction

4 H

Bonds break.

2 O

Bonds form.

Product

$2 H_2O$

VOCABULARY

chemical reactions—processes of making new substances by breaking bonds and forming new bonds

reactants—the starting materials in a chemical reaction

products—the substances that are the result of a chemical reaction

EQUATIONS

An **equation** is the way scientists write changes in the arrangement of atoms during a chemical reaction. This is the chemical equation for the formation of water.

$$2\ H_2 \quad + \quad O_2 \quad \longrightarrow \quad 2\ H_2O$$

Reactant   Reactant   Product

Two hydrogen molecules combine with one oxygen molecule and form two molecules of water.

CONSERVATION OF MASS

The word *equation* comes from the word *equal*. Chemical reactions rearrange atoms into new **compounds.** However, the total number of each kind of atom stays the same. Look at the water equation. You can see that there are the same number and kinds of atoms before and after the reaction.

This is called the **conservation of mass.** The total amount of mass is always the same, both before and after a chemical reaction.

The products of burning wood include ash and smoke. ▼

(**TALK AND SHARE**) **With your partner, use the words** *reactants* **and** *products* **in a sentence about the conservation of mass.**

Energy in Reactions

It takes **energy** to break bonds. When new bonds form, energy is released. Energy is added and released in every chemical reaction. That happens because bonds break and form in every chemical reaction.

- It always takes energy to break a chemical bond.
- Making a chemical bond always releases energy.

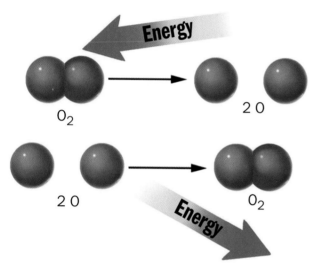

O_2

$2 O$

$2 O$

O_2

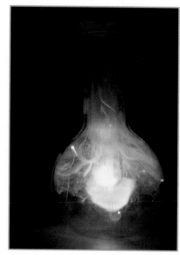

▲ The reaction of sodium and chlorine releases energy.

THERMAL ENERGY AND REACTIONS

Reactions that release **thermal energy** are called **exothermic.** For example, when gasoline burns in an engine, the process gives off energy. In this reaction, the amount of energy released by making new bonds is greater than the amount it takes to break bonds.

In some reactions, energy must be added to break bonds. These are called **endothermic** reactions. For example, **dissolving** salt in water is endothermic.

Sometimes reactions happen on their own. Other times, reactions need energy to get started. You can put gasoline in a car, but the engine won't work without a spark from a spark plug to start the chemical reaction.

Science, Technology, and Society

Explosions

Chemical reactions take place at different speeds. In an explosion, energy from a reaction is released very quickly. When you see fireworks, you see a rapid chemical reaction. When a firework is lit, it explodes and releases energy in the form of heat, sound, and light. The result is a beautiful and noisy display.

VOCABULARY

energy—the power to make something change
thermal energy—the energy of moving atoms
exothermic—releasing thermal energy
endothermic—taking in thermal energy
dissolving—breaking into component parts

CONSERVATION OF ENERGY

Energy is not lost or gained in a chemical reaction. Energy simply changes from one form to another form.

For example, to start a gas engine you need a battery to provide **electrical energy.** This becomes **chemical energy** in the chemical reaction between gasoline and oxygen. The energy that makes the engine move is **kinetic energy.** The engine releases thermal energy.

This is the principle called the **conservation of energy.** It states that the kind of energy in a system can change, but the total amount of energy cannot change.

(TALK AND SHARE) **With a partner, make a list of 4 things that give off energy. Then discuss how this energy might have been released by a chemical reaction.**

▲ What types of energy make this engine work?

Summary

Molecules form when atoms bond to each other by exchanging or sharing electrons. A chemical reaction takes place whenever bonds form or break. Energy and matter move in chemical reactions, but their amounts always stay the same.

VOCABULARY

electrical energy—the energy of moving electrons
chemical energy—the energy produced by chemical reactions
kinetic energy—the energy of motion
conservation of energy—the principle stating that energy is not created or destroyed; it is only changed from one kind to another

Explaining

Explaining a Chemical Reaction

When you explain something, you make it easier to understand.

This picture shows a rusty object. Rust is a compound called *iron oxide*. Iron oxide is shown as Fe_2O_3. The picture shows evidence of a chemical reaction, because the object's color has changed from gray to orange. Here is the reaction equation.

$$4 \, Fe + 3 \, O_2 \rightarrow 2 \, Fe_2O_3$$

Use a chart to put this equation into words.

Chart

Equation	4 Fe	+	3 O₂	→	2 Fe₂ O₃
explanation words	4 atoms iron	plus	3 molecules oxygen	make	2 molecules iron oxide
explanation sentence	4 atoms of iron added to 3 molecules of oxygen results in 2 molecules of rust.				

Practice Explaining

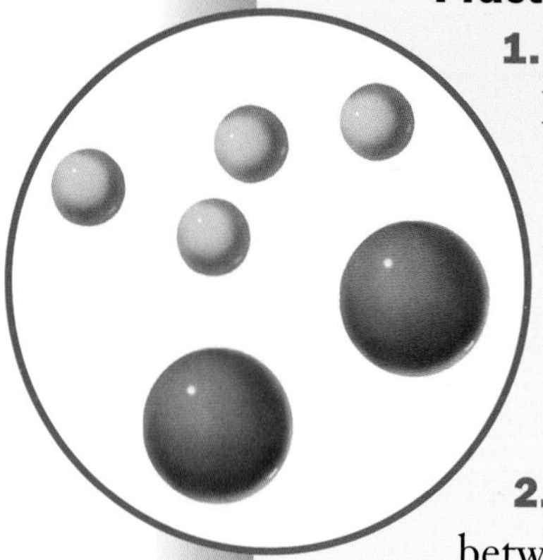

1. Draw At the left are 4 hydrogen atoms and 2 oxygen atoms. Explain what happens when the atoms make molecules and when the molecules make water. With a partner, draw an equation for using these atoms to form water. You may copy it from page 251. Use symbols or draw the atoms and molecules you need. Trade drawings with another pair and talk about the drawings.

2. Write Write the equation for the reaction between hydrogen and oxygen to make water. Then write one or two sentences to explain each step of the chemical reaction. A Chart like the one above and words from the Word Bank can help you.

Word Bank

atoms
molecule
reaction

combine
break
produce
react

Activities

Grammar Spotlight

Using *must* and *have to* When it is necessary to do something, we say "I must do it" or "I have to do it." Both *must* and *have to* mean "it is necessary." *Have to* is more common. *Must* is stronger and more formal.

Affirmative	Negative
You must have your license to drive.	You must not drive without your license.
I have to go to school tomorrow.	I don't have to go to school tomorrow.

Write two sentences about chemical reactions. Write one with *must* and one with *have to*.

Oral Language

Talking Chemistry The equation for making table salt is Na + Cl → NaCl. The science name for table salt is sodium chloride. Work with your partner or group to explain the equation in words.

Hands On

Make Molecule Models In your group, roll pieces of notebook paper into balls and use tape to form two models of a water molecule. Then use your models to show the class how bonds break and form in the chemical reaction for water.

Partner Practice

Infer from Evidence Imagine that you walk up to a school bus soon after the driver has started the engine. With your partner, talk about the clues to a chemical change you can detect. Think about clues such as the formation of a gas (do you smell anything?) and temperature changes. List the evidence you find for a chemical reaction taking place in the engine of the bus. Then talk about what you can infer from this evidence.

Understanding

Energy

Here you'll learn about how energy changes from one form to another. You'll also learn how to think about systems and practice relating the parts of a system.

▲ Sometimes I feel like I could dance all night. My mom says she wishes she had that much energy.

■ **What kinds of energy can you see here?**

■ **Where does energy come from?**

■ **What does energy feel like to you?**

Energy can change from one form to another form. When the form of energy changes, the amount of energy stays the same. Often, when there is an energy change, some thermal energy is given off.

1 Forms of Energy

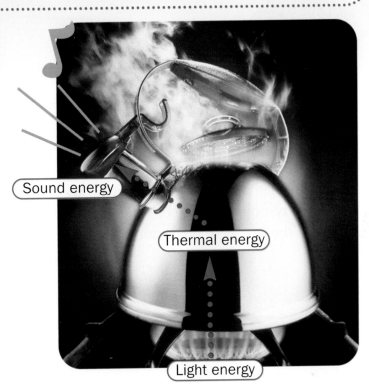

Sound energy

Thermal energy

Light energy

2 Energy changes forms.

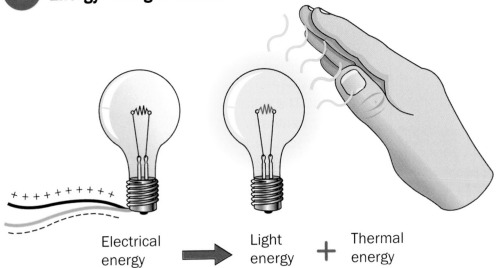

Electrical energy → Light energy + Thermal energy

Key Concepts

potential energy   position   kinetic energy   motion

Potential energy is stored energy. It is contained inside something, such as a rock resting at the top of a hill. It is called the energy of **position.**

Kinetic energy is the energy of **motion.** It is the energy something has because it is moving. Potential energy changes to kinetic energy when the rock begins rolling down the hill.

Making Electricity

Electricity is a form of energy. A coal-burning power plant changes the chemical energy in coal to electrical energy.

Power Plant

1. Burning coal releases thermal energy.

2. The thermal energy heats water. The water turns to steam. The steam turns turbines. Thermal energy becomes kinetic energy.

Turbines

Think About Systems

In a system, many parts work together. Think of a baseball game as a system. Where is energy in this system? Imagine the pitcher throwing and the ball flying. Visualize the batter running and an outfielder catching. Think about the way energy affects each part of the system as it goes into action.

Thinking About Systems

- Imagine the whole system.

- Pick a place to begin. Then list the individual parts of the system in order.

- Describe how the parts relate to each other and work together.

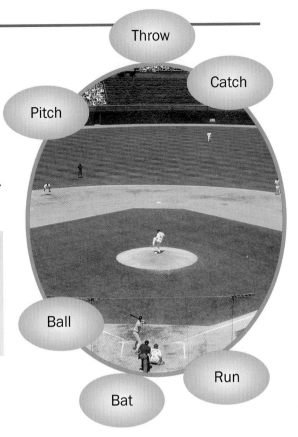

Throw

Catch

Pitch

Ball

Run

Bat

Power Lines

Appliances

3. Turbines connect to electrical generators that make electricity. Electricity flows through wires to homes, offices, and factories.

4. Appliances, such as computers, turn electricity into other forms of energy.

Understanding Energy

There are many forms of energy. Energy can change from one form to another form. The total amount of energy in a system always stays the same. Many times when energy changes form, some thermal energy is given off.

What Is Energy?

All matter has **energy.** Energy is the ability to do work. Energy can make something change. To understand the two basic kinds of energy, think about a baseball game.

POTENTIAL ENERGY

The batter is ready to swing. The batter's energy is stored and ready to use. This is **potential energy,** or the energy of **position.**

▲ Before the batter swings at the baseball, his energy is stored as potential energy.

The waiting catcher is full of potential energy. ▶

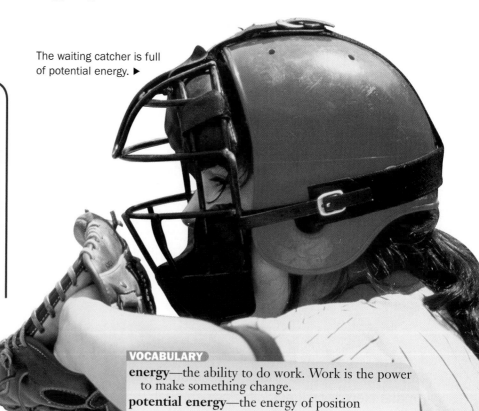

Language Notes

Homophones
These words sound alike but they have different spellings and meanings.

- **to:** a preposition used before a verb

- **two:** the number 2

- **too:** an adverb meaning also

VOCABULARY
energy—the ability to do work. Work is the power to make something change.
potential energy—the energy of position
position—the place where something is

KINETIC ENERGY

When the batter swings the bat and hits the ball, the ball flies through the air. The moving ball has **kinetic energy,** the energy of **motion.** As the batter runs toward first base, the batter has kinetic energy, too.

A glass that is near the edge of a table has potential energy. It is in a position where it can fall. If it falls off the table, it will have kinetic energy.

TOTAL ENERGY

The total energy an object has is its potential energy plus its kinetic energy. Together, these two kinds of energy are called **mechanical energy.**

There are many forms of energy, but they all consist of potential energy, kinetic energy, or both.

(TALK AND SHARE) **Imagine a bird sitting in a nest. What kind of energy does it have? The bird gets up and flies away. What kind of energy does it have now? Discuss your answers with a partner.**

▲ Once the batter, the bat, and the ball start moving, they have kinetic energy.

Energy Changes

In any system, energy can change from potential to kinetic and back again. The total amount of energy in a system always stays the same. However, energy can exist in many **forms.**

▲ How many forms of energy can you find in this picture?

FORMS OF ENERGY

- *Thermal energy*—the total kinetic energy in the particles of a substance. An increase in thermal energy warms a room.

- *Solar energy*—the energy that comes from the sun.

- *Light energy*—the energy carried by light **waves.** Energy from a light bulb lights a room.

- *Sound energy*—the energy carried by sound waves. A radio sends out sound energy.

- *Electrical energy*—the energy produced by electrical charges in matter. Electrical energy provides power for **appliances** in your home.

- *Chemical energy*—the energy stored in chemical bonds. Soda contains chemical energy that causes it to fizz when opened.

- *Nuclear energy*—the energy contained in the **nuclei** of atoms. When people split the nuclei of atoms, huge amounts of energy are released. This is what powers an atomic bomb.

TRANSFORMATION

Each form of energy can change into another form of energy. When something causes an energy change, we say that it **transforms** the energy. The name for the change is *transformation*.

For example, plants change, or transform, solar energy into chemical energy. After you eat, your body transforms some of the chemical energy in food into thermal energy. You can feel this energy during hard exercise.

When an energy transformation takes place, the amount of energy stays the same. Also, when energy changes form, some thermal energy usually is given off. You can easily see this happen with a light bulb. Electrical energy turns to light energy as a wire in the bulb glows. The light bulb also gets hot.

(**TALK AND SHARE**) **With your partner, name at least 4 forms of energy you can observe right now from where you are sitting.**

Chemical energy

Thermal energy

◄ The body can turn chemical energy into thermal energy.

▲ This kind of picture, called a thermogram, shows which parts of the hand are hottest and coldest. Red is hottest, yellow is warm, green is cool, and blue is coldest.

Energy, Temperature, and Heat

Scientists use the terms *energy*, *temperature*, and *heat* with very specific meanings.

ENERGY

Whether a substance is a gas, a liquid, or a solid, all its particles are moving. The particles have kinetic energy. Thermal energy is the amount of kinetic energy in all the particles of a substance. The more kinetic energy the particles have, the more thermal energy the substance has.

Substances with more particles have more thermal energy. For example, a gallon of warm water has more thermal energy than a cup of warm water.

TEMPERATURE

Temperature is the measure of how fast the particles in a substance are moving. A substance with rapidly moving particles has a high temperature. The gallon of water and the cup of water can have the same temperature, even though the gallon has more thermal energy.

Science, Technology, and Society

Motion Detectors

Have you ever been to a building with a motion detector? When a person moves in front of a motion detector, the detector makes a light go on or a **siren** go off.

Some motion detectors detect thermal energy. A person's body gives off thermal energy as radiation. When a person moves in front of the detector, the detector senses a change in the radiation around it. The detector responds by sending an electrical signal to other parts of its system. This electrical energy turns on the light or operates the siren.

VOCABULARY

temperature—a measure of how fast the particles in a substance are moving
siren—a machine that makes a loud, wailing sound

HEAT

Heat is the transfer of thermal energy from one object to another. The energy always goes from the object with a higher temperature to the object with a lower temperature. This can happen in 3 ways.

1. **Radiation** is the transfer of energy in waves. If you hold your hands near a fire, the waves of energy reach your hands and you feel the heat.

2. **Conduction** is the transfer of energy through things that touch each other. If you leave a metal spoon in a hot pan, the spoon gets hot. The heated atoms in the bottom of the pan move rapidly. They bump into the atoms around them. Then those atoms move faster. The process continues until the bottom of the pan and the spoon are the same temperature.

3. **Convection** is the transfer of energy through a moving liquid or gas. In a pot of boiling water, the water near the bottom gets hot. Atoms move faster and farther apart. As hot water rises to the top, cooler water moves to the bottom. It also heats up. In this way, heat moves through all the water in the pan.

Convection moves water in a heated pot. ▼

(TALK AND SHARE) With your partner, name examples of heat that you experienced today.

Summary

Energy changes from one form to another, yet the total amount stays the same. Heat is the transfer of thermal energy from one object to another.

VOCABULARY
heat—the movement of energy from a warmer object to a cooler object
radiation—the movement of energy in waves
conduction—the movement of energy through things that touch each other
convection—the movement of energy through a moving liquid or gas

Relating

Relating Parts of a System

When you relate two or more things, you show how they connect and how they affect each other. Use a Web to relate the parts of a system to each other. With a Web, you can tell what happens in the whole system.

- Think of a whole system. Put its name in the center of the Web.

- Identify the parts of the system. Then name them in the circles around the center.

- Relate each part of the system to one or more other parts. You can number the parts to put them in order by steps.

Web

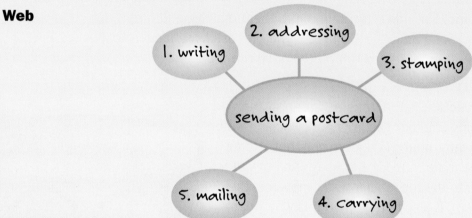

1. writing
2. addressing
3. stamping
sending a postcard
5. mailing
4. carrying

Practice Relating

1. Draw Think of a person jumping on a trampoline. When someone jumps on a trampoline, different forms of energy are involved. Draw the places where energy changes from potential energy to kinetic energy and back again as the person jumps.

Trampoline ▼

2. Write Write a paragraph that relates the parts of a system, such as kicking a ball, heating water on a fire, or some other action. Tell where potential energy changes to kinetic energy. Then exchange your paragraph with a partner and check each other's writing.

Check Your Writing

Make sure you
- ☐ Use complete sentences.
- ☐ Use a period at the end of each sentence.
- ☐ Spell all the words correctly.

Activities

Grammar Spotlight

The 5 W's   The science process always begins with asking questions. Questions that start with *Who, What, When, Where,* and *Why* help you gather basic information. From answers to your questions, you can form a hypothesis.

The 5 W's	Examples
Use *who* to ask about a person.	*Who* will do the experiment?
Use *what* to ask about a thing or event.	*What* makes the light bulb light?
Use *when* to ask about a time.	*When* will we see a change?
Use *where* to ask about a location.	*Where* does the electricity go?
Use *why* to ask about a reason or cause.	*Why* does the bowling ball hit the pins?

Ask one question about energy that uses *who, what, when, where,* or *why.*

Oral Language

Think About Systems   In a small group, describe how you got to school. Then name the main form of energy involved in each action you took to get from your home to the school. Talk about how the parts of this energy system worked together to get you to school.

Hands On

Play On!   Have each person in your group choose a favorite musical instrument or song. Then ask each person to play an imaginary instrument or sing the song to show how potential and kinetic energy are part of making music.

Partner Practice

Where Energy Goes   With your partner, roll a ball or a pencil along the desk, a table, or the floor. Discuss where the energy comes from to roll the object. Then discuss where you think the energy goes as the object rolls and comes to a stop.

Force and

Motion

Here you'll learn about forces and the way they make things move. You'll also learn how scientists ask questions and practice predicting an outcome.

▲ I like to play tug of war with my dog!

■ **What makes something move?**

■ **What forces are at work here?**

■ **When have you had to move because of a force?**

A force is a push or a pull. Forces, such as gravity and friction, affect the way things move. Forces can also change the shape of an object. Motion is a change in position. Isaac Newton wrote 3 laws of motion.

1 Force

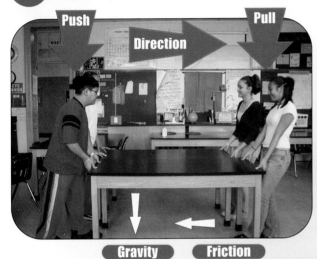

Push Pull

Direction

Gravity Friction

2 Motion

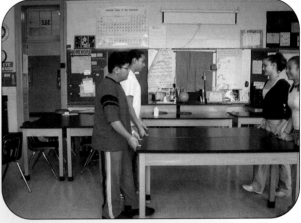

Change in position

3 Newton's Laws of Motion

Law 1: An object moves because of a force.

Law 2: The amount of force determines acceleration.

Law 3: For every action there is a reaction.

Key Concepts

rate   speed   velocity

A **rate** is a measure of how fast something happens. It is change per unit time—for example, 3 jugs of orange juice capped per second.

Speed is a kind of rate. Speed is how fast something is moving through space. It is distance per unit of time—6 feet per second.

Velocity includes both the speed and the direction of a motion—6 feet per second to the right.

Simple Machines

You do work when you apply force to an object and the object moves. Simple machines make work easier.

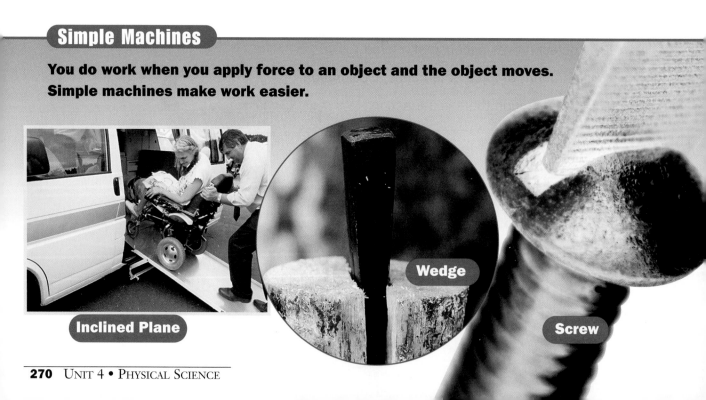

Inclined Plane

Wedge

Screw

Ask Questions

Scientists ask questions to find more information. They think of possible answers and form hypotheses.

When you ask questions, you look for information that will help you understand the things you observe. Your questions can also help you make a hypothesis you can test.

Asking Questions

☐ Decide what event or object you want to know more about.

☐ List questions about it.

☐ If you decide to investigate a question, imagine answers and make a hypothesis you can test.

For example, machines are often easy to observe. You can ask lots of questions about them. Look at the chart.

Machine Questions

- Which turns faster, a big wheel or a small wheel?
- Can an inclined plane be too steep to work?
- What is the best length of lever to use for pulling nails?

Wheel and Axle

Pulley

Lever

Force and Motion

▲ A person can press clay into different shapes by using a force.

When you push or pull something, you use a force. A force, such as gravity or friction, can change the shape of an object and the way it moves. When something moves, it changes position according to Newton's laws of motion.

Forces

A **force** is a push or pull. It can change the movement and the shape of an object. The effects of some forces are easy to see. When you squeeze a piece of soft clay in your hand, the force makes the clay change shape and **ooze** through your fingers.

All objects have forces acting on them—even objects that are not moving. When you sit in a chair, your body pushes on the chair. The chair also pushes against your body.

HOW TO MEASURE FORCE

Objects usually have forces acting on them from more than one direction. The **net force** on an object is the sum of all the forces acting on it. We measure force in units called **newtons (N).** Sometimes forces act in the *same* direction. Study the photograph.

◄ You and a friend are moving a heavy object. You pull in one direction with a force of 20 N. Your friend pushes in the same direction with a force of 10 N. To find the net force, add the forces together.
20 N + 10 N = 30 N

10 N

20 N

VOCABULARY
force—a push or a pull
ooze—move slowly through small holes or spaces
net force—the sum of all forces acting on an object
newtons (N)—the units for measuring force

▲ Team A has 3 people and pulls on a rope with a force of 30 N. Team B has 3 people and pulls in the opposite direction with a force of 40 N. To find the net force, subtract the numbers.

40 N – 30 N = 10 N in the direction of team B

It's easy to move an object when forces act in the same direction. What if people are not working together? In a tug of war, teams pull in *opposite* directions. Study the photograph above. Note the net force used in a tug of war.

BALANCED AND UNBALANCED FORCES

When a net force is greater than zero, the forces are *unbalanced*. That means an object that is sitting still will begin to move. If it is already moving and we add more force (such as an extra member for team B), it will move faster.

What if team A gets another member and pulls with 40 N? Then the forces on the rope are *balanced*. The net force is zero, and the rope will not move.

TALK AND SHARE Describe to your partner a person rowing a boat. Decide together what forces are balanced and what forces are unbalanced when a person rows a boat.

Language Notes

Multiple Meanings
These words have more than one meaning.

■ **force**
1. the cause that produces or stops the movement of an object
2. power or strength
3. make someone act against his or her will
4. a group of people working together, such as a police force

■ **net**
1. the final amount, after adding and subtracting are done
2. an object used to trap animals
3. a loosely woven material

▲ Gravity causes skydivers to fall to the ground.

▲ Gravity also holds the moon in its orbit around Earth.

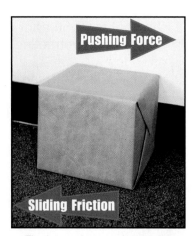

Pushing Force

Sliding Friction

▲ The box resists moving against the floor. If you put a box on the floor and push it, the force of friction causes the floor to push the box back toward you.

Gravity and Friction

If you drop a ball, it falls to the ground. The force of **gravity** pulls the ball toward Earth. Gravity is the force that pulls objects together.

The strength of gravity depends on the mass of objects and the **distance** between them. The greater the mass of an object, the greater its pull of gravity. Gravity becomes weaker as objects get farther apart. The ball falls to Earth because Earth has more mass than the ball.

Friction is the force that makes objects **resist** moving against each other. The amount of friction between two things depends on what they are made of and how they are shaped. Something slippery like oil causes less friction than rough or sticky substances, like sandpaper and glue.

The amount of friction also depends on mass. It is more difficult to move a big table across the floor than to move a little desk. The big table creates more friction against the floor.

(TALK AND SHARE) **Ask your partner how friction affects a boat as it moves through the water. Then tell your partner why you think the design of a boat reduces friction.**

VOCABULARY

gravity—the force that pulls objects together
distance—the amount of space or time between two things
friction—the force between objects that affects how easily they move past each other
resist—work against

Motion

Everything moves. Motion is a change in an object's **position.** Motion involves **speed,** direction, **velocity,** and **acceleration.** You can see all of these by studying a roller coaster.

- *Speed* is the distance an object travels in a certain amount of time. If a roller coaster is moving one mile every minute, you could also say the roller coaster moves at 60 miles per hour.

- *Velocity* is the speed and the direction an object is moving. If the speed or direction of an object changes, the velocity changes. The roller coaster does not travel in a straight line. The velocity changes with each change in direction.

- Because of gravity, the roller coaster goes faster as it gets closer to the ground. Its speed or velocity changes. *Acceleration* is the change of velocity in a unit of time. When a roller coaster starts moving, it's accelerating.

(TALK AND SHARE) **Imagine riding on a bus that is turning a corner. Talk with your partner about what it feels like when the bus changes velocity.**

The brakes on the roller coaster use friction to make it slow down and stop. ▼

> **VOCABULARY**
> **position**—the place where something is
> **speed**—the distance something travels in a period of time, such as miles per hour (mph)
> **velocity**—the combination of speed and direction
> **acceleration**—the change in velocity over a unit of time

Newton's Three Laws of Motion

In the 1600s, Isaac Newton explained the relationship between force and motion. He developed 3 **scientific laws** to explain the movement of all objects. To understand Newton's laws, think about a jet plane.

Newton's First Law of Motion: *An object that is not being pushed or pulled will stand still. If it is moving, it will keep moving at the same speed in a straight line unless a force is applied.*

A jet is big and heavy. It will move only if another **vehicle** pulls it or if the engines turn on and make it move. It will keep moving until the force of its brakes makes it stop.

Newton's Second Law of Motion: *The greater the force applied to an object, the more the object will accelerate. It takes more force to accelerate an object with a lot of mass than to accelerate something with very little mass.*

Jet engines push air out with great force. The more force the engines create, the more the jet accelerates. It takes much more force for a big passenger jet to take off than for a small plane to take off.

▲ Sitting still

▲ Taking off

VOCABULARY

scientific laws—ideas or hypotheses that have been tested over and over and have been supported by each test

vehicle—a machine used to carry people or things. Cars and trucks are vehicles.

Newton's Third Law of Motion: *For every action, there is an equal and opposite reaction.*

As the engines on the jet push air out the back of the engine, the plane moves forward with equal force.

(TALK AND SHARE) **Answer this question with your partner. If you put a ball on a plate and quickly push the plate forward, what happens to the ball? Use Newton's laws to explain your thinking.**

What Keeps an Airplane in the Air?
Air can push on objects such as birds, balls, and airplanes. The objects also push on air. An airplane wing forces air down, an action. Air forces the wing up, a reaction. The net force on the wing is called **lift.** Lift keeps the plane in the air.

Summary

A force is a push or a pull. Forces, including gravity and friction, make things change shape and position. Newton's laws explain the relationship between force and motion.

VOCABULARY
lift—a net force that pushes up on an object

Predicting

Predicting an Outcome

When you make a prediction, you think ahead. Based on what you know, you say what you think will happen in the future. You can use your knowledge of force and motion to predict what happens when you apply a force. A Prediction Organizer can help.

- First, observe and name the forces that act on an object.

- Next, decide which laws of motion may apply to the situation.

- Finally, use what you know about Newton's laws to predict the motion that will result from the forces.

For example, imagine swinging on a swingset.

Prediction Organizer

Observations +	Knowledge 	My Prediction
• push of body on swing • push of air against body	Newton's First Law: An object will keep moving at the same speed until a force is applied.	The force of air will make the swinging stop if no one pushes the swing.

Practice Predicting

1. Draw Look at this picture of an athlete. Based on what you know about force and motion, predict what will happen to the soccer ball. Explain to a partner why it will happen. Put pictures into an organizer to show the forces at work as the player kicks the ball. Add a picture showing where you think the ball will go.

2. Write Write a paragraph that predicts what will happen to the soccer ball if it hits someone's head. Identify the forces at work on the ball. Decide which of Newton's laws can explain what is happening. Then tell what will happen next. Words from the Word Bank can help you.

Word Bank

speed
direction
action
reaction
force
mass
friction
distance

Activities

Grammar Spotlight

Prepositions for Place The position of an object is the place it is located. Words such as *at*, *on*, and *in* tell where something is located.

Rule	Example
Use *at* for places and times.	*We had a tug of war at school yesterday.*
Use *on* for street names or when something touches a surface.	*The ridges on the screw help pull it.* *The wheel is on the wagon.*
Use *in* for towns, cities, states, countries, and continents.	*The family lives in Brazil.*

Now write 3 sentences, using a preposition in each one.

Hands On

Balancing Forces With a partner, take turns observing the events listed below. After each event, decide together what forces are at work and whether the forces are balanced or unbalanced.

1. Hold your textbook in the air by its front cover.

2. Crumple a piece of notebook paper.

3. Throw an eraser into the air.

Oral Language

Asking Questions In your group, write one question you have about each of these words: *running, pulling, rolling*. Then give your questions to someone else in the group. Take turns trying to answer the questions you received.

Partner Practice

Force and Friction Ask your partner to write a sentence with a pencil. Then take the pencil, erase your partner's sentence, and write a new sentence while your partner watches. Talk about how friction was involved in what each of you did.

Light and

Sound

Here you'll learn about light and sound. You'll also learn how to use math and practice summarizing data about waves.

▲ I love to watch the lightning light up the whole sky at night.

- **Where does light come from?**
- **How does sound travel?**
- **What are some of your favorite sounds?**

1 Light Waves

2 Sound Waves

Key Concepts

wave   space   time   medium

These waves move energy through the medium of water. The energy goes from one place in the water to another place. The energy also takes time to move from one place to another.

A **wave** is moving energy. The energy in a wave moves through **space.** That means it goes from one place to another. The energy in a wave also moves through **time.**

Some waves need a medium through which to move. Light waves do not need a medium. A **medium** is any substance, like water, air, or walls.

Eyes and Ears

To *detect* means to notice or discover something. Your eyes and ears can detect light and sound. Your eyes detect visible light waves.

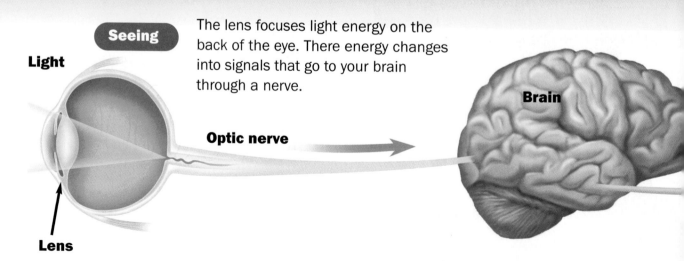

Seeing

Light

The lens focuses light energy on the back of the eye. There energy changes into signals that go to your brain through a nerve.

Brain

Optic nerve

Lens

Use Math

Scientists often talk about events by saying how much time they take to happen. For example, when you study light and sound, you learn that what you see and hear is related to time. Every wave has a frequency, or number of waves per unit of time. The higher the number of waves per unit of time, the more energy the waves are moving.

As you study waves, practice using units of time.

Talking About Time

- Choose a unit of time, such as a second or minute.
- Count or learn the number of waves in a unit of time.
- State the wave frequency as the number of waves per unit of time.

Example: frequency = 10 waves per second

Your ears detect sound waves.

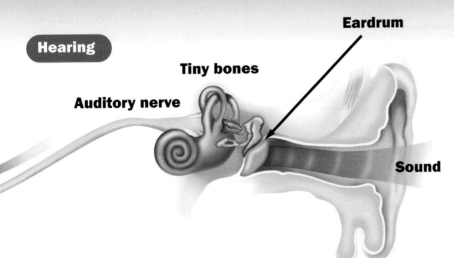

Hearing

Tiny bones

Auditory nerve

Eardrum

Sound

The outer ear collects waves and sends them toward your eardrum. The waves make the eardrum move back and forth, or vibrate. The vibrations move tiny bones that send signals to your brain through a nerve.

Light and Sound

Waves carry energy from one place to another. Light energy and sound energy both travel in waves.

▲ A ripple in water is a wave.

Waves

A **wave** is a back-and-forth or up-and-down motion. Waves are around us all the time, even if we cannot see them. For example, both solar energy and water move in waves. Waves often begin when something moves back and forth, or **vibrates.** In a wave, that movement back and forth continues on and on.

With waves, matter does not move. Only the energy moves. A boat in open water goes up and down on top of a wave, but when the wave is gone the boat is in the same place.

KINDS OF WAVES

There are two kinds of waves. When you tie a rope to a doorknob and shake the other end up and down, you create a **transverse wave.** The wave moves up and down, like the rope.

If you quickly push one end of a **spring,** you will create a **longitudinal wave.** The wave moves to the side, from coil to coil.

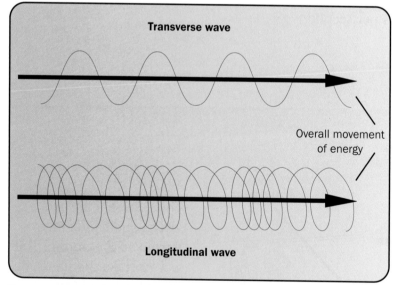

Transverse wave

Overall movement of energy

Longitudinal wave

▲ The two kinds of waves

WAVE PARTS AND PROPERTIES

Transverse waves have a top called a **crest** and a bottom called a **trough.** In between they have a resting point. Longitudinal waves have tight spots called **compressions** and loose spots called **rarefactions.**

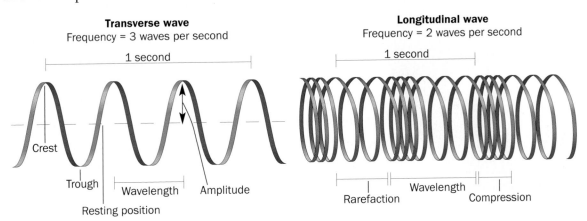

Transverse wave
Frequency = 3 waves per second

1 second

Crest

Trough

Wavelength   Amplitude

Resting position

Longitudinal wave
Frequency = 2 waves per second

1 second

Rarefaction   Wavelength   Compression

The **wavelength** is the distance from crest to crest or from compression to compression. The longer the wavelength, the lower the energy of the wave.

The **frequency** of the wave is the number of crests or compressions in an amount of time. As the wavelength gets shorter, the frequency increases. The higher the frequency, the more energy the wave has.

The **amplitude** of a transverse wave is the distance the wave rises above its resting position. The amplitude of a longitudinal wave relates to the amount of force that started the wave. The larger the amplitude, the more energy the wave has.

(**TALK AND SHARE**) **Draw a transverse wave and have your partner draw a longitudinal wave. Trade drawings and mark the wavelength on your partner's drawing.**

VOCABULARY

crest—the top
trough—the bottom
compressions—tight places
rarefactions—loose places
wavelength—the distance between two similar points on waves that are next to each other

frequency—the number of waves that go by in a unit of time
amplitude—the distance above the resting point of a transverse wave, or the amount of force causing a longitudinal wave

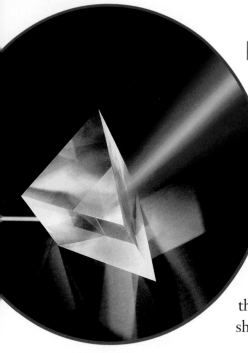

▲ A prism is a piece of cut glass that refracts, or bends back, light. Prisms show the entire color spectrum.

Light Waves

Light moves in transverse waves—that is, in up-and-down waves. Most light waves come from the sun. In science, light waves are called **electromagnetic waves.**

Nothing travels faster than light. Light waves can travel through empty space and through matter.

Light waves are part of the **electromagnetic spectrum.** A *spectrum* is a range. The electromagnetic spectrum is a range of waves. At one end of the range are low-energy waves, such as radio waves. They have long wavelengths and low frequencies. At the other end of the range are high-energy waves, such as X rays. They have short wavelengths and high frequencies.

Visible light is the part of the electromagnetic spectrum that you can see. Visible light includes all the colors. Wavelength determines the color of the light we see.

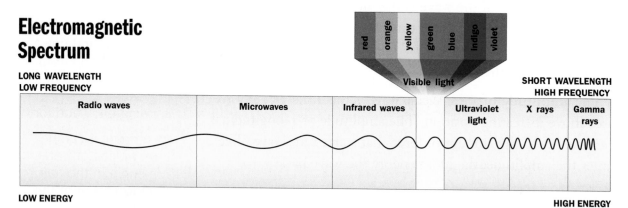

▲ The electromagnetic spectrum ranges from radio waves to gamma rays.

VOCABULARY

light—a form of energy that moves in transverse waves in empty space or through matter

electromagnetic waves—energy that can travel through empty space and matter

electromagnetic spectrum—the range of electromagnetic waves

visible light—the part of the electromagnetic spectrum that people can see

Lasers

The **laser** is an invention that makes light waves work together. A laser contains waves that move at the same frequency and in the same direction. That creates a powerful stream of light.

Laser beams can cut through steel or cut through delicate human tissue. For example, doctors use lasers for eye surgery and to remove cancers. CD players use laser beams to scan the surface of compact discs.

▲ Lasers are often used in eye surgery.

We see objects because of how they act with electromagnetic waves. Imagine you see a red car. It absorbs most of the energy from the light waves but **reflects,** or sends back, some of it. Our eyes see what the object reflects—in this case, the color red.

Different kinds of matter absorb different wavelengths of light. We see the wavelengths that are *not* absorbed. ▼

TALK AND SHARE

Discuss with your partner why you see different colors, even though light from the sun contains all the colors.

VOCABULARY

laser—light waves of the same frequency and direction
reflects—throws or bends back

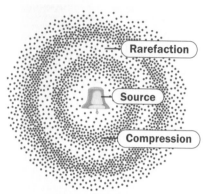

▲ Sound waves move away from the source in every direction at once.

Which is louder, the sound of using a hairbrush or the sound of hitting a drum? Why? (Hint: Think about force.) ▼

Sound Waves

Sound waves come from a vibration. That is what happens when you hit a bell. Longitudinal sound waves move through matter. That is why sound waves require a **medium**—solid, liquid, or gas—to move. Once some particles of matter vibrate, the energy travels to nearby particles that vibrate. Sound waves travel in all directions away from the source of the vibration.

PITCH AND LOUDNESS

Think of the sounds you hear every day—music, shouting, and car horns. The way you hear sound depends on the frequency and amplitude of sound waves. The faster the waves move—the higher the frequency—the higher the **pitch.** A flute and a whistle make high-pitched sounds. Slow-moving waves give low pitches, like the sound of a tuba.

What makes a sound loud? The amount of force in a longitudinal wave determines **loudness.** High amplitude, or great force, means more energy and a louder sound. Low amplitude, like the force of a whisper, means less energy and a softer sound.

VOCABULARY

sound—a form of energy that moves in longitudinal waves through matter
medium—a substance through which something moves, such as water, air, or metal (plural, *media*)
pitch—the highness or lowness of a sound
loudness—the force of a sound

SPEED AND MEDIUM

Sound travels with different speeds through different material. It moves faster through a solid than through a liquid. That is, sound travels faster in metal (a solid) than in water (a liquid). Sound moves faster through a liquid than through a gas. Sound moves 16 times faster through steel than through air. Why does sound travel at different speeds in different media?

The answer is based on how close atoms are in the different states of matter. Atoms **collide** with their neighbors when they are pushed by sound waves. The atoms in solids and liquids are closer together than the atoms in gases. Atoms that are closer together collide more quickly than atoms that are farther apart. This is why sound vibrations move fastest in solids and most slowly in gases.

Sound waves travel more slowly than light waves. Light travels through air about one million times faster than sound does. That is why you usually see lightning before you hear thunder, even though they happen at the same time.

(TALK AND SHARE) **Imagine that you and your partner are 10 meters apart. Talk about whether it would be easier to hear each other's voices under water or in a dry desert. Give a reason for your answer.**

Solid

Liquid

Gas

▲ Sound moves faster through particles that are close together than through particles that are far apart.

Summary

Both light energy and sound energy travel in waves. Waves move energy through space and time.

VOCABULARY
collide—run into

Summarizing

Summarizing Data About Waves

A summary is a short statement that gives only the main points. When you summarize, you study or review a topic, consider the main ideas about it, and state how the ideas are related.

You can summarize what you have learned about waves. For example, tell what you know about the two main properties of waves—frequency and wavelength. Then make a short statement to tell how these properties are related. A Summary Organizer can help.

Summary Organizer

Topic	Main Ideas	Summary
waves	<u>frequency</u> - the number of waves that go by per unit of time <u>wavelength</u> - the distance between similar points in two waves	Waves have two properties, wavelength and frequency.

Practice Summarizing

1. Draw Prepare a summary of how energy relates to the frequency and wavelength of a wave. First, draw a light wave. Mark its wavelength and its frequency. Draw another light wave that has a different wavelength. Tell which of your waves has more energy.

2. Write List 4 things you remember about sound waves. Then write a short paragraph that summarizes what you know about wavelength, frequency, and energy in sound waves. Use a Summary Organizer to plan what to say. When you have finished your paragraph, check your writing.

Check Your Writing

Make sure you
- Use complete sentences.

- Use a period at the end of each sentence.

- Spell all the words correctly.

Grammar Spotlight

Adverbs of Place and Time You can use adverbs to describe where and when something happens. Below are some examples. If a sentence has both an adverb of place and an adverb of time, put the adverb of place first.

Place	Time	Sample Sentence
here	now	*I am here now.*
near	soon	*The bus will be near us soon.*
far	tomorrow	*Gerardo will walk far tomorrow.*
there	then	*Suzanna will be there then.*
on	yesterday	*We put on sweaters yesterday.*

Make a sentence using one adverb of place (*near*) and one adverb of time (*yesterday*).

Hands On

Use Math With your partner or group, use crayons or other materials to make strips of each of the colors—red, orange, yellow, green, blue, indigo, and violet—of visible light. Then use math to arrange the colors in order from the longest wavelength to the shortest wavelength. Refer to page 286 for a model.

Partner Practice

Making Sound Waves Make a sound. Then have your partner describe its pitch and loudness. Next, have your partner make a sound. Describe its pitch and loudness. Finally, talk together about the frequency and amplitude of the sounds you made.

Matter in the
Universe

Here you'll learn about the universe, stars, and planets. You'll also learn how to analyze data and practice comparing and contrasting planets.

Building Background

▲ It's hard to see the stars in the city, but in the country they seem clearer.

■ **Where do you think the sun is in this picture?**

■ **Where are you in this picture?**

■ **How big do you think the universe is?**

The universe is made up of matter and space. Galaxies in the universe include billions of stars. One star is our sun. The sun is the center of our solar system. Our solar system includes 9 planets.

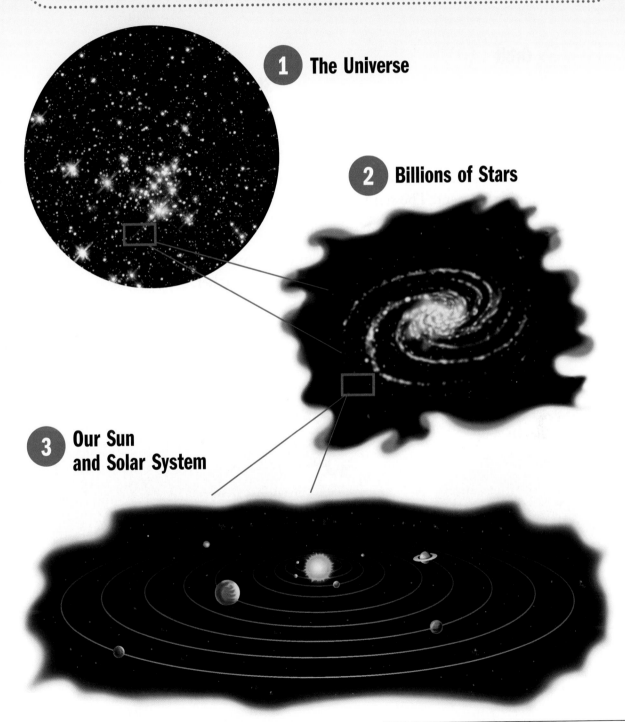

1 The Universe

2 Billions of Stars

3 Our Sun and Solar System

Key Concepts

star   planet   orbit   gravity

Planet

Orbit

Star

A **star** is made of gases. It gives off energy by changing one element into another element. The sun is a star.

A **planet** may be made of gases, liquids, and solids. Earth is a planet.

A planet travels around a star in an **orbit.** Stars hold planets in their orbits because of **gravity,** a force that pulls objects together.

Comets, Asteroids, and Meteoroids

Outer space is full of objects. Sometimes we see them flash by as they come near Earth.

Comet

Asteroid

Comets are made of dust and ice. When a comet travels close to the sun, it looks very bright.

Asteroids are very large pieces of rock or metal. Many asteroids orbit between Mars and Jupiter.

Analyze Data

Scientists collect data about matter in the universe. They organize data in a way that helps them analyze the data. For example, scientists organize data to analyze the sizes of things in the universe.

Comparing Sizes

☐ Pick a feature to analyze, such as mass or diameter.

☐ Write the data on a table or chart. Be sure measurements are all in the same units.

☐ Divide the larger number by the smaller number to find how many times bigger one object is than the other.

Look at the data for the distance across (the diameter of) the sun and Earth. Which is bigger?

Divide the larger number (1,390,180) by the smaller number (12,756). You find that the sun's diameter is about 109 times larger than that of Earth.

Object	Diameter
Sun	1,390,180 kilometers
Earth	12,756 kilometers

Other times they enter Earth's atmosphere and hit the ground.

Meteors

Meteoroids are pieces of rock that orbit the sun. Sometimes meteoroids enter Earth's atmosphere. Then we call them meteors or shooting stars.

Meteorite

A piece of a meteoroid that hits Earth is called a meteorite.

Matter in the Universe

T he universe contains matter and space. Matter in billions of stars is organized into galaxies. Our solar system contains one star (the sun), Earth, and 8 other planets.

The Universe

The **universe** consists of all the **stars, planets,** and **moons.** It also includes the empty space between them. You are part of the universe.

ORIGIN OF THE UNIVERSE

Scientists hypothesize that about 13 billion years ago, a giant explosion took place. They call it the **big bang.** Afterward, the elements helium and hydrogen formed. Over billions of years, these elements produced the stars, **galaxies,** and other elements.

SIZE OF THE UNIVERSE

The universe is too big to measure. Distances between objects in the universe are so big that scientists measure them in light-years. A **light-year** is the distance a ray of light travels in one year, or 9.5 trillion kilometers. It takes light from the star nearest our sun 4.3 years to reach Earth. That means the star is 4.3 light-years away.

▲ These lights are from galaxies, not from individual stars. A galaxy is a group of stars.

▲ People collect data about the universe by using powerful telescopes.

STUDYING THE UNIVERSE

Astronomers are people who study objects in space. They use satellites and computers to gather information about the universe. People have built powerful **telescopes** on Earth and have sent telescopes into space. With this **technology,** astronomers are learning more about the universe.

GALAXIES

The universe contains billions of galaxies. Galaxies are huge groups of billions of stars. Galaxies usually have one of 3 shapes—**elliptical, spiral,** or **irregular.**

Our own galaxy has a spiral shape. It has a bulge in the middle and arms that are called the *disk*. We can see part of its disk as a band of stars we call the **Milky Way.** Our solar system lies on one of the arms of the spiral. All of the stars you see at night are part of the Milky Way.

▲ Galaxies are large groups of stars. Earth is in a spiral-shaped galaxy.

(TALK AND SHARE) **With your partner, list these in order from smallest to largest:** *star, universe, moon, galaxy, Earth.* **Then compare your answers with other pairs of students and discuss.**

The Hubble Space Telescope

In 1990, astronomers sent the Hubble Space Telescope into space. The Hubble can take very clear pictures using visible and ultraviolet light and infrared waves. It collects millions of images that help scientists learn more about the universe. The telescope is named after Edwin Hubble, who proved there were galaxies.

VOCABULARY

astronomers—scientists who study the universe

telescopes—the tools that make faraway objects look closer and larger

technology—any invention that makes work easier

elliptical—having an oval or egglike shape

spiral—having a winding or coiled shape

irregular—having no particular shape

Milky Way—the galaxy that contains our sun

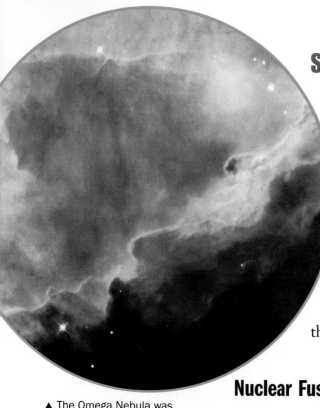

▲ The Omega Nebula was photographed by the Hubble Space Telescope. In a nebula, stars are beginning to form.

▲ Solar flares rise from the surface of the sun.

Stars

When you look up at the night sky, you see stars as twinkling dots of light. A star is really a huge, swirling ball of hot gas. **Gravity** holds a star together.

Stars form from a cloud of dust and gas called a **nebula.** The gases are mainly hydrogen and helium. Gravity pulls in more dust and gas. The pressure and temperature at the center becomes so high that **nuclear fusion** starts. In nuclear fusion, the nuclei of several atoms join together. As they do so, they give off energy.

Nuclear Fusion

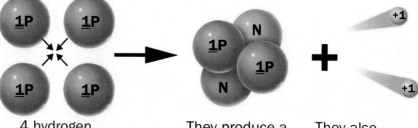

4 hydrogen nuclei fuse, or join together.

They produce a helium nucleus (2 protons, 2 neutrons).

They also produce energy, which radiates outward from the star.

Over millions of years, stars burn up their hydrogen and helium. Finally, they cool down and burn out. Some dying stars explode and become **supernovas.**

(**TALK AND SHARE**) **With a partner, discuss how energy can come out of stars and what happens when it does.**

VOCABULARY

gravity—the force that pulls objects together
nebula—a large cloud of dust and gas in space
nuclear fusion—the process in stars in which nuclei of separate atoms join in a new nucleus and energy is released
supernovas—the remains of stars that exploded when they died

The Sun and the Solar System

Our **solar system** is made up of the sun, 9 planets, and the moons of the planets. The planets and moons move in **orbits** because of gravity. The body with more **mass** holds the bodies with less mass in their orbits. The sun holds all 9 planets in their orbits. A planet may hold one or more moons in orbit.

The sun is huge. It makes up about 99 percent of the mass of our solar system. The surface of the sun is a sea of boiling gases. Huge jets of flame shoot out into space. The sun will probably stay the way it is for billions of years.

Solar System

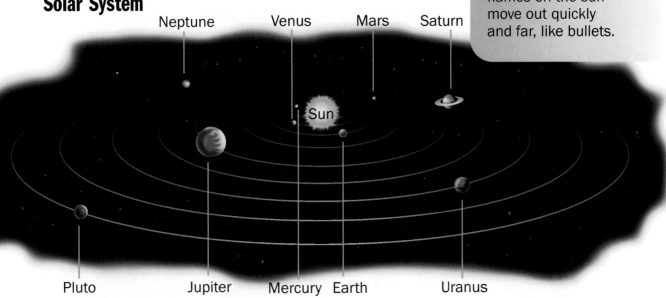

Each planet has its own orbit around the sun. The sun's gravity holds the planets in their orbits.

TALK AND SHARE With your partner, look at the diagram of the solar system above. Decide which planet is pulled most strongly by the sun's gravity. Then decide which planet is pulled least strongly.

VOCABULARY
solar system—the sun and 9 planets in orbit around it
orbits—paths made around objects of larger mass by objects of smaller mass. (The verb *orbit* means to move along such a path.)
mass—the total amount of matter in an object

Kinds of Planets

Our solar system has two main kinds of planets. Some are mostly gas. Others are rocky. Pluto is different from all the other planets. Some scientists think Pluto might be an asteroid and not a planet at all, but it is still included in our solar system.

▲ Pluto

GAS GIANTS

The outer planets of our solar system—Jupiter, Saturn, Uranus, and Neptune—are called **gas giants.** They have tiny cores of rock but are made mostly of gases and liquids. They have no solid surface.

Jupiter is by far the largest planet in our solar system. It has twice as much mass as all the other planets put together. All the gas giants have rings around them. Saturn is most famous for its rings. They are the largest and most easy to see. Small pieces of icy rock make up the rings.

▲ Jupiter

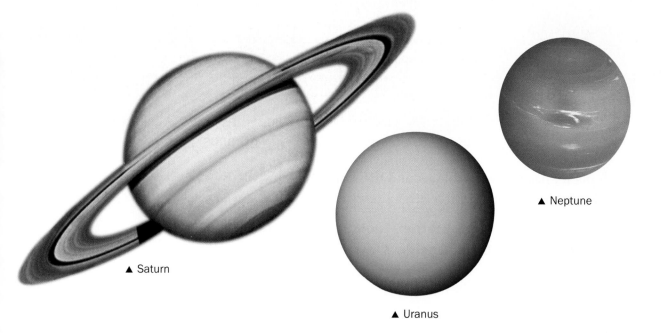

▲ Saturn

▲ Uranus

▲ Neptune

TERRESTRIAL PLANETS

The 4 planets closest to the sun are called **terrestrial planets.** Mercury, Venus, Earth, and Mars are the terrestrial planets. They have rocky surfaces and cores made from iron.

Mercury has almost no **atmosphere.** Venus has a thick yellow atmosphere made of **sulfuric acid** gas. Its surface is like a hot desert. It is similar in size to Earth. Mercury and Venus are very hot because they are so close to the Sun.

Earth has a feature not found anywhere else in the solar system. Earth has water. As a result, Earth is the only planet that we know of that can support life. Mars is much colder than Earth. It is called the "red planet" because of its red rocks and dust. Astronomers are looking to see if there used to be water and life of some kind on Mars.

▲ Mercury

▲ Venus

▲ Earth

(TALK AND SHARE) **Work with your partner to list the planets in order based on their distance from the sun. How does the distance from the sun relate to the pull of the sun's gravity?**

Summary

All matter and space make up the universe. The universe contains billions of galaxies that are made of stars. Our sun is a star. Our solar system includes the sun and 9 planets.

▲ Mars

VOCABULARY

terrestrial planets—the inner planets, Mercury, Venus, Earth, and Mars. The word *terrestrial* comes from *terra*, the Latin word for earth or ground.
atmosphere—a layer of gas that surrounds a planet
sulfuric acid—a substance made of the elements hydrogen, sulfur, and oxygen. Sulfuric acid burns and can cut metals.

Comparing and Contrasting

Comparing and Contrasting Planets

When you compare, you point out things that are the same. When you contrast, you say how things are different. Comparing and contrasting are helpful when you analyze data about objects in space.

To compare and contrast, use a Venn Diagram.

1. Record data about two or more things. Make sure any measurements are in the same units.

2. Look for similarities. List them in the center.

3. Put the differences in the outside of the diagram.

Venn Diagram

Jupiter

Different
- gas giant
- 5th planet from the sun

The Same
- planet
- orbits the sun

Earth

Different
- terrestrial planet
- 3rd planet from the sun

Practice Comparing and Contrasting

1. Draw Use the data below to draw a Venn Diagram for Venus and Earth. Then talk with your partner about whether the two planets are alike or different.

2. Write Use the data below and everything else you know about Venus and Earth to write a short paragraph. Compare and contrast the two planets. Words from the Word Bank can help you.

Word Bank

terrestrial
closer
farther

orbit
atmosphere
surface

Planet	Distance from the Sun	Atmosphere	Kind of Planet	Diameter
Venus	108,000,000 kilometers	Sulfuric acid gas	Terrestrial	12,104 kilometers
Earth	150,000,000 kilometers	Air	Terrestrial	12,756 kilometers

Grammar Spotlight

Yes/No Questions with *am, is,* and *are* When you ask present-tense *yes* or *no* questions with the verb *be*, put *am, is,* or *are* before the subject.

Subject	Use	Example
I	am	*Am I correct?*
you, they, we	are	*Are you the teacher?*
		Are they all planets?
		Are we part of the solar system?
he, she, it	is	*Is he an astronomer?*
		Is she a student?
		Is it cold, like Mars?

Write two yes/no questions about the universe. Use the correct form of the verb *be* in each sentence.

Oral Language

Describe a Planet Have each person in your group choose one or two planets to describe to the rest of the group. Tell about appearance, distance from the sun, and anything else he or she knows or can find out about the planet.

Partner Practice

Analyze Data With a partner, use an encyclopedia or the Internet to collect data on how far each planet in the solar system is from the sun. Then divide each distance by the distance for Mercury, the planet closest to the sun. Write a sentence for each planet saying how much farther away it is from the sun than Mercury.

Hands On

Solar System With a partner, create a model of the solar system. Refer to the diagram on page 299. Use paper, styrofoam balls, string or wire, and any other materials you think will work. As you make your model, talk about what each planet is like.

References

Metric Prefixes, Units, and Conversions

Common Metric Prefixes	
milli-	1/1000
centi-	1/100
deci-	1/10
hect-	x 100
kilo-	x 1000

Units

Quantity	Metric Unit	U.S. Unit
Length, distance	meter (m)	inch, foot, yard, mile
Capacity, volume	liter (L)	cup, pint, quart, gallon
Mass	gram (g)	ounce

Metric-U.S. Conversions

To change	Multiply by	To change	Multiply by
cm to in	0.40	in to cm	2.54
m to yard	1.09	yard to m	0.91
km to mile	0.62	mile to km	1.61
g to ounce	0.04	ounce to g	28.35
kg to pound	2.21	pound to kg	0.45

Science Word Parts

Science words can be difficult to understand and remember. Knowing the word parts will help you understand the meaning of complicated words.

Key		
Word followed by dash	**=**	**prefix**
Word preceded by dash	**=**	**suffix**
Word without dash	**=**	**root word or combining form**

A

	Meaning	Example
a-	not	asexual
-able	able, can do	renewable
-al	of, like	musical
alt-	high	altitude
alter	other	alternative
amphi-	both	amphibian

▲ A frog is an **amphibian** because it lives *both* on land and in water.

A

annu	year	annual
anthrop	human being	anthropology
anti-	against	antibody
astro-	star	astronomy
aud	hear, listen	auditory
auto-	self	autoimmune

B

bi-	two	bicycle
bio	life	biome

C

	Meaning	Example
cardio	heart	cardiovascular
carni-	meat	carnivore
chloro-	green	chloroplast

Chloroplasts contain chlorophyll, the *green* pigment in plants. ▶

chron	time	chronology
cide	killer, killing of	pesticide
circ-	around	circulatory
co-	together	cooperate
cycle	circle, wheel	bicycle
cyto-	cell	cytoplasm

D

de-	opposite of	decomposer
derm	skin	epidermis
dict	say	predict

E

endo-	inside	endothermic
epi-	over, above	epithelial
equi	equal	equivalent
-er	one who	carrier
eu-	true	eukaryote
exo-	outside	exothermic

F

flect	bend back	reflect
flu	flowing	fluid
fore-	before, in front of	foreleg

F	**Meaning**	**Example**
fract	break	fraction
-ful	full of	helpful
G		
gen	birth, produce	genetics
geo	of Earth	geology

▲ **Geology** is the *study of Earth*.

G		
grad	step, go	gradual
-graph	write, draw, record	photograph
gravi-	heavy	gravity
H		
hab	live	habitat
hemi-	half	hemisphere
hetero	different	heterogenous
herb-	plant	herbivore
homo	same	homogenous
hydr	water	hydroelectric
I		
-ic	like	prokaryotic
ign-	fire	igneous

I	**Meaning**	**Example**
-ily	in some way	readily
in-	not, opposite of	independent
infra-	below	infrared
inter-	between	interact
-ion	act of, state of	radiation
-ist	one who	geologist
J		
ject	throw	project
L		
-less	without	careless
-logy	study of	geology
lum	light	illuminate
luna	moon	lunar

The *moon* looks red during a **lunar** eclipse because it is in shadow. ▶

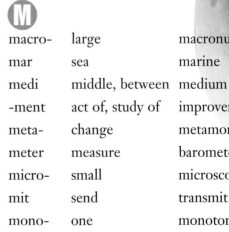

M		
macro-	large	macronutrient
mar	sea	marine
medi	middle, between	medium
-ment	act of, study of	improvement
meta-	change	metamorphic
meter	measure	barometer
micro-	small	microscope
mit	send	transmit
mono-	one	monotone

A **microscope** is a *tool for seeing small* things. ▶

M	Meaning	Example
morph	shape	metamorphic
multi	many	multicellular
N		
nat	to be born	innate
-ness	state of	goodness
neur	nerve	neuron
non-	not	nonrenewable
nov	new	supernova
numer	number	numerous
O		
omni-	all	omnivore
-ous	having, full of	populous
P		
ped	foot	pedestrian
phon	sound	telephone
photo	light	photosynthesis
poly-	many	polymer
pop	people	population
post-	after	postscript
pre-	before	predict
pro-	before	prokaryote
proto	first	prototype
R		
re-	again	recycle
rupt	break	interrupt
S		
scope	tool for seeing	telescope
script	write	subscript
sed-	settle	sediment
semi-	half, partly	semicircle
sol	sun	solar

S	Meaning	Example
spec	look	inspect
sphere	ball	atmosphere
spir	breath	respiration
sub-	under, below	submarine
syn	put together	photosynthesis
T		
tact, tag	touch	contagious
tele	distant	television
tempo	time	temporary
tens	stretch, strain	tension
terra	Earth	terrestrial
therm	heat	thermal
tom	cut	anatomy

A **telescope** is a *tool for seeing distant* objects. ▼

▲ A **television** allows you to *see* images from a *distant* source.

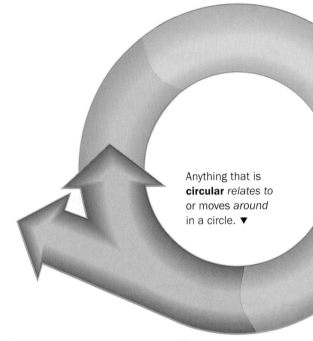

Anything that is **circular** *relates to* or moves *around* in a circle. ▼

T	Meaning	Example
tox	poison	toxic
trans-	across, over	transform
tri-	three	triangle
-tude	condition, quality	amplitude

U		
-ular	relating to	circular
ultra-	beyond	ultraviolet
un-	not	unbalanced
under-	below	underwater
uni-	one	unicellular

V		
vac	empty	vacuole
vas-	vessel	vascular
vers	turn	reverse
vis	see	vision
viv	life	revive
voc	call	vocalize
vor	eat	carnivore

W	Meaning	Example
-ward	in the direction of	inward

Y		
-y	containing, full of	salty

Z		
zoo	animal	zoology

Lions are **carnivores** because they *eat meat.* ▼

GLOSSARY

Pronunciation Key

ă	pat	ĭ	pit	ôr	core	ŭ	cut
ā	pay	ī	bite	oi	boy	ûr	urge
âr	care	îr	pier	ou	out	th	thin
ä	father	ŏ	pot	ŏŏ	took	*th*	this
ĕ	pet	ō	toe	ŏŏr	lure	zh	vision
ē	be	ô	paw	ōō	boot	ə	about

absorb (əb sôrb′) *v.* take in or soak up. *Use a sponge to **absorb** the water you spilled.* (p. 108)

acceleration (ăk sĕl′ ə rā′ shən) *n.* the change in velocity over a unit of time. (p. 275)

acid rain *n.* polluted precipitation. (p. 107)

adapt (ə dăpt′) *v.* fit a situation. *A species may **adapt** to changes in its environment.* (p. 200)

adaptation (ăd′ ăp tā′ shən) *n.* a change or changes that help an organism survive and reproduce in its habitat. (p. 198)

advantage (ăd văn′ tĭj) *n.* a benefit, such as something that improves the chances of survival. *Long necks give giraffes an **advantage** in reaching leaves high on trees.* (p. 198)

affect (ə fĕkt′) *v.* change. *If you don't do your homework, it will **affect** your final grade.* (p. 20)

air mass *n.* a big area of air that has the same temperature and amount of water (humidity). (p. 72)

alternate (ôl′ tər nāt′) *v.* take turns. *My brother and I **alternate** who takes out the trash every Tuesday.* (p. 80)

amphibian (ăm fĭb′ ē ən) *n.* a member of a class of animals that are born in water but can also live on land, such as frogs, toads, and salamanders. (p. 133)

amplitude (ăm′ plĭ tōōd′) *n.* the distance above the resting point of a transverse wave, or the amount of force causing a longitudinal wave. (p. 285)

analyze (ăn′ ə līz′) *v.* think about data and decide what they mean. *We'll write a report after we **analyze** our observations.* (p. 24)

anatomy (ə năt′ ə mē) *n.* the structure of a living thing. (p. 204)

ancestor (ăn′ sĕs′ tər) *n.* from whom one is descended. *Parents, grandparents, and great-grandparents are all **ancestors**.* (p. 205)

ancient (ān′ shənt) *adj.* from a time long past. *The pyramids in Egypt were built by an **ancient** civilization.* (p. 204)

angle (ăng′ gəl) *n.* a corner. *A triangle has 3 **angles**.* (p. 46)

antibiotic (ăn′ tĭ bī ŏt′ ĭk) *n.* a drug that can kill disease-causing organisms. (p. 132)

antibody (ăn′ tĭ bŏd′ ē) *n.* a blood protein that recognizes certain germs or viruses. (p. 181)

appliance (ə plī′ əns) *n.* a machine, used in homes, that is powered by gas or electricity. *A refrigerator is an **appliance**.* (p. 262)

artery (är′ tə rē) *n.* a blood vessel that carries blood away from the heart. (p. 157)

arthropod (är′ thrə pŏd′) *n.* a member of the phylum of animals without backbones that includes insects, spiders, and crustaceans. (p. 133)

asexual (ā sĕk′ shōō əl) *adj.* without sex. Each offspring of asexual reproduction has only one parent. (p. 188)

assemble (ə sĕm′ bəl) *v.* put together. *The instructions told me how to **assemble** my new bicycle.* (p. 168)

astronomer (ə strŏn′ ə mər) *n.* someone who studies objects in space. (p. 297)

atmosphere (ăt′ mə sfîr′) *n.* the layer of air that surrounds Earth. (p. 68)

atom (ăt′ əm) *n.* the smallest part of an element that has properties of that element. (p. 95)

atomic number *n.* the number of protons in the nucleus of one atom of an element. (p. 238)

attract (ə trăkt′) *v.* pull toward. *If you don't put a lid on the garbage can, it will **attract** mice.* (p. 214)

automatic (ô′ tə măt′ ĭk) *adj.* happens without thinking. *Blinking is an **automatic** response to bright light.* (p. 179)

axis (ăk′ sĭs) *n.* an imaginary line through the middle. (p. 78)

bacteria (băk tîr′ ē ə) *n.* living things made of just one cell (singular, *bacterium*). (p. 119)

balance (băl′ əns) **1.** *n.* a measuring device in which a beam is brought to equilibrium when the masses on each end are the same. (p. 212) **2.** *n.* stability; the condition of all forces being equal.

bare (bâr) *adj.* not covered. *In the summer, I like to take off my shoes and walk around in my **bare** feet.* (p. 58)

bed (bĕd) *n.* one set of layers of sedimentary rock. (p. 60)

behavior (bĭ hāv′ yər) *n.* way of acting. *The students were on their best **behavior** while the teacher was away.* (p. 200)

big bang *n.* a huge explosion that may have created the universe. (p. 296)

binary fission *n.* the bacterial process of dividing in half to reproduce. (p. 188)

biomass (bī′ ō măs′) *n.* a renewable resource that comes from living things. (p. 94)

blood vessel *n.* a tube that carries blood. (p. 157)

boil (boil) *v.* heat to a high temperature. When water boils, it changes into water vapor. (p. 71)

boiling point *n.* the temperature at which a liquid changes to a gas. Water boils at 100 °Celsius. (p. 227)

bounce (bouns) *v.* spring back after hitting something. *If you throw the ball against the wall, it will **bounce** back to you.* (p. 20)

brain (brān) *n.* the control center of an animal body. (p. 153)

bundle (bŭn′ dl) *n.* a group of things held together. *Carmen brought a **bundle** of sticks to build a campfire.* (p. 153)

calcium (Ca) (kăl′ sē əm) *n.* a mineral found in some vegetables and in dairy products, such as milk and cheese, that helps build bones. (p. 168)

Calorie (kăl′ ə rē) *n.* 1,000 calories (a kilocalorie); unit of energy supplied by food. (p. 162)

cancer (kăn′ sər) *n.* a disease in which cell division is out of control. (p. 144)

capillary (kăp′ ə lĕr′ ē) *n.* a small blood vessel that connects arteries and veins. (p. 157)

capture (kăp′ chər) *v.* take and hold. (p. 141)

carbohydrate (kär′ bō hī′ drāt′) *n.* an energy-releasing nutrient (such as sugar and starch), made of carbon, hydrogen, and oxygen. (p. 167)

carbon (C) (kär′ bən) *n.* an element that is part of many living and nonliving things on Earth. (p. 119)

carbon dioxide (CO$_2$) *n.* a molecule made of one carbon atom and two oxygen atoms. (p. 118)

cardiovascular system *n.* another name for the animal circulatory system. (p. 156)

category (kăt′ ĭ gôr′ ē) *n.* a group of things put together because they have the same characteristics. (p. 126)

cell (sĕl) *n.* the basic unit of life. (p. 129)

cell cycle *n.* the life cycle of a cell, including resting, growing, and dividing. (p. 138)

cell division *n.* the process by which cells make copies of themselves and increase in number. (p. 138)

cell membrane *n.* the covering that controls what enters the cell and what leaves the cell. (p. 140)

cell wall *n.* the tough outer case of a plant cell. (p. 140)

cellular respiration *n.* the process by which cells break down food to make energy. (p. 166)

cement (sĭ mĕnt′) *v.* stick together. (p. 48)

centimeter (sĕn′ tə mē′ tər) *n.* a unit of length. (p. 212)

characteristic (kăr′ ək tə rĭs′ tĭk) *n.* a quality that defines something. (p. 126)

chemical (kĕm′ ĭ kəl) *n.* a material, made of atoms and molecules, found in Earth and around Earth. (p. 44)

chemical bond *n.* an attraction that holds atoms together. (p. 246)

chemical change *n.* a change in matter that results in the formation of a new substance. (p. 240)

chemical energy *n.* the energy produced by chemical reactions. (p. 253)

chemical equation *n.* a sentence made of symbols and words that tells what happens when atoms participate in a chemical reaction. (p. 164)

chemical property *n.* the way an element or compound behaves with other elements. (p. 234)

chemical reaction *n.* a process in which atoms gain, lose, or share electrons. (p. 217)

chemical symbol *n.* an abbreviation for an element, usually made of one or two letters from the beginning of its name. Sometimes the abbreviation comes from a Latin name, such as Fe for iron, which in Latin is *ferrum*. (p. 238)

chemical weathering *n.* a change in the materials that make up rock. (p. 56)

chloroplast (klôr′ ə plăst′) *n.* an organelle in plant cells that makes food from energy. (p. 141)

chromosome (krō′ mə sōm′) *n.* the structure in the cell nucleus that contains plans for the cell and the entire organism. (p. 143)

circulatory system *n.* the body system that carries blood. (p. 155)

classify (klăs′ ə fī′) *v.* put into groups based on characteristics. *Scientists **classify** living things into 6 kingdoms.* (p. 126)

climate (klī′ mĭt) *n.* a pattern of temperature and precipitation that remains for a long time in a big area. (p. 66)

cloud (kloud) *n.* a group of tiny water drops or pieces of ice that hangs in the air. (p. 70)

coal (kōl) *n.* a resource that comes from dead land plants. (p. 92)

code (kōd) *n.* a system of rules or signals. (p. 190)

cold front *n.* a place where cold air pushes up warm air. (p. 72)

collide (kə līd′) *v.* run into. *The wet road caused the two cars to **collide**.* (p. 35)

comfortable (kŭm′ fər tə bəl) *adj.* having all needs met. *My mother always makes visitors feel very **comfortable** in our home.* (p. 104)

community (kə myōō′ nĭ tē) *n.* in science, all of the species living together in the same environment. (p. 116)

complex carbohydrate *n.* a carbohydrate, such as those in pasta and bread, that releases energy over time. (p. 167)

compound (kŏm′ pound′) *n.* matter made by two or more elements that cannot be separated physically. (p. 217)

compress (kəm prĕs′) *v.* squeeze or press together. *I had to* **compress** *the pillows to fit them in the suitcase.* (p. 46)

compression (kəm prĕsh′ ən) *n.* a tight place in a longitudinal wave. (p. 285)

conclusion (kən klo͞o′ zhən) *n.* a report of what happened. (p. 25)

condensation (kŏn′ dən sā′ shən) *n.* the process of turning from a vapor, or gas, to a liquid. (p. 71)

condense (kən dĕns′) *v.* turn from gas to liquid. (p. 227)

conduction (kən dŭk′ shən) *n.* the movement of energy through things that touch each other. (p. 265)

conductor (kən dŭk′ tər) *n.* a material that allows heat and electricity to pass through. (p. 239)

conservation of energy *n.* the principle stating that energy is not created or destroyed; it is only changed from one kind to another. (p. 253)

conservation of mass *n.* the principle stating that in a chemical reaction, matter is not created or destroyed, only changed. (p. 251)

conserve (kən sûrv′) *v.* use carefully so that some is left. **Conserve** *the paper by writing on both sides.* (p. 97)

consist of *v.* have, are made up of. *Chocolate milk* **consists of** *chocolate and milk.* (p. 129)

consumer (kən so͞o′ mər) *n.* a living thing that eats other living things for food. (p. 120)

continent (kŏn′ tə nənt) *n.* a very large area of land. (p. 33)

control (kən trōl′) *n.* a factor in an experiment that is kept the same. (p. 23)

convection (kən vĕk′ shən) *n.* the movement of energy through a moving liquid or gas. (p. 265)

core (kôr) *n.* the hot center of Earth. (p. 30)

covalent bond *n.* the sharing of one or more electrons between two atoms. (p. 248)

crest (krĕst) *n.* the top. (p. 285)

crop (krŏp) *n.* a plant that people grow for a purpose, such as to eat or to make clothing. (p. 104)

crust (krŭst) *n.* the cooler, outer part of Earth. (p. 30)

crystal (krĭs′ təl) *n.* a tiny structure with flat sides and angles. (p. 46)

cubic (kyo͞o′ bĭk) *adj.* having 3 equal dimensions. If something is one cubic centimeter, its length, height, and width are each one centimeter. (p. 212)

cure (kyo͝or) *v.* stop a disease. *Penicillin will* **cure** *some infections.* (p. 144)

cycle (sī′ kəl) *n.* a set of regularly repeating events. *Spring, summer, winter, and fall make up the* **cycle** *of seasons.* (p. 48)

cytoplasm (sī′ tə plăz′ əm) *n.* the jellylike fluid that fills a cell. (p. 140)

data (dā′ tə) *n.* the facts collected in an experiment (singular, *datum*). (p. 24)

daughter cell *n.* one of two cells that results when a parent cell divides. (p. 143)

decay (dĭ kā′) *v.* rot and break apart. *The walls of the building were so old, they began to* **decay.** (p. 204)

decomposer (dē′ kəm pō′ zər) *n.* a living thing that breaks down dead material for food. (p. 120)

decrease (dĭ krēs′) *v.* make smaller or lower in number. *I can't afford to buy the computer until they* **decrease** *the price.* (p. 226)

defend (dĭ fĕnd′) *v.* protect from danger. *A skunk will* **defend** *itself by spraying a smelly liquid.* (p. 180)

delta (dĕl′ tə) *n.* a large area of sediment put down where water flows into a lake or an ocean. (p. 60)

density (dĕn′ sĭ tē) *n.* mass per unit volume (D = m/v). (p. 228)

deposition (dĕp′ ə zĭsh′ ən) *n.* the process of building up the surface of Earth by putting down rock. (p. 54)

descend (dĭ sĕnd′) *v.* come down. *The airplane will descend after the pilot is told it's safe to land.* (p. 203)

desert (dĕs′ ərt) *n.* a very dry area on Earth. (p. 104)

design (dĭ zīn′) *v.* plan. *I learned how to design a website in my computer science class.* (p. 22)

develop (dĭ vĕl′ əp) *v.* form over time. *Scientists constantly develop new drugs to fight disease.* (p. 202)

digestive system *n.* the body system that breaks down food. (p. 154)

disappearing trait *n.* a characteristic that is being lost over time. (p. 205)

dissolve (dĭ zŏlv′) *v.* break apart in liquid. *The sugar will dissolve in your cup of hot tea.* (p. 56)

distance (dĭs′ təns) *n.* the amount of space or time between two things. *The distance from the east coast of the United States to the west coast is 3,000 miles!* (p. 274)

distinctive (dĭ stĭngk′ tĭv) *adj.* having qualities that set one thing apart from others. *The man was easy to remember because he had a very distinctive voice.* (p. 229)

disturb (dĭ stûrb′) *v.* upset, unsettle, put out of order. *If you don't turn the music down, it will disturb the sleeping baby.* (p. 176)

diversity (dĭ vûr′ sĭ tē) *n.* differences. *When our class discussed politics, there was a large diversity of opinion.* (p. 126)

DNA *n.* a chemical in the cell that stores genes. (p. 190)

dominant gene *n.* a gene that is greater in power. A dominant gene will "win" and the offspring will have the trait it carries. (p. 193)

dump (dŭmp) *n.* a place where many people put their garbage. (p. 106)

earthquake (ûrth′ kwāk′) *n.* a sudden release of energy caused by breaking and moving rock. (p. 37)

eclipse (ĭ klĭps′) *n.* a shadow caused by Earth on the moon or vice versa. (p. 85)

ecology (ĭ kŏl′ ə jē) *n.* the science of how living things and their environment interact. (p. 114)

ecosystem (ē′ kō sĭs′ təm) *n.* an environment and everything that lives in it. (p. 114)

egg (ĕg) *n.* a female sex cell. (p. 189)

electrical energy *n.* the energy of interacting electrons. (p. 253)

electricity (ĭ lĕk trĭs′ ĭ tē) *n.* a form of energy used to heat and light buildings. (p. 92)

electromagnetic spectrum *n.* the range of electromagnetic waves. (p. 286)

electromagnetic wave *n.* energy that can travel through empty space and matter. (p. 286)

electron (ĭ lĕk′ trŏn′) *n.* a negatively charged particle that travels around the nucleus of an atom. (p. 213)

element (ĕl′ ə mənt) *n.* a substance that cannot be split into simpler substances. Each element is made of just one kind of atom. (p. 96)

elliptical (ĭ lĭp′ tĭ kəl) *adj.* having an oval or egg-like shape. (p. 297)

endangered species *n.* a group of living things that could become extinct. (p. 117)

endothermic (ĕn′ dō thûr′ mĭk) *adj.* taking in thermal energy. (p. 252)

energy (ĕn′ ər jē) *n.* the ability to do work. Work is the power to make something change. (p. 68)

ensure (ĕn shŏŏr′) *v.* make certain. *We left the house early to ensure we would get to school on time.* (p. 202)

environment (ĕn vī′ ərn mənt) *n.* all the living and nonliving things that surround you or affect you. (p. 102)

epithelial (ĕp′ ə thē′ lē əl) *adj.* relating to the type of cells and tissues that cover the outside of the body and line the inside of the body. (p. 154)

equation (ĭ kwā′ zhən) *n.* in science, a statement that shows how reactants turn into products during a chemical reaction. (p. 251)

equator (ĭ kwā′ tər) *n.* an imaginary line around Earth's middle. (p. 68)

equilibrium (ē′ kwə lĭb′ rē əm) *n.* a state of being in balance. (p. 174)

erosion (ĭ rō′ zhən) *n.* the process of moving rock from place to place. (p. 54)

eukaryotic (yōō′ kâr′ ē ôt′ ĭk) *adj.* having a nucleus. (p. 130)

evaporate (ĭ văp′ ə rāt′) *v.* turn from a liquid to a vapor. (p. 70)

evidence (ĕv′ ĭ dəns) *n.* information and facts you can use to support a hypothesis. (p. 24)

exothermic (ĕk′ sō thûr′ mĭk) *adj.* releasing thermal energy. (p. 252)

expand (ĭk spănd′) *v.* get bigger. *A balloon will* **expand** *when you blow air into it.* (p. 57)

experiment (ĭk spĕr′ ə mənt) *n.* a set of steps for testing a hypothesis. (p. 22)

explanation (ĕk′ splə nā′ shən) *n.* a reason. *My* **explanation** *for being late was that my alarm clock was broken.* (p. 21)

express (ĭk sprĕs′) *v.* in science, turn into a trait by a gene. (p. 193)

external (ĭk stûr′ nəl) *adj.* outside. (p. 178)

extinct (ĭk stĭngkt′) *adj.* gone from Earth. (p. 117)

factor (făk′ tər) *n.* a thing that can affect what happens. *Class participation is a* **factor** *in your final grade.* (p. 23)

fat (făt) *n.* an energy-storing nutrient made of carbon, hydrogen, and oxygen. (p. 167)

fault (fôlt) *n.* a crack in Earth's crust where rock breaks and moves. (p. 37)

fertilizer (fûr′ tl ī′ zər) *n.* food added to soil to help plants grow. (p. 93)

fiber (fī′ bər) *n.* a long, thread-like structure (p. 153)

filter (fĭl′ tər) *n.* a tool used to strain and separate substances from a liquid or a gas. (p. 217)

flood (flŭd) *n.* water spilling over the sides of a river. (p. 61)

fluid (flōō′ ĭd) *n.* any liquid that flows, like water. (p. 177)

food chain *n.* a model of how energy moves from producers to consumers. (p. 121)

food web *n.* a model showing how food chains interact. (p. 121)

force (fôrs) *n.* a push or a pull. *The* **force** *of the wind was strong enough to knock over the lawn chairs.* (p. 59)

form (fôrm) *n.* a type. *Ballet is a* **form** *of dance.* (p. 262)

fossil (fŏs′ əl) *n.* the preserved parts of organisms that lived a long time ago. (p. 204)

fossil fuel *n.* an energy resource such as oil, coal, and natural gas. (p. 95)

freezing point *n.* the temperature at which a liquid changes to a solid. Water changes to ice at 0 °Celsius. (p. 227)

frequency (frē′ kwən sē) *n.* the number of waves that go by in a unit of time. (p. 285)

friction (frĭk′ shən) *n.* the force between objects that affects how easily they move past each other. (p. 274)

front (frŭnt) *n.* the place where warm and cold air masses meet. (p. 72)

fuel (fyōō′ əl) *n.* an energy resource. (p. 166)

function (fŭngk′ shən) *n.* a job. *The* **function** *of a teacher is to educate students.* (p. 150)

galaxy (găl′ ək sē) *n.* a group of billions of stars. (p. 296)

garbage (gär′ bĭj) *n.* unwanted waste material. (p. 106)

gas (găs) *n.* a state of matter with no definite shape or volume. (p. 107)

gas giants *n.* the outer planets, Jupiter, Saturn, Uranus, and Neptune. (p. 300)

gem (jĕm) *n.* a mineral valued for its beauty. (p. 48)

gene (jēn) *n.* any section of DNA from a chromosome that passes on traits from parents to offspring. (p. 186)

generation (jĕn′ ə rā′ shən) *n.* a group of individuals living during the same time and at the same stage of descent from an ancestor. *Grandparents, parents, and children are three different **generations.*** (p. 201)

genetic variation *n.* the different traits that come from new combinations of genes. (p. 192)

geologist (jē ŏl′ ə jĭst) *n.* a scientist who studies the whole Earth. (p. 60)

geothermal energy *n.* power that comes from heat inside Earth. (p. 97)

germ (jûrm) *n.* a very small living thing that can cause sickness. (p. 106)

glacier (glā′ shər) *n.* a large mass of ice that moves very slowly down a mountain or through a valley. (p. 61)

gland (glănd) *n.* a body part that makes chemicals and sends them somewhere else in the body, where they are used. (p. 177)

global (glō′ bəl) *adj.* covering the whole planet. *Email has made **global** communication easier and faster.* (p. 102)

global climate *n.* the long-term pattern of temperatures and precipitation for all of Earth. (p. 108)

gram (grăm) *n.* a unit of mass. (p. 212)

gravity (grăv′ ĭ tē) *n.* a force that pulls things together. (p. 58)

greenhouse gas *n.* a substance in the air that helps keep Earth warm. (p. 108)

groundwater (ground′ wô′ tər) *n.* the water beneath Earth's surface that fills wells and springs. (p. 107)

group (gro͞op) *n.* in science, a column in the periodic table. (p. 240)

habitat (hăb′ ĭ tăt′) *n.* the place where an organism lives and reproduces. (p. 102)

heart (härt) *n.* the animal organ that sends blood through the body. (p. 157)

heat (hēt) *n.* the transfer of energy from a warmer object to a cooler object. *You can avoid the noontime **heat** by sitting in the shade.* (p. 222)

hormone (hôr′ mōn′) *n.* a chemical released by a cell, tissue, or organ that affects body functions. (p. 155)

humidity (hyo͞o mĭd′ ĭ tē) *n.* a measure of the amount of water in the air. (p. 71)

hurricane (hûr′ ĭ kān′) *n.* a swirling storm that starts over an ocean. (p. 73)

hydroelectric power *n.* the energy that comes from fast-moving water. (p. 96)

hypothesis (hī pŏth′ ĭ sĭs) *n.* an idea that can be tested. (p. 18)

igneous (ĭg′ nē əs) *adj.* relating to fire. (p. 42)

igneous rock *n.* rock that forms when magma cools. (p. 46)

immune system *n.* the body system that can tell what is unsafe and responds to destroy it. (p. 180)

increase (ĭn krēs′) *v.* make larger or raise in number. *My boss said he would **increase** my pay if I worked hard.* (p. 200)

individual (ĭn′ də vĭj′ o͞o əl) *n.* a single object or organism. (p. 116)

infection (ĭn fĕk′ shən) *n.* a sickness that can spread from one organism to another. *Sidney cleaned and covered the cut on her knee to prevent* **infection.** (p. 180)

ingredient (ĭn grē′ dē ənt) *n.* one of the parts that make up something. *The main* **ingredient** *in these cookies is sugar.* (p. 164)

inherit (ĭn hĕr′ ĭt) *v.* receive a set of traits from one or more parents. (p. 186)

interact (ĭn′ tər ăkt′) *v.* affect one another. (p. 114)

internal (ĭn tûr′ nəl) *adj.* inside. (p. 176)

inversion (ĭn vûr′ zhən) *n.* something that is upside down. (p. 68)

ion (ī′ ŏn) *n.* an atom or molecule that carries an electric charge. (p. 249)

ionic bond *n.* the exchanging of electrons between atoms. (p. 249)

iron (Fe) (ī′ ərn) *n.* a metal element. (p. 56)

irregular (ĭ rĕg′ yə lər) *adj.* having no particular shape. (p. 297)

kinetic energy *n.* the energy of motion. (p. 225)

landslide (lănd′ slīd′) *n.* many rocks moving fast downhill. (p. 59)

laser (lā′ zər) *n.* light waves of the same frequency and direction. (p. 287)

lava (lä′ və) *n.* melted rock on the surface of Earth. (p. 36)

layer (lā′ ər) *n.* one thickness that lies on top of or under another one. *Earth is made up of 4* **layers.** (p. 32)

leaf (lēf) *n.* a part of a plant that takes in sunlight to make food (plural, *leaves*). *Each* **leaf** *changes color in the fall.* (p. 150)

lift (lĭft) *n.* a net force that pushes up on an object. *A feather can float in the air because of* **lift.** (p. 277)

light (līt) *n.* a form of energy that moves in transverse waves in empty space or through matter. *The sun produces Earth's* **light.** (p. 286)

light-year (līt′ yîr′) *n.* the distance a ray of light travels in one year. (p. 296)

link (lĭngk) *n.* in science, a trait that is similar in two species. (p. 205)

liquid (lĭk′ wĭd) *n.* a state of matter with definite volume but no definite shape. *Water and juice are both* **liquid** *at room temperature.* (p. 224)

liter (lē′ tər) *n.* a unit of volume. One liter equals 1,000 cubic centimeters. (p. 212)

liver (lĭv′ ər) *n.* one part of the body that produces chemicals that break down food. (p. 143)

longitudinal wave *n.* a wave that moves in compressions and rarefactions, in the same direction as the overall movement of energy. (p. 284)

loudness (loud′ nəs) *n.* the force of a sound. (p. 288)

lunar eclipse *n.* the shadow made on the moon when Earth comes between the moon and the sun. (p. 85)

machine (mə shēn′) *n.* an object that makes work easier to do. (p. 93)

magma (măg′ mə) *n.* melted rock inside Earth. (p. 36)

mammal (măm′ əl) *n.* a member of a class of animals with backbones that have fur or hair. (p. 133)

manage (măn′ ĭj) *v.* control or give direction. *The people who* **manage** *this restaurant tell the cooks and servers what to do.* (p. 94)

mantle (măn′ tl) *n.* the thick, warm middle layer of Earth. (p. 30)

mass (măs) *n.* the total amount of matter in something. (p. 210)

material (mə tîr′ ē əl) *n.* a substance used to make something. (p. 93)

materials scientist *n.* a person who finds new ways to use elements and compounds. (p. 240)

matter (măt′ ər) *n.* anything that has mass and takes up space. (p. 117)

measurement (mĕzh′ ər mənt) *n.* a number plus a unit, such as 2 cm. A measurement must always have a number and a unit. (p. 24)

mechanical energy *n.* the energy an object has because of its position and motion. (p. 261)

mechanical weathering *n.* changes in the size and shape of rock. (p. 57)

medium (mē′ dē əm) *n.* a substance through which something moves, such as water, air, or metal (plural, *media*). (p. 282)

meiosis (mī ō′ sĭs) *n.* cell division that produces 4 sex cells, each with half the number of chromosomes of the parent cell. (p. 191)

melting point *n.* the temperature at which a solid changes to a liquid. (p. 227)

metal (mĕt′ l) *n.* an element that is usually a solid, shiny conductor. (p. 233)

metallic bond *n.* the sharing of electrons among many atoms. (p. 248)

metalloid (mĕt′ l oid′) *n.* an element with some properties of metals and some properties of nonmetals. (p. 233)

metamorphic (mĕt′ ə môr′ fĭk) *adj.* relating to change. (p. 42)

metamorphic rock *n.* rock that has been changed by heat and pressure. (p. 47)

method (mĕth′ əd) *n.* a way of doing something. (p. 22)

mid-ocean ridge *n.* a line of volcanoes on the bottom of an ocean. (p. 45)

Milky Way *n.* the galaxy that contains our sun. (p. 297)

mineral (mĭn′ ər əl) **1.** *n.* a hard, nonliving substance made in Earth. (p. 48) **2.** *n.* a nutrient from food that helps support structures in the body. (p. 168)

mitochondrion (mī′ tə kŏn′ drē ən) *n.* the organelle that makes energy from food (plural, *mitochondria*). (p. 141)

mitosis (mī tō′ sĭs) *n.* the set of stages in the division of a cell nucleus. (p. 144)

mixture (mĭks′ chər) *n.* a combination of two or more substances that can be separated physically. *Chicken soup is a **mixture** of broth, chicken, noodles, and vegetables.* (p. 217)

model (mŏd′ l) *n.* a copy of an object or a system. *A globe is a **model** of Earth.* (p. 22)

moisture (mois′ chər) *n.* wetness. (p. 69)

molecule (mŏl′ ĭ kyōol′) *n.* a pair or group of atoms held together by one or more chemical bonds. (p. 177)

monoculture (mŏn′ ə kŭl′ chər) *n.* the growing of a single crop in an area. (p. 192)

moon (mōon) *n.* an object that orbits a planet. (p. 84)

motion (mō′ shən) *n.* a change in position. (p. 222)

mountain (moun′ tən) *n.* a part of Earth's crust that is taller than the surrounding crust. (p. 34)

mucus (myōo′ kəs) *n.* a liquid protective material in the body. (p. 180)

multicellular (mŭl′ tē sĕl′ yə lər) *adj.* having two or more cells. (p. 130)

muscle (mŭs′ əl) *n.* a tissue that makes a body part move. (p. 153)

natural gas *n.* a fossil fuel that is invisible, with no definite shape or volume. (p. 96)

natural resource *n.* a thing found on Earth that helps meet people's needs. (p. 92)

natural selection *n.* the process by which traits that improve the chances for survival pass to new generations in increasing numbers. (p. 198)

nebula (nĕb′ yə lə) *n.* a large cloud of dust and gas in space. (p. 298)

nervous system *n.* the body system that receives and sends information from the environment. It includes the brain, spinal cord, nerves, and sense organs. (p. 178)

net force *n.* the sum of all forces acting on an object. (p. 272)

neutral (nōō′ trəl) *adj.* having no charge, because positive charges equal negative charges. (p. 214)

neutron (nōō′ trŏn′) *n.* a particle in a nucleus of an atom that has no charge. (p. 213)

newton (N) (nōōt′ n) *n.* a unit for measuring force. (p. 272)

nitrogen (N) (nī′ trə jən) *n.* an element that helps living things grow. (p. 119)

noble gas *n.* an element that does not react with other elements. (p. 239)

nonmetal (nŏn mĕt′ l) *n.* an element that is usually dull and easy to break and that does not conduct heat and electricity. (p. 233)

nonrenewable (nŏn rĭ nōō′ ə bəl) *adj.* impossible to completely replace. (p. 90)

nonrenewable resource *n.* something of which there is a limited supply, so that if you run out, there is no more. (p. 94)

nuclear energy *n.* power that comes from a change in the nuclei of atoms. (p. 95)

nuclear fusion *n.* the process in stars in which nuclei of separate atoms join in a new nucleus and energy is released. (p. 298)

nucleus (nōō′ klē əs) *n.* **1.** the center part (plural, *nuclei*). (p. 96) **2.** the cell organelle that contains chemicals needed to reproduce. (p. 129) **3.** the center of an atom that contains protons and neutrons. (p. 213)

nutrient (nōō′ trē ənt) *n.* a substance that living things need to survive and grow. (p. 117)

observe (əb zûrv′) *v.* notice. *You can* **observe** *objects in space through a telescope.* (p. 20)

ocean (ō′ shən) *n.* a large area of salty water. (p. 33)

offspring (ôf′ sprĭng′) *n.* one or more organisms born of a parent. (p. 186)

ooze (ōōz) *v.* move slowly through small holes. *Jelly* **oozed** *out of the sandwich when I bit into it.* (p. 272)

orbit (ôr′ bĭt) **1.** *n.* the path made around objects of larger mass by objects of smaller mass. (p. 294) **2.** *v.* revolve in a way that is controlled by gravity. (p. 82)

organ (ôr′ gən) *n.* a part of the body that performs special functions. *The eyes, stomach, heart, and skin are all* **organs.** (p. 154)

organelle (ôr′ gə nĕl′) *n.* a part inside a eukaryotic cell with a special job. (p. 140)

organism (ôr′ gə nĭz′ əm) *n.* a living thing. (p. 131)

organize (ôr′ gə nīz′) *v.* put in order. *I decided to* **organize** *the books by author name to make them easier to find.* (p. 24)

organ system *n.* a group of organs that work together in the body. (p. 155)

overcome (ō′ vər kŭm′) *v.* break. (p. 227)

ovule (ŏv′ yōōl) *n.* the part of a plant that contains the female sex cell. (p. 189)

oxygen (O) (ŏk′ sĭ jən) *n.* a colorless gas that most living things need to survive. *Plants send* **oxygen** *into the air.* (p. 118)

parent cell *n.* the cell that is going to divide. (p. 143)

particle (pär′ tĭ kəl) *n.* a very small piece of something. *The builders wore safety glasses so that dust* **particles** *didn't get into their eyes.* (p. 213)

pattern (păt′ ərn) *n.* a repeating order. (p. 48)

perceive (pər sēv′) *v.* notice; become aware of. (p. 178)

period (p'r' ē əd) *n.* in science, a row in the periodic table. (p. 240)

periodic table *n.* a chart that organizes elements by their properties. (p. 238)

pesticide (pĕs' tĭ sīd') *n.* a substance used to kill living things that eat crops. (p. 106)

petroleum (pə trō' lē əm) *n.* a resource that comes from dead ocean plants. (p. 92)

phase (fāz) *n.* a regular change in how the moon looks from Earth. (p. 84)

phosphorus (P) (fŏs' fər əs) *n.* an element that humans need for energy and to form teeth and bones. (p. 168)

photosynthesis (fō' tō sĭn' thĭ sĭs) *n.* the process in which plant cells turn sunlight into food. (p. 141)

physical (fĭz' ĭ kəl) *adj.* **1.** using the body or tools. *Running is a physical activity.* (p. 217) **2.** observable. *Color is a physical property of matter.* (p. 228)

physical change *n.* a change in matter that does not result in new substances. (p. 226)

physical property *n.* a characteristic of matter that you can observe without changing the matter. (p. 234)

pitch (pĭch) *n.* the highness or lowness of sound. (p. 288)

planet (plăn' ĭt) *n.* a solid object that moves in a path around a star. *Earth is a planet that moves around the sun.* (p. 294)

plasma (plăz' mə) *n.* a state of matter, common in stars, in which particles have broken up. (p. 229)

plate (plāt) *n.* a large, thick piece of rock that moves. (p. 30)

plate tectonics *n.* the way Earth's plates move. (p. 34)

poison (poi' zən) **1.** *v.* harm, make unsafe. (p. 106) **2.** *n.* a harmful substance. (p. 107)

polar (pō' lər) a*dj.* cold and dry. (p. 69)

pollen (pŏl' ən) *n.* the part of a plant that contains the male sex cell. (p. 189)

pollution (pə lōō' shən) *n.* dirty air, water, or land. (p. 106)

population (pŏp' yə lā' shən) *n.* a group of the same kind of living things. (p. 105)

position (pə zĭsh' ən) *n.* the place where something is. (p. 258)

potential energy *n.* the energy of position. (p. 258)

precipitation (prĭ sĭp' ĭ tā' shən) *n.* water in the form of fog, snow, rain, or sleet. (p. 69)

predator (prĕd' ə tər) *n.* an organism that hunts, catches, and eats another organism. (p. 201)

prediction (prĭ dĭk' shən) *n.* a guess about what will happen. (p. 21)

preserve (prĭ zûrv') *v.* keep whole and safe. *We must preserve these tomatoes if we want to eat them next year.* (p. 109)

pressure (prĕsh' ər) *n.* a push. (p. 45)

primary (prī' mĕr'ē) *adj.* happening first. (p. 120)

producer (prə dōō' sər) *n.* a living thing that makes its own food. (p. 120)

product (prŏd' əkt) *n.* the substance that is the result of a chemical reaction. (p. 250)

prokaryotic (prō' kâr ē ŏt' ĭk) *adj.* without a nucleus. (p. 129)

property (prŏp' ər tē) *n.* a characteristic of something that makes it what it is. (p. 215)

protect (prə tĕkt') *v.* keep from being damaged or harmed. *Sunglasses protect your eyes from the sun.* (p. 109)

protein (prō' tēn') *n.* a substance the body uses for growth and repair, made of carbon, hydrogen, oxygen, and nitrogen. (p. 168)

proton (prō' tŏn') *n.* a particle in the nucleus of an atom that has a positive charge. (p. 213)

Punnett square *n.* a diagram used to show possible gene combinations. (p. 192)

R

radiation (rā′ dē ā′ shən) *n.* energy made by particles shooting out of the nuclei of atoms. (p. 108)

radioactive (rā′ dē ō ăk′ tĭv) *adj.* sending out high-energy radiation (p. 239)

radioisotope (rā′ dē ō ī′ sə tōp′) *n.* an atom whose nucleus sends out particles. (p. 156)

rarefaction (râr′ ə făk′ shən) *n.* a loose place in a longitudinal wave. (p. 285)

rate (rāt) *n.* a measure of how fast something happens. (p. 270)

ray (rā) *n.* a stream of particles shooting out of the nuclei of atoms. (p. 214)

react (rē ăkt′) *v.* change chemically. (p. 237)

reactant (rē ăk′ tənt) *n.* one of the starting materials in a chemical reaction. (p. 250)

rearrange (rē′ ə rānj′) *v.* put in a new order. (p. 165)

recessive gene *n.* a gene having less power. A recessive gene can only produce a trait when there is no dominant gene for the same trait. (p. 193)

recognize (rĕk′ əg nīz′) *v.* realize or identify something that was known before. *Dana has been gone so long that I hope I **recognize** her!* (p. 181)

recycle (rē sī′ kəl) *v.* use a material again. (p. 109)

reflect (rĭ flĕkt′) *v.* bend or turn back. *A mirror will **reflect** your image.* (p. 108)

reflex (rē′ flĕks′) *n.* an automatic response to a stimulus. (p. 179)

release (rĭ lēs′) *v.* set free. *Once the bird's wing is healed, they will **release** it back into the wild.* (p. 118)

remains (rĭ mānz′) *n.* a dead body. (p. 204)

renewable (rĭ nōō′ ə bəl) *adj.* possible to replace. (p. 90)

renewable resource *n.* something that can be used again and again without running out. (p. 94)

reproduce (rē′ prə dōōs′) *v.* make a copy. (p. 116)

reptile (rĕp′ tīl′) *n.* a class of air-breathing animals with backbones that includes snakes, lizards, turtles, alligators, and crocodiles. (p. 133)

resist (rĭ zĭst′) *v.* work against. *Our dog **resists** our efforts to give him a bath.* (p. 274)

resistant to *adj.* able to defend itself against. (p. 202)

resource (rē′ sôrs′) *n.* anything you use. (p. 90)

respond (rĭ spŏnd′) *v.* react to a stimulus. (p. 176)

response (rĭ spŏns′) *n.* an action that follows a stimulus. (p. 174)

restore (rĭ stôr′) *v.* put back or make as good as new. (p. 109)

result (rĭ zŭlt′) *n.* something that happens. *Good grades are a **result** of hard work.* (p. 18)

reverse (rĭ vûrs′) *n.* the opposite. *I thought Greenland was a warm place, but the **reverse** is true.* (p. 227)

revolve (rĭ vŏlv′) *v.* travel around something. (p. 78)

rock (rŏk) *n.* a hard material that makes up Earth's crust and mantle. (p. 32)

rock cycle *n.* the way rocks change and become different rocks. (p. 48)

root (rōōt) *n.* the part of a plant that takes in nutrients and water. (p. 150)

rotate (rō′ tāt) *v.* turn on an axis. (p. 78)

runoff (rŭn′ ôf′) *n.* water that moves over the top of the ground. (p. 70)

rust (rŭst) *v.* change by reacting with air or water. (p. 56)

S

scarce (skârs) *adj.* very hard to find. *Some wild animals have a hard time surviving in the winter because food is **scarce**.* (p. 201)

scientific law *n.* an idea or hypothesis that has been tested over and over and has been supported by each test. (p. 276)

scientific name *n.* genus name plus species name. The first letter of the genus name is always capitalized, the species name is all in lowercase, and the whole name is written in italic letters. (p. 128)

scrape (skrāp) *v.* rub hard. *Before I paint the fence, I have to scrape off the old paint.* (p. 37)

sea level *n.* the height of ocean water where it meets the land. (p. 108)

seafloor spreading *n.* the way rock is added to Earth's crust on the bottom of an ocean. (p. 45)

season (sē′ zən) *n.* summer, fall, winter, or spring. (p. 82)

secondary (sĕk′ ən dĕr′ ē) *adj.* happening second. (p. 120)

sediment (sĕd′ ə mənt) *n.* small pieces of rock, shell, and bone. (p. 46)

sedimentary rock *n.* the type of rock made when sediment is squeezed together. (p. 46)

seep (sēp) *v.* drip down slowly. *The crack in the window causes water to seep in every time it rains.* (p. 70)

sense (sĕns) *n.* sight, taste, touch, smell, and hearing. (p. 20)

settle (sĕt′ l) *v.* come to rest. *The ball will roll down the hill and settle at the bottom.* (p. 37)

sex cell *n.* a specialized cell that carries traits from parents. (p. 189)

sexual (sĕk′ shoo əl) *adj.* involving two parents. (p. 189)

shell (shĕl) *n.* an imaginary path around the nucleus of an atom in which electrons move. (p. 237)

siren (sī′ rən) *n.* a machine that makes a loud, wailing sound. *The ambulance turned on its siren to warn cars to let it pass.* (p. 264)

smog (smôg) *n.* dirty air made of smoke and fog. (p. 68)

soil (soil) *n.* a mixture of rock pieces, water, and air in which plants can grow. (p. 56)

solar eclipse *n.* the shadow made on Earth when the moon comes between Earth and the sun. (p. 85)

solar energy *n.* energy from the sun. (p. 68)

solar system *n.* the sun and 9 planets in orbit around it. (p. 299)

solid (sŏl′ ĭd) *n.* a state of matter with a definite shape and volume. (p. 224)

sound (sound) *n.* a form of energy that moves in longitudinal waves through matter. (p. 288)

space (spās) *n.* a blank or empty area. *There is not enough space in the kitchen for that huge table.* (p. 282)

specialize (spĕsh′ ə līz′) *v.* have one particular job. *My parents are both doctors who specialize in the care of children.* (p. 130)

species (spē′ shēz) *n.* a group of similar living things that can reproduce. (p. 116)

speed (spēd) *n.* how fast something is moving through space. *The car's speed was 60 miles (37 kilometers) per hour.* (p. 270)

sperm (spûrm) *n.* a male sex cell. (p. 189)

spill (spĭl) *v.* fall out. *The drink will spill if you don't hold the cup properly.* (p. 36)

spiral (spī′ rəl) *adj.* having a winding or coiled shape. *A snake will curl its body into a spiral shape when resting.* (p. 297)

spring (sprĭng) *n.* **1.** a place where underground water flows to the surface of Earth. (p. 70) **2.** a coil of metal that returns to its original shape after being pushed. (p. 284)

squint (skwĭnt) *v.* close the eyes partway. *The sun was so bright it made me squint.* (p. 178)

stable (stā′ bəl) *adj.* balanced and not easy to change. (p. 237)

star (stär) *n.* a large object, made of gas, that gives off energy. (p. 294)

starch (stärch) *n.* a substance plants use to store energy. (p. 167)

state (stāt) *n.* the physical form of something. Solid, liquid, and gas are 3 states of matter. (p. 224)

stem (stĕm) *n.* the part of the plant that moves nutrients and water. (p. 150)

stimulus (stĭm′ yə ləs) *n.* something an organism can sense (plural, *stimuli*). (p. 174)

strain (strān) *n.* a group within a species that has a special set of traits. (p. 202)

structure (strŭk′ chər) *n.* anything made out of parts. (p. 150)

sublimation (sŭb′ lə mā′ shən) *n.* the process of changing from a solid directly to a gas. (p. 227)

substance (sŭb′ stəns) *n.* a particular kind of matter. Water, air, and wood are all substances. (p. 215)

sugar (shŏŏg′ ər) *n.* **1.** a food made of carbon, oxygen, and hydrogen atoms. (p. 119) **2.** a nutrient that usually has a sweet taste. (p. 165)

sulfuric acid *n.* a substance made of hydrogen, sulfur, and oxygen. Sulfuric acid burns and can cut metal. (p. 301)

supernova (sōō′ pər nō′ və) *n.* the remains of a star that exploded when it died. (p. 298)

support (sə pôrt′) *v.* make stronger. (p. 18)

surface (sûr′ fəs) *n.* outside. *The **surface** of the car looked clean, but it was a mess inside.* (p. 33)

survey (sər′ vā) *n.* a list of questions to ask. *A woman came to our house to conduct a **survey** about what people watch on TV.* (p. 22)

survival (sər vī′ vəl) *n.* the ability to continue living. (p. 202)

swamp (swŏmp) *n.* a very wet area with lots of trees. (p. 95)

system (sĭs′ təm) *n.* a group of structures that work together. (p. 152)

table salt *n.* salt used to flavor food. The name for table salt in science is *sodium chloride*. (p. 249)

technology (tĕk nŏl′ ə jē) *n.* the use of science to solve problems. (p. 22)

telescope (tĕl′ ĭ skōp′) *n.* a tool that makes faraway objects look closer and larger. (p. 297)

temperate (tĕm′ pər ĭt) *adj.* having a cycle of cold and hot temperatures. (p. 69)

temperature (tĕm′ pər ə chŏŏr′) *n.* a measure of the amount of motion of particles. You can measure temperature with a thermometer. (p. 68)

terrestrial planets *n.* the inner planets, Mercury, Venus, Earth, and Mars. The word *terrestrial* comes from *terra*, the Latin word for earth or ground. (p. 301)

test (tĕst) *v.* try or experiment. (p. 18)

theory (thē′ ə rē) *n.* an explanation with evidence to support it. (p. 34)

thermal energy *n.* the energy of moving atoms. (p. 222)

tide (tīd) *n.* the daily change in the height of water along coasts. (p. 84)

tilt (tĭlt) *v.* slant; tip. *All afternoon I watched the plant slowly **tilt** toward the sunlight.* (p. 82)

time (tīm) *n.* a movement from the past through the present to the future. Time is measured in units such as minutes, hours, and years. (p. 282)

tissue (tĭsh′ ōō) *n.* a group of cells that work together to do a job. (p. 153)

tornado (tôr nā′ dō) *n.* a twisting storm with very fast winds that forms over land. (p. 73)

trait (trāt) *n.* a feature that can be controlled by genes, such as eye color, hair color, and height. (p. 186)

transfer (trăns′ fər) *n.* movement. *Elvio was in charge of the family's* **transfer** *to a new school district.* (p. 225)

transform (trăns fôrm′) *v.* change from one kind to another kind. *The children tried to* **transform** *themselves into superheroes.* (p. 263)

transport system *n.* an organized way of carrying material from one place to another. (p. 156)

transverse wave *n.* a wave that moves up and down, at right angles to the overall movement of energy. (p. 284)

trench (trĕnch) *n.* a deep, long, low area. (p. 34)

tropical (trŏp′ ĭ kəl) *adj.* always warm and wet, near Earth's equator. (p. 69)

trough (trôf) *n.* bottom. (p. 285)

tumor (tōo′ mər) *n.* a group of cells that may contain cancer cells. (p. 144)

unicellular (yōo′ nĭ sĕl′ yə lər) *adj.* having one cell. (p. 129)

unique (yōo nēk′) *adj.* unlike anything else. *Every snowflake has a* **unique** *shape.* (p. 215)

universe (yōo′ nə vûrs′) *n.* outer space and everything in it. (p. 296)

unstable (ŭn stā′ bəl) *adj.* ready to fall apart. *Don't stand on that pile of books because it is* **unstable.** (p. 214)

valley (văl′ ē) *n.* a low place between hills or mountains. (p. 61)

vapor (vā′ pər) *n.* a gas, such as air. (p. 71)

variable (vâr′ ē ə bəl) *n.* a factor in an experiment that can change. (p. 23)

variation (vâr′ ē ā′ shən) *n.* a small difference among organisms of the same type. (p. 202)

variety (və rī′ ĭ tē) *n.* different kinds. *He asked me to pick my favorite flavor, but I like a* **variety** *of flavors.* (p. 128)

vascular system *n.* a system for moving food and water. (p. 156)

vascular tissue *n.* groups of cells that work together to move food and water. (p. 157)

vehicle (vē′ ĭ kəl) *n.* a machine used to carry people or things. *A car or truck is a vehicle.* (p. 276)

vein (vān) *n.* a blood vessel that carries blood to the heart. (p. 157)

velocity (və lŏs′ ĭ tē) *n.* the combination of speed and direction. (p. 270)

vibrate (vī′ brāt′) *v.* move back and forth very quickly. *Manny's cell phone is set to* **vibrate** *instead of ring.* (p. 225)

virus (vī′ rəs) *n.* a nonliving particle that reproduces in healthy cells and causes infection. (p. 180)

visible light *n.* the part of the electromagnetic spectrum that people can see. (p. 286)

vitamin (vī′ tə mĭn) *n.* a carbon-containing molecule that helps cells do work. (p. 168)

volcano (vŏl kā′ nō) *n.* a place where melted rock comes out of Earth's surface. (p. 36)

volume (vŏl′ yōom) *n.* the amount of space something takes up, measured in liters or cubic centimeters. (p. 210)

warm front *n.* a place where warm air blows into cold air. (p. 72)

water cycle *n.* the pattern of water moving between air and the ground. (p. 70)

wave (wāv) *n.* a regular change that moves through a system. (p. 262)

wavelength (wāv′ lĕngkth′) *n.* the distance between two similar points on waves that are next to each other. (p. 285)

weather (wĕ*th*′ ər) *n.* a pattern of temperature and humidity that covers a small area for a short time. (p. 66)

weathering (wĕ*th*′ ər ĭng) *n.* the process of being broken apart by water, air, or ice. (p. 48)

weight (wāt) *n.* the measure of the force of gravity on an object's mass. (p. 210)

white blood cell *n.* a body cell that destroys germs. (p. 181)

wise (wīz) *adj.* careful and thoughtful. *Our grandmother seems to be a very **wise** person.* (p. 94)

wrinkle (rĭng′ kəl) *v.* squeeze into high places and low places. (p. 35)

zone (zōn) *n.* an area or region that has special characteristics. (p. 69)

zygote (zī′ gōt′) *n.* the cell produced when a sperm and an egg combine. (p. 189)

INDEX

A

acceleration, 275, 276
acid rain, 107
adaptation, 197, 198, 200–201, 202, 207
advantage, 198, 201, 202
agriculture, 102–103
air mass, 72
air pollution, 107
alpha rays, 214
amphibians, 133
amplitude, 285, 288
anatomy, 155, 204, 205
ancestor, 205
animal cells, 137, 141, 142
animals, 118–121, 125, 133
    endangered species of, 117
    resources from, 93
antibiotic-resistant bacteria, 202
antibiotics, 132, 202
antibodies, 181
archaebacteria, 125, 131
arteries, 157
arthropods, 133
asexual reproduction, 188
asteroids, 294
astronomers, 297, 301
astronomy, 76–87, 292–303
atmosphere, 65, 68, 108, 301
atomic number, 238
atoms
    classification of, 234–235, 237–241
    collisions of, 289
    differences among, 214, 248
    matter and, 117, 209, 213–214
    nuclear energy and, 95
    nucleus of, 213, 237
attraction, 246
axis, 78, 80

B

bacteria, 119, 125, 131, 180
    antibiotic-resistant, 202
balanced forces, 273
beach, 58, 62
bed, sedimentary, 60
behaviors, 200
    changing, 201
beta rays, 214
big bang theory, 296
binary fission, 188

biomass, 94, 95
biomes, 114–115
    desert, 104, 115, 116
    forest, 114
    freshwater, 115
    grassland, 114
    marine, 114
    tundra, 115
birds, 133
blood cells, 126, 150–151, 153, 158, 181
blood vessels, 150, 157
boiling point, 227
bonds, 245, 246
    chemical, 248
    covalent, 248
    ionic, 249
    metallic, 248
brain, 153, 179, 282–283
bundles
    muscle fibers, 153
    vascular tissue, 157

C

calcium, 168
calendars, 83
Calories, 162, 163, 169
cancer, 144, 214
capillaries, 157
carbohydrates, 163, 167, 169, 170, 171
carbon, 118, 119, 215, 241, 243, 246
carbon cycle, 119
carbon dioxide, 118, 119, 160, 164–166
carbon dioxide–oxygen cycle, 118
cardiac muscle, 149, 153
cardiovascular system, 156
categories, 126
cell(s), 126, 129, 149
    animal, 137, 141, 142
    defined, 138
    eukaryotic, 130, 132–133, 137, 140, 142, 148–155
    muscle, 149, 154
    parts of, 136–147
    plant, 137, 140, 141, 142, 156
    prokaryotic, 129–131
    sex, 189, 191
    specialized, 130, 153
    structure and function in, 136–143, 153
cell cycle, 138, 143

cell division, 136, 137, 138, 143, 144, 145
cell membrane, 137, 140, 141, 142, 146, 147
cellular respiration, 166
cell wall, 137, 140, 141, 142, 146
Celsius scale, 223
chalk, 57
charges, electric, 210–211, 213, 214
chemical bonds, 248
chemical change, 240, 244–253
    detection of, 246–247
chemical energy, 253, 262
chemical levels, balancing, 177
chemical properties, 234, 236
chemical reactions, 217, 245, 250–255
chemicals, 44, 107, 177
chemical symbol, 238
chloroplasts, 137, 141, 142, 146, 165
chromosomes, 143–145, 190–192
circulatory system, 149, 155, 156, 158
class, 128
classification, 126, 128–132, 133, 134, 229
climate, 66
    global, 108
    polar, 69
    temperate, 69, 104
    tropical, 69
climate zones, 65, 69, 75
clouds, 72
coal, 89, 90, 92, 95, 96, 98
cold air, 67, 68, 72
cold front, 72
comets, 294
communities, 116
competition, 113
complex carbohydrates, 167
compounds, 209, 217, 251
compressions, 285
conclusion, 25, 26
condensation, 71, 75, 226, 227
conduction, 265
conductors, 238
conservation
    of energy, 253
    of mass, 251
    of resources, 89, 97, 99, 109
consumers, 120–121, 123
continental plate, 33, 35
continents, 29, 33

INDEX

night, 80–81
nitrogen, 119, 215
nitrogen cycle, 119
noble gases, 239, 240
nonmetals, 234–235, 239, 240, 241
nonrenewable resources, 89, 90, 95
North Pole, 69, 80
nuclear energy, 95, 96, 98, 262
nuclear fusion, 298
nucleus, 96, 129
    atomic, 96, 213, 237
    cell, 129, 137, 140, 141, 142,
      143–145, 147
nutrient cycles, 118–119
nutrients, 113, 117, 118–121, 138,
    154, 160–171

O

observations, 50, 51, 127, 135
obsidian, 46
ocean plate, 33, 35
oceans, 29, 33, 54, 62, 65, 69, 70,
    71, 118
    effect of, on climate, 69
    rock formation under, 45
offspring, 186, 189
oil, 95, 104
orbit, 82, 294
order, 128
organelles, 140–144, 146, 147
organs, 149, 154, 155, 158, 179
organ systems, 149, 152, 154–157
ovule, 187, 189
oxygen, 118, 161, 209, 214–216,
    234, 248, 250–252, 254
oxygen cycle, *see carbon
    dioxide–oxygen cycle*

P

parent cell, 143–145
particles, 213
penicillin, 132
people, effect of, on Earth, 100–108
peregrine falcon, 117
periodic table, 232–241
    patterns in, 240–241
periods, 240, 241
pesticides, 106
petroleum, 91, 92, 96, 98
phases of the moon, 78–79, 84
phloem, 157
phosphorus, 168

photosynthesis, 141, 164, 165
phylum, 128
physical change, 226
physical properties, 228–229,
    234, 236
physical science, 208–303
pitch, 288
planets, 294, 296
    kinds of, 300–301
plant cells, 137, 140, 141, 142
plants, 114–115, 118–121, 125,
    133, 150
    reproduction in, 187, 189
    resources from, 93
    response to light stimulus, 178
    role of, in making food, 165
    vascular tissue in, 157
plasma, 229
plates, 33, 45
    movement of, 29, 34–35, 45
plate tectonics, theory of, 31,
    34–35, 38, 39
Pluto, 300
poisons, 131
polar climate, 69, 115
pollen, 187, 189
pollination, 113, 187
pollution, 94, 101, 106–107
    air, 107
    land, 106
    water, 107
population, 116, 123, 200
    human, 105
position, energy of, 258, 260, 275
potential energy, 258, 260
precipitation, 69, 70, 71, 107, 226
predators, 201
predictions, 21, 25, 27, 74, 175
primary consumers, 120
producers, 120, 121, 123, 132, 161
products, 250
prokaryotic cells, 129–131
properties, 215
    chemical, 234, 236
    physical, 228–229, 234, 236
proteins, 163, 168, 181
protists, 125, 132, 180
protons, 213, 237
pulley, 271
Punnett square, 192, 193

R

radiation, 214, 265

radioisotopes, 156
rarefactions, 285
rate, 270
reactants, 250
reactions, 217, 246, 250–253
    energy in, 245, 252
reactivity, 236
recessive genes, 193
recycling, 109
reflection, 287
reflexes, 179
renewable resources, 89, 90, 94
reproduction, 139, 184–195
    asexual, 188
    sexual, 189, 191
reproductive system, 155
reptiles, 133
resources, 90
    conservation of, 89, 97, 109
respiratory system, 155
response, 172–183
results, 18, 23
    communicating, 25
revolution, 78
ribosome, 142
river delta, 60
rivers, 55, 58, 61, 62, 63
rock, 40–49, 93
    formation of, 41, 44–45
    igneous, 41, 42, 46, 48, 49
    metamorphic, 41, 42, 47, 48, 49
    sedimentary, 41, 42, 46, 48, 49, 60
rock cycle, 48–49, 51
rotation, 78, 80
runoff, 70
rust, 56, 234, 254

S

sapphires, 48
Saturn, 300
science process, 16–27
scientific name, 128
scientist, being a, 16–17, 20–25
seafloor spreading, 45
sea levels, 108
seasons, 82–83, 86
secondary consumers, 120
sedimentary rock, 41, 42, 43, 46,
    48, 49, 60
sediments, 46, 50, 57, 58, 60, 61
seed, 187, 189
seeing, 282
senses, 20, 174, 178, 179

SKILLS AND FEATURES

SKILLS AND FEATURES

Acknowledgments

PHOTO CREDITS

4 *top* ©Getty Images *lower left* © Layne Kennedy/CORBIS *center left* © Dan Guravich/CORBIS *center right* © Royalty-Free/CORBIS *lower right* © Royalty-Free/CORBIS **5** *top* ©Royalty-Free/ CORBIS *bottom* ©William Manning/CORBIS **6** *top* ©Kevin R. Morris/ CORBIS *bottom* ©Eckhard Slawik/ Science Photo Library **7** *top* ©Royalty-Free/CORBIS *center* © Stocktrek *bottom* ©Mark E. Gibson/ CORBIS **8** *top* © Gary W. Carter/CORBIS *bottom* ©Stone/Getty Images *bottom right* ©Charles & Josette Lenars/ CORBIS **9** *top* ©Eileen Ryan Photography, 2004 *center right* © Joubert/Photo Researchers, Inc. *bottom center* ©Andrew Syred/ Photo Researchers *bottom right* ©Getty Images **10** *top* ©2004 Dynamic Graphics, Inc. *bottom left* ©Creatas *bottom right* ©Royalty-Free/CORBIS **11** *bottom right* ©Getty Images *bottom* ©Chase Swift/CORBIS **12** *top* © Getty Images *bottom* ©Royalty-Free/CORBIS **13** *top* ©Royalty-Free/CORBIS *center right* ©Sinclair Stammers SCIENCE PHOTO LIBRARY *bottom left* ©Leland Bobbé/ CORBIS *bottom right* ©Charles D. Winters/ Photo Researchers, Inc. **14** *top left* ©Howard Sochurek/ CORBIS *top right* ©Getty Images *bottom* ©Michael S. Yamashita/ CORBIS **15** *top* ©Royalty-Free/CORBIS *bottom* ©NASA **16** *left* ©John Schaefer, Director, Children's Media Workshop *center* ©Jonathan Blair/ CORBIS **17** ©Eileen Ryan Photography, 2004 **18** *top right* ©Getty Images *bottom left* © Getty Images *top left* © Lightscapes Photography, Inc./CORBIS *center right* © Royalty-Free/ CORBIS *bottom right* ©Royalty-Free/CORBIS **19** *bottom left* ©Layne Kennedy/ CORBIS *bottom center* ©Dan Guravich/ CORBIS *bottom right* ©Royalty-Free/CORBIS *far bottom right* ©Royalty-Free/CORBIS **20** *top* ©Images.com/ CORBIS *left* © Getty Images *right* ©Eileen Ryan Photography, 2004 **21** ©Eileen Ryan Photography, 2004 **22** *top* ©Eileen Ryan Photography, 2004 *bottom* ©Royalty-Free/CORBIS **23** *top* ©Eileen Ryan Photography, 2004 *center* ©Getty Images **24** ©Eileen Ryan Photography, 2004 **25** *top* © Getty Images *bottom* ©Eileen Ryan Photography, 2004 **26** © Getty Images **27** ©John Schaefer, Director, Children's Media Workshop **28** *left* ©John Schaefer, Director, Children's Media Workshop *center* ©Royalty-Free/CORBIS **32** ©Stocktrek/ CORBIS **33** *top* ©Courtesy of NASA **34** ©Tibor Bognár/ CORBIS **36** *bottom right* ©Simon Fraser/ Photo Researchers, Inc. **37** *bottom* ©Grant Smith/CORBIS **38** ©Royalty-Free/ CORBIS **39** ©John Schaefer, Director, Children's Media Workshop **40** *left* ©John Schaefer, Director, Children's Media Workshop *center* ©Greg Probst/ CORBIS **41** *top* ©Darrell Gulin/ CORBIS *center* ©Simon Fraser/ Photo Researchers, Inc. *bottom* ©Steve Austin; Papilio/CORBIS **42** *bottom right* ©Royalty-Free/CORBIS **43** *top* ©Biophoto Associates/ Photo Researchers, Inc. *bottom left* ©Roger Ressmeyer/CORBIS *bottom right* ©Roger Ressmeyer/ CORBIS **44** *top* Digital image © 1996 CORBIS; Original image courtesy of NASA/CORBIS *bottom* ©Roger Ressmeyer/ CORBIS **46** *top* ©Eileen Ryan Photography, 2004 *bottom* ©Doug Sokell/ Visuals Unlimited **47** *top* ©Eileen Ryan Photography, 2004 *bottom* ©Ric Ergenbright/ CORBIS **48** *top* ©Eileen Ryan Photography, 2004 *bottom* © Sukree Sukplang/Reuters/Corbis **50** *top* Charles D. Winters/Photo Researchers, Inc. *bottom* © Royalty-Free/CORBIS **51** ©John Schaefer, Director, Children's Media Workshop **52** *left* ©John Schaefer, Director, Children's Media Workshop *center* ©Owaki-Kulla/

CORBIS **53** *left* ©Royalty-Free/CORBIS *center* © Derek Croucher/CORBIS **54** *left* ©Courtesy of NASA *center* ©Owaki-Kulla/ CORBIS *right* ©Gerald & Buff Corsi/ Visuals Unlimited **55** *top right* ©Bjorn Backe; Papilio/ CORBIS *top left* ©Jay Dickman/ CORBIS *bottom left* ©Royalty-Free/ CORBIS *bottom right* ©Richard T. Nowitz/ CORBIS **56** *top* ©Royalty-Free/ CORBIS *bottom* © Massimo Mastrorillo/ CORBIS **57** *top* ©Kevin Flemming/ CORBIS *bottom* ©Nik Wheeler/ CORBIS **58** ©Royalty-Free/ CORBIS **59** © Reuters/CORBIS **60** ©Tom Bean/ STONE *bottom* ©William Manning/CORBIS **61** *top* ©Michael Kevin Daly/ CORBIS *bottom* ©Royalty-Free/CORBIS **63** ©John Schaefer, Director, Children's Media Workshop **64** *left* ©John Schaefer, Director, Children's Media Workshop *center* ©Cydney Conger/ CORBIS **65** *center* ©Royalty-Free/ CORBIS *left* ©Royalty-Free/ CORBIS *right* ©Michael S. Yamashita/ CORBIS *bottom left* ©Royalty-Free/ CORBIS *bottom right* ©Ariel Skelley/ CORBIS **66** *bottom left* ©Dave G. Houser/ CORBIS *bottom right* ©Kevin R. Morris/ CORBIS **67** *bottom left* ©Elizabeth Opalenik/ CORBIS *bottom right* ©Carl & Ann Purcell/ CORBIS **68** *top* ©Royalty-Free/ CORBIS *bottom* ©Randy Faris/CORBIS **69** *top* ©Royalty-Free/CORBIS *center* ©James L. Amos/CORBIS *bottom* ©Royalty-Free/CORBIS **71** *top* ©Royalty-Free/CORBIS *bottom* ©Royalty-Free/CORBIS **73** *top* ©Jim Reed/ CORBIS **74** ©Getty Images **75** ©John Schaefer, Director, Children's Media Workshop **76** *left* ©John Schaefer, Director, Children's Media Workshop *top* ©Joseph Sohm; ChromoSohm Inc./ CORBIS *bottom* ©Joseph Sohm/ CORBIS **77** *center left* ©Royalty-Free/CORBIS *center right* ©Richard Cummins/ CORBIS *bottom left* ©Alan Schein Photography/ CORBIS *bottom right* ©Noeleen Lowndes in Australia **78-79** *bottom* ©Eckhard Slawik/ Science Photo Library **80** *bottom* © Stone/Getty Images **81** *top left* © Tim McGuire/CORBIS *top right* ©Jose Luis Pelaez, Inc/ CORBIS *bottom right* ©Jose Luis Pelaez, Inc/ CORBIS *far bottom* ©Donald C. Johnson/ CORBIS **82** ©Donna Disario/ CORBIS **83** ©Royalty-Free/CORBIS **84** *top* ©Franz-Marc Frei/ CORBIS *bottom* ©Dallas and John Heaton/ CORBIS **85** ©Roger Ressmeyer/ CORBIS **87** ©John Schaefer, Director, Children's Media Workshop **88** *left* ©John Schaefer, Director, Children's Media Workshop *top left* Royalty-Free/CORBIS *top right* ©Creatas *bottom left* ©Bob Gomel/ CORBIS *bottom right* ©Josef Scaylea/ CORBIS **89** *left* ©Creatas *right* ©Creatas *bottom* ©Mark E. Gibson/ CORBIS **90** *left* ©Raymond Gehman/ CORBIS *center* ©Michael S. Yamashita/ CORBIS *right* ©Creatas **91** *left* ©Amos Nachoum/ CORBIS *right* ©David Oliver/ Stone **92** *top* ©Roy Morsch/CORBIS *bottom* ©Jeff Albertson/ CORBIS **93** *top* ©Royalty Free/CORBIS *center* ©Royalty-Free/CORBIS *bottom* ©Royalty-Free/CORBIS **94** *left* ©Creatas *right* ©Creatas **95** *top* ©Royalty-Free/CORBIS *bottom* ©Creatas **96** *bottom* ©Lester Lefkowitz/ CORBIS **97** ©NREL/ US Department of Energy/ Science Photo Library **99** ©John Schaefer, Director, Children's Media Workshop **100** *left* ©John Schaefer, Director, Children's Media Workshop *center* ©Ricardo Azoury/ CORBIS **101** *top* ©Premium Stock/ CORBIS *center* ©Lester Lefkowitz/ CORBIS *bottom* © Jonathan Blair/ CORBIS **102** *top left* ©Getty Images *top right* ©Getty Images *center right* ©Pam Gardner; Frank Lane Picture Agency/CORBIS *bottom left* ©Patrick Johns/ CORBIS *bottom right* ©Bill Stormont/ CORBIS **103** *top* ©Getty Images *bottom left* ©Royalty-Free/CORBIS *bottom right* ©Richard Hamilton Smith/ CORBIS **104** ©Dave G. Houser/CORBIS **106** *top* ©Royalty-Free/CORBIS *bottom* ©Wolfgang Kaehler/ CORBIS **107** *top* ©Vince Streano/ CORBIS *bottom* ©Jonathan Blair/ CORBIS **109** *top* ©Chris Jones/ CORBIS **111** ©John Schaefer, Director, Children's Media Workshop **112** *left* ©John Schaefer,

Director, Children's Media Workshop *center* ©Charles & Josette Lenars/ CORBIS *bottom* ©Staffan Widstrand/ CORBIS
113 *top left* ©Sharna Balfour; Gallo Images/ CORBIS *top right* ©Joe McDonald/ CORBIS *center left* ©Gary W. Carter/ CORBIS *center right* ©W. Perry Conway/ CORBIS *bottom left* ©Creatas
114 *bottom left* ©James A. Sugar/ CORBIS *bottom center* ©David Keaton/ CORBIS *bottom left* ©Royalty-Free/CORBIS
115 *bottom left* ©David Muench/ CORBIS *bottom center* ©Royalty-Free/CORBIS *bottom right* ©Charles Mauzy/ CORBIS
116 ©Royalty-Free/ CORBIS **117** ©Creatas **119** ©Getty Images
120 *top* ©ImageState **122** ©Getty Images **123** ©John Schaefer, Director, Children's Media Workshop **124** *left* ©John Schaefer, Director, Children's Media Workshop *center* ©Gilbert S. Grant/ Photo Researchers, Inc. **125** *top left* ©Wolfgang Baumeister/ Science Photo Library *center* ©Dr. Kari Lounatmaa/ Science Photo Library *top right* ©Jeffrey L. Rotman/ CORBIS *bottom left* ©Simon Fraser/ Science Photo Library *bottom center* ©Vaughan Fleming/ Science Photo Library *bottom right* ©Getty Images **126** *bottom left* ©Stone/Getty Images *bottom right* ©Kelly-Mooney Photography/ CORBIS **127** *top* ©Imagebank/Getty Images *bottom left* ©RNT Productions/ CORBIS *bottom right* ©Japack Company/CORBIS
128 *top* ©Jon Feingersh/ CORBIS *bottom* ©Getty Images
129 ©A. B. Dowsett/ Science Photo Library **130** ©CNRI/ Science Photo Library **131** *top* ©Dr. Kari Lounatmaa/ Science Photo Library *bottom* ©Scimat **132** *left* ©Royalty-Free/CORBIS *right* ©Eric V. Grave *bottom* ©Biophoto Associates **133** *top* ©Adam Jones/Photo Researchers, Inc. *bottom* ©Index Stock Imagery, Inc. **134** ©J. R. Planck **135** *top* ©Richard T. Nowitz/ Photo Researchers, Inc. *bottom* ©John Schaefer, Director, Children's Media Workshop **136** *left* ©John Schaefer, Director, Children's Media Workshop *center* ©Stem Jems/ Photo Researchers, Inc.
138 *bottom left* ©Getty Images *bottom right* ©Jose Luis Pelaez, Inc./ CORBIS **139** *top* ©Eileen Ryan Photography, 2004 *bottom left* ©Jon Feingersh/ CORBIS *bottom right* ©Ariel Skelley/ CORBIS
140 ©Dr. Dennis Kunkel/ Visuals Unlimited **141** *top* ©George Chapman/ Visuals Unlimited *bottom* ©Dr. Donald Fawcett/ Visuals Unlimited **143** ©Joubert/Photo Researchers, Inc. **144** *top* ©Biophoto Associates/ Photo Researchers, Inc. *bottom* ©Cnri/ Photo Researchers, Inc. **146** ©Getty Images **147** ©John Schaefer, Director, Children's Media Workshop **148** *left* ©John Schaefer, Director, Children's Media Workshop *center* ©Richard Bailey/ CORBIS **149** *center left* ©Science Photo Library /Photo Researchers, Inc. *center* ©Innerspace Imaging/ Science Photo Library *bottom left* ©Science Photo Library/Photo Researchers, Inc.
150 *bottom left* ©National Cancer Institute/ Science Photo Library *bottom right* ©Susumu Nishinaga/ Science Photo Library
151 *bottom left* ©Duomo/ CORBIS *bottom right* ©Deb Yeske/ Visuals Unlimited **152** *left* ©Ralf-Finn Hestoft/ CORBIS *right* ©Ed Bock/ CORBIS **153** *top* ©National Cancer Institute/ Science Photo Library *bottom* ©Science Photo Library **156** *center* ©Royalty-Free/CORBIS *bottom* ©Dr. Gary Gaugler/Visuals Unlimited **157** *top* ©Susumu Nishinaga/ Science Photo Library *bottom* ©Andrew Syred/ Photo Researchers **159** ©John Schaefer, Director, Children's Media Workshop **160** *left* ©John Schaefer, Director, Children's Media Workshop *center* ©Royalty-Free/CORBIS **162** *top* © Michael Keller/CORBIS *bottom left* ©James Noble/ CORBIS *bottom center* ©Jose Luis Pelaez, Inc./ CORBIS *bottom right* ©Creatas **163** *left* ©CORBIS *center* ©Nathan Benn/ CORBIS *right* ©Royalty-Free/CORBIS
164 *top* ©Larry Rana/ USDA *bottom* © Mark E. Gibson/CORBIS **165** *left* ©Dr. Kari Lounatmaa / Science Photo Library *right* © Getty Images **166** *left* ©Getty Images *center* © Dr. Donald Fawcett / Visuals Unlimited *right* ©Creatas **167** *top left* ©Taxi/Getty Images *bottom* ©Rob Lewine/ CORBIS **168** *top left*

©Royalty-Free/CORBIS *center* ©Creatas *bottom left* ©Royalty-Free/CORBIS *bottom right* ©Royalty-Free/CORBIS
169 ©Royalty-Free/CORBIS
171 ©John Schaefer, Director, Children's Media Workshop
172 *left* ©John Schaefer, Director, Children's Media Workshop *center* ©Getty Images **173** *top left* © Royalty-Free/CORBIS *top right* ©Royalty-Free/CORBIS *bottom left* ©O. Alamany & E. Vicens/ CORBIS *bottom right* ©Tom Brakefield/ CORBIS **174** *top* © Jonathan Blair/CORBIS *bottom* ©Dr. Jeremy Burgess / SCIENCE PHOTO LIBRARY
175 ©Dr. Jeremy Burgess / SCIENCE PHOTO LIBRARY
176 *top* ©Creatas *bottom* ©Tom Brakefield/ CORBIS
177 ©Royalty-Free/ CORBIS **178** *top* ©W. Perry Conway/ CORBIS *bottom* ©Stone **180** *top* ©Lowell Georgia/ Photo Researchers, Inc. *left* ©Science VU/ Visuals Unlimited *bottom right* ©Jose Luis Pelaez, Inc./ CORBIS **183** ©John Schaefer, Director, Children's Media Workshop **184** *left* ©John Schaefer, Director, Children's Media Workshop *center* ©Royalty-Free/CORBIS **185** *top* ©Roy Morsch/CORBIS *bottom* © Tony Hamblin; Frank Lane Picture Agency/CORBIS **186** *top* ©Getty Images *bottom* ©Royalty-Free/CORBIS **187** *top* ©Yann Arthus-Bertrand/ CORBIS *bottom* ©Mark Cassino/SuperStock **188** *top* © Stephen Frink/CORBIS *bottom* ©A. B. Dowsett/ SCIENCE PHOTO LIBRARY
189 *left* ©Wolfgang Kaehler/ CORBIS *right* ©IT Stock Free/ PictureQuest *center* ©Dynamic Graphics, Inc.
190 ©Nigel Cattlin/ Photo Researchers, Inc. **192** *top* ©Royalty-Free/CORBIS *bottom* ©CORBIS **194** ©Paul Barton/ CORBIS **195** ©John Schaefer, Director, Children's Media Workshop **196** *left* ©John Schaefer, Director, Children's Media Workshop *center* ©Getty Images
197 ©Getty Images **200** *top* ©Kevin Schafer/ CORBIS *bottom* ©Chase Swift/ CORBIS **201** *top* Jennifer Almeida Scalo *bottom* Ralph A. Clevenger/CORBIS **202** ©Dr. Kari Lounatmaa / SCIENCE PHOTO LIBRARY **204** *top* ©Richard Cummins/ CORBIS *bottom* ©Getty Images
206 ©Getty Images **207** ©John Schaefer, Director, Children's Media Workshop **208** *left* ©John Schaefer, Director, Children's Media Workshop *center* ©Royalty-Free/CORBIS **209** *top* ©Royalty-Free/ CORBIS
210 ©Aaron Horowitz/ CORBIS **211** ©Paul A. Souders/ CORBIS **212** *top* ©Royalty-Free/CORBIS *right* ©Royalty-Free/CORBIS *bottom left* ©Annie Griffiths Belt/ CORBIS
214 ©Walter Hodges/CORBIS **215** ©Royalty-Free/CORBIS **216** ©Stuart Westmorland/ CORBIS
217 ©Royalty-Free/CORBIS **219** ©John Schaefer, Director, Children's Media Workshop **220** *left* ©John Schaefer, Director, Children's Media Workshop *center* ©Vince Streano/CORBIS **221** ©Royalty-Free/CORBIS **222** *bottom left* ©Getty Images *bottom center* © Mark A. Johnson/CORBIS **223** *center* ©Getty Images *right* ©Owen Franken/ CORBIS **224** *top* ©Imagebank/Getty Images *bottom* ©Royalty-Free/CORBIS *right* ©Getty Images **226** *top* ©Lindsay Hebberd/ CORBIS **227** *top* ©Royalty-Free/CORBIS *bottom* ©Jeff Daly/ Visuals Unlimited **228** *top* ©Royalty-Free/CORBIS *bottom* ©Creatas **229** *top* ©Jose Luis Pelaez, Inc./CORBIS **231** ©John Schaefer, Director, Children's Media Workshop **232** *left* ©John Schaefer, Director, Children's Media Workshop *center* ©Owaki - Kulla/CORBIS **233** *right* © Royalty-Free/CORBIS **234** *bottom left* ©Royalty-Free/CORBIS *bottom center* ©Royalty-Free/CORBIS *bottom right* ©George Bernard / SCIENCE PHOTO LIBRARY *far bottom left* ©Sinclair Stammers / SCIENCE PHOTO LIBRARY

235 *bottom left* ©Walter Hodges/ CORBIS *bottom center* ©Charles D. Winters/ Photo Researchers, Inc. **236** ©Bob Rowan; Progressive Image/ CORBIS **240** Royalty-Free/CORBIS **242** ©Getty Images **243** ©John Schaefer, Director, Children's Media Workshop **244** *left* ©John Schaefer, Director, Children's Media Workshop *center* ©Richard H. Cohen/CORBIS **245** *top left* ©Andrew Lambert Photography / SCIENCE PHOTO LIBRARY *top right* ©Andrew Lambert Photography / SCIENCE PHOTO LIBRARY *bottom right* ©Kevin Schafer/CORBIS **246** *left* ©Leland Bobbé/ CORBIS *right* ©Creatas **247** *top* ©Al Francekevich/ CORBIS *bottom left* Martyn F. Chillmaid / SCIENCE PHOTO LIBRARY *bottom right* ©BAZUKI MUHAMMAD/ Reuters Newmedia Inc/ CORBIS **248** *top* ©2004 PunchStock *bottom left* ©Royalty-Free/ CORBIS **249** *top* ©Ted Spiegel/ CORBIS *bottom* ©Creatas **250** *top* ©Catherine Karnow/ CORBIS **251** ©James L. Amos/CORBIS **252** *top* ©Andrew Lambert Photography / SCIENCE PHOTO LIBRARY *bottom* ©Royalty-Free/CORBIS **253** © Royalty-Free/CORBIS **254** *top* ©Lee Snider; Lee Snider/CORBIS **255** ©John Schaefer, Director, Children's Media Workshop **256** *left* ©John Schaefer, Director, Children's Media Workshop *center* ©Michelle Chaplow/ CORBIS **257** *top* ©James Noble/ CORBIS **258** *left* ©Carlos Dominguez/ CORBIS *right* ©Lester Lefkowitz/ CORBIS **259** *top* ©Joseph Sohm; Chromosohm Inc./ CORBIS *bottom left* ©Creatas *bottom right* ©Charles Gupton/ CORBIS **260** *top* ©Tim Kiusalaas/ CORBIS *bottom* ©Duomo/ CORBIS **261** ©Royalty-Free/CORBIS **262** *top* ©2004 PunchStock *bottom* ©Getty Images **263** *top* © Royalty-Free/CORBIS *bottom* © Royalty-Free/CORBIS **264** *top* ©Howard Sochurek/ CORBIS *bottom* ©Steve Chenn/ CORBIS **266** ©Kevin Fleming/CORBIS **267** ©John Schaefer, Director, Children's Media Workshop **268** *left* ©John Schaefer, Director, Children's Media Workshop *center* ©David H. Wells/ CORBIS **269** *left* ©Eileen Ryan Photography, 2004 *right* ©Eileen Ryan Photography, 2004 *bottom* ©Getty Images **270** *top* ©Royalty-Free/ CORBIS *bottom left* © Richard Olivier/CORBIS *bottom center* ©Royalty-Free/CORBIS *bottom right* ©Getty Images **271** *center right* ©Richard Cummins/ CORBIS *center left* ©Kevin Flemming/ CORBIS *bottom center* ©Michael S. Yamashita/ CORBIS **272** *top* ©Tom Stewart/ CORBIS *bottom* ©Eileen Ryan Photography, 2004 **273** *top* ©Eileen Ryan Photography, 2004 *bottom* ©Torleif Svensson/ CORBIS **274** *top* ©Tom Sanders/ CORBIS **275** ©Michele Westmorland/ CORBIS **276** *left* ©George Hall/ CORBIS *right* ©David Lawrence/ CORBIS **277** *center* ©Paul A. Souders/ CORBIS *right* © Royalty Free/CORBIS **278** ©Pete Stone/ CORBIS **279** ©John Schaefer, Director, Children's Media Workshop **280** *left* ©John Schaefer, Director, Children's Media Workshop *center* ©A & J Verkaik/CORBIS **281** *top* ©Royalty-Free/CORBIS *bottom* ©Creatas **282** *top* ©Royalty-Free/ CORBIS **283** ©Don Hammond/ CORBIS **284** ©Creatas **286** ©Clayton J. Price/ CORBIS **287** *top* ©National Institutes of Health/ Science Photo Library *bottom* ©LWA-Dann Tardif/CORBIS **288** *left* ©Creatas *right* ©John Dakers; Eye Ubiquitous/ CORBIS **291** ©John Schaefer, Director, Children's Media Workshop **292** *left* ©John Schaefer, Director, Children's Media Workshop *center* ©Dennis di Cicco/CORBIS **293** ©NASA **294** *left* ©NASA *right* ©Roger Ressmeyer/ CORBIS **295** *left* ©NOAO *right* ©Jonathan Blair/ CORBIS **296** *top* ©Nasa *center* ©NASA/ Roger Ressmeyer/ CORBIS *bottom* ©Getty Images

297 *top* ©NASA/ Roger Ressmeyer/ CORBIS *center* ©NASA **298** *top* ©NASA *bottom* ©Getty Images **300** *top left* ©Getty Images *top right* ©NASA *bottom left* ©Getty Images *bottom center* ©NASA/Roger Ressmeyer/CORBIS *bottom right* ©Getty Images **301** *far top* ©US Geological Survey *top* ©Getty Images *center* ©NASA *bottom* ©Phil James (Univ. Toledo), Todd Clancy (Space Science Inst., Boulder, CO), Steve Lee (Univ. Colorado), and NASA **303** ©John Schaefer, Director, Children's Media Workshop **304** *center* ©Eileen Ryan Photography, 2004 **305** *center* ©Getty Images **306** *left* ©Getty Images *right* ©Dr. Kari Lounatmaa / Science Photo Library **307** *left* ©NASA *center right* ©Roger Ressmeyer/ CORBIS *bottom right* ©Royalty-Free/CORBIS **308** ©Getty Images **309** *top* ©Jose Luis Pelaez, Inc./CORBIS *bottom* ©O. Alamany & E. Vicens/ CORBIS

Cover *Foreground*: frog: ©Getty Images; prism: ©Getty Images; stars: ©Photodisc/ Getty Images *Background:* ©Photodisc/ Getty Images; ©BrandX/ Getty Images. Based on a system of labeling the columns A through J and the rows 1 through 18, the following background images were taken by the following photographers: A8, A10, A13, A16, A18, C9, C11, C13, C14, C16, C17, D5, D7, D8, D11, D13, D15, D18, E1, E8, E12, E15, E16, E17, E19, E20, F1, F2, F5, F6, F11, F13, F17, F19, G9, G10, G12, H2, H3, H12, H13, H17, I1, I8, I9, I11, I14, I16, I18, I19, J2, J4, J5, J6, J8, J12, J13, J17, J19: Philip Coblentz/ Getty Images; A5, E7: Steve Allen/ Getty Images; F16: Sexto Sol/ Getty Images; B19: Spike Mafford/ Getty Images; B12: Philippe Colombi/ Getty Images; J1: Albert J Copley/ Getty Images

ILLUSTRATION CREDITS

9 *bottom* © Jonathan Massie **11** ©Linda Howard Bittner
15 © Jonathan Massie **18** ©Carla Kiwior **29** © John Lambert
30 © John Lambert **30–31** *bottom* ©Linda Howard Bittner
32 © John Lambert **33** © John Lambert **34** © John Lambert
35 © John Lambert **36** © John Lambert **37** © John Lambert
42 © John Lambert **45** © John Lambert **48** © John Lambert
54 ©Carla Kiwior **66** ©Carla Kiwior **68** © Jonathan Massie
69 © Jonathan Massie **70** © John Lambert **72** © John Lambert
77 © George Hamblin **78** ©Carla Kiwior **79** © George Hamblin
80 © George Hamblin **82** © George Hamblin **83** © George
Hamblin **85** © George Hamblin **86** © George Hamblin
90 ©Carla Kiwior **96** © Jonathan Massie **98** © Jonathan Massie
108 © George Hamblin **113** © Linda Howard Bittner
114 ©Carla Kiwior **118** © Linda Howard Bittner **119** © Linda
Howard Bittner **120** © Linda Howard Bittner **121** © Linda
Howard Bittner **137** © Linda Howard Bittner **138** ©Carla Kiwior
141 © Linda Howard Bittner **142** © Linda Howard Bittner
143 ©Carla Kiwior **145** © Linda Howard Bittner **149** *top*
©Jonathan Massie *bottom right* ©Carla Kiwior **150** ©Carla Kiwior
154 ©Carla Kiwior **156** ©Carla Kiwior **158** ©Carla Kiwior
161 ©Linda Howard Bittner **174** © Linda Howard Bittner
175 ©Linda Howard Bittner **179** ©Carla Kiwior **181** ©Catherine
Twomey**186** ©Linda Howard Bittner **187** ©Linda Howard Bittner
190 ©Catherine Twomey **191** ©Catherine Twomey
197 ©Carla Kiwior **198** ©Carla Kiwior **198-199** ©Linda
Howard Bittner **202** ©George Hamblin **203** ©Linda Howard
Bittner **205** ©Carla Kiwior **209** ©Catherine Twomey
210 ©Carla Kiwior **213** ©Catherine Twomey **214** ©Catherine
Twomey **215** ©Catherine Twomey **216** ©Catherine Twomey
218 *top* ©Catherine Twomey *bottom left* ©Catherine Twomey
bottom right ©Catherine Twomey **221** ©Jonathan Massie **222**
©Carla Kiwior **223** ©Jonathan Massie **225** ©Jonathan Massie
226 ©George Hamblin **228** ©Jonathan Massie **234** ©Carla Kiwior
237 ©Catherine Twomey **241** ©Catherine Twomey
245 ©Catherine Twomey **246** ©Carla Kiwior **248** ©Catherine
Twomey **249** ©Catherine Twomey **250** ©Catherine Twomey
252 ©Catherine Twomey **254** ©Catherine Twomey **257** ©John
Lambert **258** ©Carla Kiwior **265** © John Lambert **274** ©George
Hamblin **281** © Jonathan Massie **282** ©Catherine Twomey
283 ©Catherine Twomey **284** ©Jonathan Massie **285** ©Jonathan
Massie **286** ©Jonathan Massie **288** ©Jonathan Massie
289 ©Catherine Twomey **293** ©George Hamblin
294 ©George Hamblin **298** ©Catherine Twomey
299 ©George Hamblin **308** © Catherine Twomey **309** © Carla
Kiwior

TEXT CREDITS

310 Pronunciation Key, Copyright © 2003 by Houghton Mifflin
Company. Reproduced by permission from The American Heritage
Student Dictionary.

The editors have made every effort to trace the ownership of
all copyrighted selections found in this book and to make full
acknowledgment for their use. Omissions brought to our attention
will be corrected in a subsequent edition.